‹ **W9-AFE-212**

DATE DUE		
MAY 0 8 1997		

Washington, D.C.

COMPARATIVE AMERICAN CITIES

A series edited by Joe T. Darden

Washington, D.C.

Inner-City Revitalization and

Minority Suburbanization

Dennis E. Gale

Temple University Press · Philadelphia

Temple University Press, Philadelphia 19122
Copyright © 1987 by Temple University
All rights reserved
Published 1987
Printed in the United States of America
∞ The paper used in this publication meets the minimum
requirements of American National Standard for Information
Sciences—Permanence of paper for Printed Library Materials,
ANSI Z39.48-1984

Library of Congress Cataloging-in-Publication Data
Gale, Dennis E.
  Washington, D.C. : inner-city revitalization and minority
suburbanization.
  (Comparative American cities)
  Includes index.
  1. Urban renewal—Washington (D.C.) 2. Central
business districts—Washington (D.C.)   3. Suburbs—
Washington (D.C.)   4. Minorities—Washington (D.C.)
I. Title. II. Series.
HT177.W3G35   1987   307.3′42′0973   87-10001
ISBN 0-87722-496-X (alk. paper)

To Susan and Charlie,
who conferred on me my proudest titles,
husband and father

Contents

List of Maps and Tables

Maps

Tables

Preface

No matter how extensively one analyzes the shifting forces of urban decline and revitalization in Washington, nothing so impresses the mind as personal experience. I recall visits to Washington during my youth in the late 1950s and early 1960s, in which the old downtown, Georgetown, Capitol Hill, and other neighborhoods still presented what seemed a uniformly frayed and sometimes shabby appearance. Later, on leave from graduate school as a summer intern in the U.S. Department of Housing and Urban Development, I witnessed the Great Society fervor in the capital. With the 1968 riots in Washington only a year behind, my class of interns was treated to a bus tour of some of the city's problem areas, including some of those involved in the Federal Urban Renewal Program. Little did we realize that some sections of the city termed "blighted" and considered by Washington's planners to be ripe for higher-density development were already beginning to attract young professional people, mostly whites, who were buying old dwellings and renovating them. Some of us, just a few years from the threshold of adult careers, would later become a part of this "gentrification" movement. At that transitional period, however, few of us believed that there was much hope for revitalizing Washington's declining neighborhoods through other than massive government intervention. However much we may have deplored the worst excesses of the federal Urban Renewal Program, most of us were firmly convinced that if left to private market forces, without public planning, regulatory controls, and subsidies, America's older inner-city neighborhoods, for the most part, would be doomed.

Many Americans recalled President Nixon's admonitions about the high crime rate in the nation's capital. Demonstrations against the war in Vietnam and civil rights marches were commonplace. People fought urban renewal and highway plans, which threatened to destroy neighborhood identity. Tensions between black and white, affluent and poor, politically active and politically apathetic were woven throughout much of the fabric of life in the nation's capital.

Just as certain as central Washington's troubles though, were contrasting conditions of life in Washington's surrounding suburban communities. As elsewhere in the nation during the 1950s and 1960s, they were populated largely by middle- and upper-class families. Prince George's and Montgomery counties in Maryland, as well as Arlington County and the city of Alexandria across the Potomac River in Virginia, were dotted with subdivision after subdivision of single-family detached homes wrapped around curly cul-de-sacs. Farther out, Fairfax County, Virginia, was already emerging as the frontier of rapid new growth. Farm fields were falling prey to the lure of new "tax ratables" and the gospel of real estate development. The opening of the Capital Beltway, a circumferential interstate highway, laced these jurisdictions together forming a loosely assembled metropolitan area.

Even by the mid-1960s, however, a visitor to the suburbs would look long and hard to find more than a handful of blacks or other racial minorities in the schools, swimming pools, or shopping centers. Where blacks did appear, they were often inhabitants of small post-bellum hamlets settled by freed slaves and sharecroppers. Suburban blacks then, although *in* the suburbs, were not *of* the suburbs.

When I eventually returned to Washington and settled there, I could look back on periods of residency in Boston and Philadelphia. I had become a city planner and had developed a professional perspective about American communities. Fifteen years have passed since then, and today I look upon the city's core with astonishment. For the central business district—including the federal mall area—and much of the surrounding stratum of older residential neighborhoods are well along the path toward a rather startling transformation. Few who witnessed the continual drubbing endured by America's older central cities, especially in the wake of the urban riots of the 1960s, could fail to be impressed by Washington today. In considerably less than two decades, much of the fabric of the city's historical center has been rewoven.

Just as astonishing to me, however, is the racial transformation of parts of the inner suburbs of Washington. While still in its early stages, the trend is manifested in many ways. For example, a visit to a suburban shopping mall near the beltway in Prince George's County brings the lesson home. Fifteen years ago black faces were few in number. Today some shopping centers are frequented by more blacks than whites. In others there is a reasonably healthy racial balance among both shoppers and store personnel. While less extensive in other suburban communities, the presence of blacks is noticeable in large areas of the inner suburbs. It is only when one visits the metropolitan fringe areas that one realizes how few blacks have settled in the new suburbs.

Tragically, there has been nothing unique about Washington's predominantly black and declining core nor about its largely white and middle-class outer suburban ring. These conditions have been all too common in metropolitan areas throughout the nation. Happily, there is nothing unique about signs of their reversal either. We are now aware that dozens of central cities have begun to experience revitalization and their suburbs, minority suburbanization. Yet, as the following pages show, the nation's capital has probably progressed further in both directions than have all but a handful of metropolitan areas in the country.

From my point of view, this (and other factors) makes Washington's very recent history instructive. Because inner-city revitalization and minority suburbanization have progressed as far as they have, Washington's experience to date may offer insights about the future of such trends in other urban areas. If one assumes that different metropolitan areas will progress at different rates in these two directions, then their relatively advanced state in the Washington area may provide helpful lessons about their later effects elsewhere. But it is important to emphasize that although Washington's experience may be instructive, it is not prophetic. Not all metropolitan areas have experienced noteworthy levels of core revitalization or suburban minority population growth. And not all will do so in the future. It is evident, though, that in many metropolitan areas—for example, Atlanta, New York, Philadelphia, San Francisco, Los Angeles, St. Louis, and New Orleans—these dynamics are already underway. In the final analysis, nevertheless, this book, part of a series on major metropolitan areas in the United States, speaks only for the Washington area. Other volumes in the series will provide perspectives that, together with the views in the present volume, contribute to a fuller understanding of the American metropolitan condition today and tomorrow.

Typically, any effort at research leaves many debts in its wake. This book is no exception to the rule. Drawing primarily on research monographs and papers, government reports, newspaper articles, and statistical files, its documentary lineage is complex and its obligations are many. Most important of all, however, has been the time for scholarly pursuits provided me by George Washington University. I am indebted to the university and especially to the Department of Urban and Regional Planning and the School of Government and Business Administration for their support during the lengthy research and writing of this book. Part of my writing was completed during a sabbatical leave in the autumn of 1985. The Center for Washington Area Studies at the university offered a quiet haven for certain periods of my work, and colleagues there stimulated my thinking as my research unfolded. The university's Gelman Library, especially the

Washingtoniana section of its Special Collections Division, provided several volumes of out-of-print material that would have been difficult, if not impossible, to obtain elsewhere.

Almost without exception, area local governments were responsive and cordial in their attempts to satisfy my seemingly endless request for documents and data sources. The District of Columbia government and its public school system, as well as the governments and school systems in Prince George's, Montgomery, Arlington, and Fairfax counties and the city of Alexandria, were generous with their time and their talent. Especially helpful were the Metropolitan Washington Council of Governments and the Greater Washington Research Center. Both institutions have enriched knowledge of public affairs in the Washington area; both were extremely helpful with the task at hand. Several documents were secured from the National Capital Planning Commission as well.

Much that was important to the subject of this book, however, could not be found in organized studies and reports. Rather, the daily newspaper was the most appropriate source from which to draw insights. In this regard I have been lucky. The *Washington Post*, with its talented staff of reporters and columnists, has supplied a wellspring of information about matters (especially political matters) of importance to my research. Most of all, it has been a source of day-to-day observations about the unfolding of life in the national capital area. As has been the case with too many American cities, however, Washington has become essentially a one-newspaper town. The other major newspaper, the *Evening Star*, folded in the early 1980s. The *Washington Times* arose in its wake, but its coverage of local news is sorely limited. Thus, to some readers perhaps, I have relied too heavily on the *Post* for coverage of certain matters such as political trends. I hope my book does not suffer too greatly from this constraint.

Finally, I am indebted to Dr. Joe T. Darden, Dean of Urban Affairs at Michigan State University and the editor of the series of which this book is a part. He has offered numerous and thoughtful suggestions and given freely of his time and insights as the various drafts of my manuscript have evolved. His patience with the tedious process of research and writing has now stretched out over three years, and his confidence in my work has been a continuous source of encouragement. To him, and to David M. Bartlett, Janet M. Francendese, Charles de Kay, JoAnne Mottola, and Joan Polsky Vidal of Temple University Press, I am indeed grateful.

SERIES PREFACE

The Comparative American Cities series grew out of a need for more comparative scholarly works on America's urban areas in the post-World War II era. American cities are storehouses of potential assets and liabilities for their residents and for society as a whole. It is important that scholars examine the nation's metropolitan areas to assess trends that may affect economic and political decision-making in the future.

The books have a contemporary approach, with the post-World War II period providing historical antecedents for current concerns. Each book generally addresses the same issues, although the peculiarities of the local environments necessarily shape each account. The major areas of concern include uneven regional development, white middle-class suburbanization, residential segregation of races and classes, and central-city issues such as economic disinvestment, black political power, and the concentration of blacks, Hispanics, and the poor. Each city in the series is viewed within the context of its metropolitan area as a whole. Taken together, these studies describe the spatial redistribution of wealth within the metropolises—the economic decline of central cities and the economic rise of the suburbs—a redistribution facilitated by the massive construction of interstate highways in the 1950s, 1960s, and 1970s.

Since World War II the metropolitan areas included in this series have been increasingly affected by uneven economic and social development and by conflict between cities and suburbs and between the white majority and the growing nonwhite minority. The central cities of each metropolitan area have also been losing jobs to the suburbs. There has been a tendency toward growing income inequality between cities and suburbs and between blacks and whites. Economic growth and decline have followed closely the racial composition of neighborhoods—that is, black neighborhoods have declined, while white neighborhoods have generally grown.

All of these studies assess the ways central-city governments have responded to these issues. In recent years most central-city elected officials have attempted to provide services and employment opportunities on a more equitable basis and to implement a more balanced and progressive economic development agenda. Most central-city mayors have been elected with the strong support of minorities, and the mayors have often cooperated with the business elite in attempts to stimulate more economic growth and to save the cities from further economic decline. Since this decline is related to structural changes in the economy within the context of uneven development, however, attempts at preventing the flow of jobs to the suburbs have largely failed, and the economic and social gap continues to widen.

There are no quick solutions to the economic, racial, and political problems of the cities in these studies. Though high-technology industries may play a part in each city's future, it is unlikely that they will produce as many jobs as are needed, or reduce the racial differences in unemployment rates. Blacks and other minorities who have limited spatial access to the areas of high-tech industries may not receive a fair share of their benefits.

Each city's plight is deeply rooted in America's problems of free-market economic investment, racial prejudice and discrimination, and the outmoded political structure that continues to separate the city from the suburbs, one suburb from another, the rich from the poor, and blacks from whites. As long as this structure remains, there is a strong probability that the situation will worsen, as population mobility continues to reinforce patterns of economic, social, and racial inequality, contributing to more racial and class conflict.

The problems of urban America require the immediate attention of government officials and the citizenry of this nation. New solutions involving changes in the political structure are long overdue. Our hope is that comparative studies such as these might provide the impetus for informed decisions and policies that will address the underlying problems besetting America's major urban areas.

Joe T. Darden, Series Editor
Comparative American Cities

Washington, D.C.

1

Introduction: Inner-City Revitalization and Minority Suburbanization

For generations American scholars have struggled to define the nature and character of American urban life. Their viewpoints, of course, have depended largely on their academic discipline, their research, and their experiences. Nonetheless, most have defined the assets and liabilities of cities and their suburbs according to circumstances of their populations, their economic foundations, or their physical environments. For example, sociologists, social historians, social geographers, demographers, and anthropologists have tended to emphasize demographic characteristics, settlement patterns, behavioral conditions, or cultural dynamics. Economists, economic geographers, and economic historians, on the other hand, have examined such matters as resource supply and demand, employment structures, and fiscal conditions in urban and metropolitan markets. Architects, architectural historians, environmental designers, landscape architects, and urban and regional planners tend to concentrate on the functional and aesthetic aspects of the built and natural elements of urbanizing areas; to a lesser extent, they may concern themselves with relationships between these matters and the populations and economic systems of particular sites, neighborhoods, communities, or regions.

It is probably beyond the reach of any single volume to combine the myriad perspectives necessary to portray the true richness and complexity of urban conditions in America. Even within a single metropolitan area, emancipated from the burden of nationwide generalizations, the scholar finds the task of capturing the most critical trends and conditions a frustrating one. Therefore, no matter how accurate a rendering he or she presents, the final product must necessarily be disappointing for its omissions, if not for its commissions.

With these thoughts in mind, I deliberately circumscribed the subject of this book in terms that render it anything but a broad sweep across the various disciplines. For example, although its geographic focus is the

Washington, D.C., metropolitan area, it makes no pretense at addressing critical matters such as intrametropolitan fiscal flows, transportation patterns, or environmental relationships. Topics such as criminal justice and public health, likewise, are absent from this book.

Rather, the purpose here is to grapple with two issues that seem central to answering the question, Why study the Washington metropolitan area at all? The first is central-city revitalization, and the second is minority suburbanization. But to fully appreciate these concerns, one must recall the characterizations of American metropolitan areas such as Washington's that had become almost routine by 1970. By that time, a quarter-century had lapsed since the end of World War II, and a massive out-migration was underway from central cities to suburbs. To be sure, we know that the urban-to-suburban flow of population was underway long before 1945, but a combination of forces converged in the late 1940s and 1950s to accelerate the pace of urban out-migration and contribute to the suburban population explosion. Theories that attempt to explain the causes of this exodus and its effects on central cities and metropolitan communities abound. But two of the most popular characterizations are the following:

1. In central cities, particularly the larger cities, out-migration of middle-class, white families was due in part to their desire to escape conditions that they deemed negative and to secure those that they felt were desirable. Among conditions viewed as undesirable were deteriorating housing and neighborhoods, the in-migration of blacks from southern rural areas, shaky property values, rising crime rates, increasing congestion and noise, parking problems, and poor schools. The departure of white families, of course, only helped to accelerate these conditions. Among the positive attributes of suburban life they expected to find were more modern and spacious housing, federal government assistance in housing finance, predominantly (if not, entirely) white populations, rising property values, low crime rates, open space and greenery, plentiful parking, and effective schools.

2. As whites secured suburban enclaves and dominated their governments and economies, it became difficult, if not impossible, for racial minorities to move to these areas. At first, they were excluded through tactics such as the inclusion of racial covenants in property deeds. After these were declared unconstitutional, other techniques prevailed, such as the practices of "steering" by real estate agents and "redlining" by lending institutions and insurance companies and the unwillingness of suburban governments to build publicly subsidized housing. On top of these, the institution of exclusionary zoning (that is, land-use policies that preclude construction of less-expensive medium- and high-density housing) further

discouraged minorities from pursuing the same suburban attributes that white families had. These conditions, in concert with the relatively high cost of suburban housing, effectively denied the large majority of minority households freedom of choice in housing.

Of course, not all whites had negative feelings about the city, and not all wanted to exclude minorities from the suburbs. Similarly, not all urban minorities brought with them the worst social problems, and many had no interest in moving to the suburbs. But as a general pattern—true far more often than not—these characterizations prevailed. As a result, by the time the United States had fought two more wars abroad, the depiction of the American metropolitan area was firmly fixed. Most of the larger central cities were continuing to lose white population to the suburbs and to gain disproportionately large minority and poverty populations. This was especially true of cities in the eastern and midwestern parts of the country. Most suburban communities, on the other hand, were characterized as overwhelmingly composed of whites of working- and middle-class backgrounds, with at most only a scintilla of residency by blacks. Certainly, Washington and most of its suburban communities conformed to these parameters.

But even as the stereotypes were reaching lapidarian proportions, the dynamics of metropolitan racial migration were already shifting in the national capital area. It took the results of the U.S. decennial census in 1980, however, to confirm the full extent of these changes. Therefore, the first mission of this volume is to explore demographic shifts and their implications for future racial settlement patterns in Washington and its suburbs. In particular, we will be concerned with the growing revitalization of Washington's core, largely by whites, and the rising presence of minorities in the metropolitan suburbs.

Underlying our interest in documenting these rather remarkable departures from earlier patterns is a curiosity about their import for future conditions in the national capital metropolitan area. In particular, it is worth probing some of the political implications of minority suburbanization and white-led revitalization. To what extent, for example, is there evidence of shifting power relationships in Washington's local political structure? What roles are minorities playing in suburban political systems? How receptive are both settings to these changes?

If politics and government are the most propitious vehicles for expressing differing racial expectations about community life, then certainly the character and quality of local public services are among the primary measures of these expectations. In particular, this study centers on public education, arguably the single most critical public service by which families (that is, households with children present) evaluate their alternatives for household location. Elements of the public school systems in Washington and some of its suburban communities are examined in studies of the differing outcomes of public policy in racially changing areas. In particular, though, the public schools are the primary crossroads at which white and minority children (and less directly, their parents) are likely to meet. The social and economic circumstances of these interactions are an important barometer of the success of both white-led, inner-city revitalization and minority suburbanization. The book is organized around these concerns.

Chapter 2 describes the primary population and demographic trends in the Washington metropolitan area between 1970 and 1980, with special attention to suburban/central-city dynamics. It includes data on the evolving employment structure, a necessary foundation for understanding socioeconomic and settlement patterns among minorities and whites. Following Chapter 2, Part One examines the deterioration and resurgence of the city's core—its business and governmental center and the surrounding ring of older neighborhoods. A brief history of decline and revitalization is presented, and recent data on the social and economic effects of revitalization are analyzed. Part One concludes with an exploration of the implications of revitalization for the city's public schools.

Part Two is concerned with the migration primarily of black, Asian, and Hispanic households to Washington's suburban counties. Earlier exclusionary tendencies are outlined, and the shifting demographic flows that became evident in the 1970s are discussed. Following these considerations is an exploration of the experiences several suburban communities have had with rising minority enrollment in the public schools. Again, the success with which school systems have coped with rapid racial and ethnic change is a focal point.

Part Three begins with a summation of the characteristics of the metropolitan area's social geography and its evolving form. It then centers on the interaction of race and politics in Washington and in one of its suburbs, Prince George's County. These case studies examine recent election results and voting systems, as well as racial balances in the memberships of elected bodies. The implications of these trends for public school policy are discussed. Chapter 12 briefly assesses the overall effect of the Washington metropolitan area's racial, socioeconomic, migratory, and political shifts. It concludes with some thoughts about future directions of change in the Washington metropolitan area.

As the following pages indicate, both inner-city revitalization and minority suburbanization have advanced about as far in the Washington metropolitan area as they have anywhere in the United States. Indeed, the national capital area is widely recognized among scholars and urban policy analysts as ranking among the nation's most experienced metropolitan areas with respect to both of these social phenomena. This fact seems to justify a study of the evidence of inner-city revitalization and minority suburbanization and their implications for the future of the Washington metropolitan area. These inquiries provide an opportunity to address the following issues: What happens when thousands of whites depart from conventional household location patterns and settle in older, declining urban neighborhoods? What happens when thousands of minorities overcome political, economic, legal, and institutional barriers and move from the central city to suburban communities? What effects do these twin conditions have on overall metropolitan form? What are some of the political and public policy outcomes?

Because the conditions of urban neighborhood decline and suburban minority exclusion have prevailed in metropolitan America for several decades, the Washington experience holds special importance. During the postwar decades many social reformers were calling for a return to the city by middle-class people and an opening up of the suburbs to blacks, Hispanics, and other disfranchised minorities. Now that these admonitions have borne fruit, it is time to assess some of the outcomes.

Of course, this is not to be construed as an argument that as goes Washington, so goes the nation. Every metropolitan area—indeed, every human settlement—is unique. Some observers feel that Washington, as the national capital, is substantially unlike other major metropolises, primarily because of its large governmental employment base and the effects this has on its economy. Indeed, as Chapter 2 points out, its share of blue-collar jobs is small, and its white-collar base is substantial. Viewed another way, however, Washington's economic base is a more advanced version of the "advanced services economies" arising in most major American metropolitan areas.[1] This condition, coupled with the Washington metropolitan area's substantial experience with inner-city revitalization and minority suburbanization, undergirds the argument that the national capital area may offer important insights into the kind of future in store for many other metropolitan areas. Thus, while no urban setting is a perfect "laboratory" from which to ponder questions about the future of American cities, Washington may be particularly revealing insofar as postindustrial metropolitan areas are concerned.

Before the reader proceeds, a few words are in order about definitions of

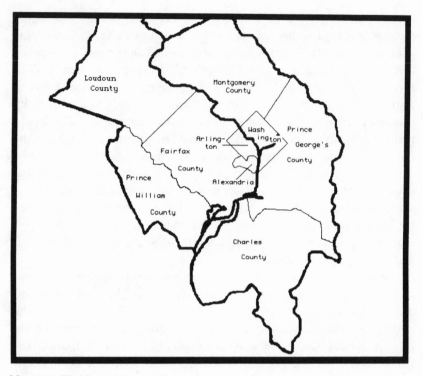

Map 1.1   Washington metropolitan area
Source: Prepared by Dennis E. Gale.

terms employed in the book. First, some people are confused about the District of Columbia (also referred to herein as the District) v. the city of Washington. While there are historical distinctions, which are interesting, they bear no importance here. Thus, the terms are used interchangeably to refer to the national capital, a central city, as defined by the U.S. Bureau of the Census.

I refer to the Standard Metropolitan Statistical Area or SMSA (now termed the Metropolitan Statistical Area by the Census Bureau) as the "metropolitan area" throughout the book (see Map 1.1). It includes not only the District of Columbia but also several suburban counties and in-corporated municipalities. The District of Columbia is located astride the boundary between Maryland and Virginia. It is abutted on its northwest, northeast, and southeast perimeters by the state of Maryland. Two coun-ties in Maryland—Montgomery and Prince George's—lie adjacent to the District. Farther south is Charles County. Across the Potomac River on Washington's southwest side is Virginia, to which the city is linked by several bridges and a set of subway tunnels. Along the Virginia side of the river are Arlington County and the city of Alexandria; encircling them is the greater expanse of Fairfax County. Like Charles County in Maryland, Loudoun and Prince William counties in Virginia are outlying jurisdictions that have been added to the Census Bureau's definition of the Washington SMSA in the past decade. Hence, while Montgomery, Prince George's, Arlington, and Fairfax counties and the city of Alexandria compose the older suburbs around Washington, Charles, Loudoun, and Prince William counties are considered the newly suburbanizing areas. The former group will be referred to as the "inner tier" suburbs and the latter group, as the "second tier" or "outer tier" suburbs.

I have made no attempt to deal with individual suburban municipalities (with the exception of the city of Alexandria) but rather have simply treated them as part of the primary form of governance around Washington, the counties. Therefore, readers will find few references to suburban communities below the level of the county. My reasoning was simply to preclude unnecessary detail and limit the length of the book to manageable proportions.

Each of the counties around Washington, in both Virginia and Maryland, is governed by an elected county council or board of supervisors. Each employs a county executive, who exercises day-to-day management over county operations. School boards are separate institutions responsible solely for local public education, and each employs a superintendent as chief executive. Alexandria, Virginia and the District of Columbia each have an elected mayor and an elected city council.

Having established these definitions, I can now begin with an overview of major population and employment trends in the Washington metropolitan area.

2

Suburban Central-City Population and Employment Trends

Historical Antecedents

The national capital was relocated from Philadelphia to the shores of the Potomac River during the early 1790s, and a plan was prepared by Frenchman Pierre Charles L'Enfant. With subsequent modifications, the plan became the authority around which decisions about the growth and development of the federal city were made. At first, Washington was overshadowed by its older and more prosperous neighbor, Georgetown. A small but successful river port, Georgetown traded primarily agricultural products with ports along the Potomac and the Chesapeake Bay. In 1828 work was begun on the Chesapeake and Ohio Canal, which, when completed, linked Georgetown to Cumberland, Maryland, 184 miles to the northeast. As elsewhere in the United States, however, the canal could not compete successfully with the railroad, and gradually Georgetown's economy eroded. Meanwhile, the federal city grew in size and economic might. With the end of the Civil War, confidence in the persistence of the national government was reinforced, many federal government buildings were constructed, and the city experienced rapid urbanization.

Washington never had significant industrial manufacturing activities and thus never became highly dependent on factory work to sustain its economy. Many of its poor and working-class citizens earned their livings in personal services, as domestics, launderers/laundresses, or gardeners, for example. It was not a city such as Boston, New York, Philadelphia, Baltimore, Chicago, or Cincinnati, each of which exported large volumes of manufactured commodities to regional or national markets. Neither did it resemble such cities in its population. While several nationalities were represented in its citizenry, their numbers were relatively small when compared with the huge communities of Irish, Italian, Jewish, German, and Polish immigrants in many of the large industrial cities.

Table 2.1   Population in the Washington metropolitan area,
1950, 1960, 1970, and 1980[a] (Number of people in thousands)

Jurisdiction	1950	1960	1970	1980
Washington SMSA	1,464.0	2,064.4	2,893.5	3,039.0
District of Columbia	802.2	764.0	756.7	638.3
Virginia				
Arlington	135.4	163.4	174.3	152.6
Alexandria	61.8	91.0	110.9	103.2
Fairfax[b]	106.0	272.7	487.1	625.8
Loudoun	—	24.5	37.2	57.4
Prince William	—	50.2	95.1	144.7
Maryland				
Montgomery	164.4	340.9	522.8	579.1
Prince George's	194.2	357.7	661.7	665.1
Charles	—	—	47.7	72.8

Source: John C. McClain and Jay Langford, "Cooperative Forecasting, Round III Summary Report—1984," Washington, D.C.; Metropolitan Washington Council of Governments, 1984, p. 5.

a. Loudoun and Prince William counties became part of the SMSA in 1960 and Charles County in 1970. Frederick, Stafford and Calvert counties, not included here, were added in 1980. Their combined population in 1980 was 189.9.

b. Includes Fairfax County, Fairfax City and Falls Church.

Both Washington's black and white populations grew steadily throughout the late nineteenth century, and rising federal employment during World War I and the New Deal attracted thousands more to settle in the national capital. Railroad and streetcar service to the Maryland suburbs from the 1860s onward extended Washington's sphere of influence. As new neighborhoods and roads were added to its perimeter with the rise of automobile commuting, the city increasingly took on many of the characteristics of other large urban centers in the United States.

This trend was especially apparent during the post–World War II era in Washington, a period that found it losing population in its central city while undergoing explosive population growth in its rapidly spreading suburbs. At least since the late 1940s, when the city's population surpassed 800,000, it has experienced varying population losses. From 1950 to 1960 approximately 5 percent of the District's population was lost, followed in the next decade by a marginal decrease of almost 1 percent (see Table 2.1)[1] But from 1970 to 1980 the rate of decline leaped forward. A net loss of 118,000 persons (16 percent) occurred, leaving the city with a population of about 638,000.

Meanwhile, suburban growth rates were moving in the opposite direction. The metropolitan-area population outside Washington rose by almost 639,000 people (96 percent) in the decade of the 1950s. In the next decade it grew by more than 836,000 persons (64 percent). Thus, for two decades the relationship of the city to its suburbs was one of moderate city decline accompanied by rapid suburban growth. But the decade of the 1970s witnessed a shifting of this relationship. For just as the District's rate of population decline increased enormously, so also did the suburban area's rate of population growth decrease. About 264,000 people (12 percent) were added to the suburban population during the decade. (Because Frederick, Stafford, and Calvert counties did not become a part of the SMSA until 1980, they were omitted from the present analysis.) In short, the city was losing population (16 percent) at a slightly faster rate than the suburbs were gaining it.

Comparable to many other SMSAs, in the 1970s the rate of growth in the capital metropolitan area declined from that of the 1960–1970 period (40.2 percent), when about 829,000 people were added. By 1980 there were 3,039,000 people living in the Washington Standard Metropolitan Statistical Area (SMSA), a gain of almost 146,000 people (5 percent). The distribution of population change, however, varied drastically from central city to suburb. As with many large central cities, the District of Columbia has been losing population while its suburban area has been gaining. By 1980 the District and Fairfax, Montgomery, and Prince George's counties each had about one-fifth of the metropolitan area's population (see Table 2.1). Arlington County and the city of Alexandria, comprising the remainder of the inner tier of suburban jurisdictions, had 5 and 3 percent, respectively. The remaining 9 percent of population was distributed in the second tier of jurisdictions, composed of Loudoun, Prince William, and Charles counties. Therefore, the District and its adjacent jurisdictions composed about 91 percent of the SMSA population in 1980.

Even though overall suburban population was growing during the 1970s, growth was differentially distributed. By 1980 Arlington and Alexandria had lost 12.4 percent and 6.9 percent, respectively, of their 1970 populations. Prince George's County gained by less than 1 percent in that period. In Montgomery County, population increased by almost 11 percent, however, and Fairfax County's population rose by almost one-third (28.5 percent). In the second tier of Virginia counties—each characterized by rapidly suburbanizing rural areas—each county's population increased by slightly more than 50 percent. The second tier of Maryland counties merge with the Baltimore metropolitan area and are not considered part of the Washington SMSA. Nonetheless, they too have experienced similarly rapid growth rates.

Therefore, the overriding population characteristic that has emerged in the national capital metropolitan region since midcentury is one of centrifugal growth pressure. The locus of rapid population growth rippled outward from the center, where it was confined until about 1950. As this dynamic peaked and was followed by population decline in Washington, the locus of rapid population growth next centered in parts of the inner tier of counties during the 1950s and 1960s. In the most recent stage, rapid population increase has left most of these jurisdictions as they struggle toward stability or perhaps (following the lead of the District) gradual decline. Drifting farther outward, the wave of rising population has reached the second tier of counties. To the south and west of this tier, plentiful agricultural land in the outlying fringe areas of Virginia guarantees the continuation of suburban spread for many years to come. But to the east of the tier, the rapidly converging Baltimore and Washington metropolitan areas—part of the "Boswash" (Boston–Washington) megalopolis—suggest a somewhat finite long-term future for the spread of the metropolitan region of the nation's capital in that direction.

Demographic Patterns

While the changing dynamics of population growth and decline present several public policy issues to Washington-area leaders, even more pressing issues are presented by some of the qualitative conditions related to the composition of the population. Among those that have brought the closest scrutiny are shifts in age structure, household size, and socioeconomic characteristics.

An Aging Population

Within the Washington metropolitan area, the shifting age structure of the population has paralleled national trends during the 1970s. Although there has been a drop in the population of children and teenagers, the adult population (that is, those over age 17) has grown significantly (see Table 2.2). The number of infants and children aged 4 or younger decreased by 26.9 percent (68,777) during the decade, while that of children aged 5 to

Table 2.2 Number of people, by age cohorts, in the Washington metropolitan area, 1970 and 1980

Jurisdiction	1970				1980			
	0–4	5–17	18–64	65+	0–4	5–17	18–64	65+
Washington SMSA	255,218	730,569	1,703,437	171,899	186,441	610,992	1,964,031	226,707
District of Columbia	59,735	164,371	461,601	70,803	34,365	109,126	420,555	74,287
Virginia								
Arlington	11,946	29,618	119,114	13,606	6,889	18,080	109,948	17,682
Alexandria	9,843	20,785	72,959	7,351	5,486	13,452	74,814	9,465
Fairfax	43,713	147,528	281,275	15,247	39,904	142,311	414,206	29,385
Loudoun	3,881	10,692	19,741	2,836	4,261	14,576	34,716	3,874
Prince William	13,776	35,359	59,199	2,768	15,743	44,305	102,016	4,601
Maryland								
Montgomery	43,074	145,935	301,181	32,619	33,374	120,937	373,837	50,905
Prince George's	69,250	176,281	388,367	26,669	46,419	148,205	433,939	36,508

Source: John C. McClain, Jr., and Roger Wentz, "Population, Households and Housing Unit Characteristics of Metropolitan Washington, 1980," COG Census Report 2, Metropolitan Washington Council of Governments, Washington, D.C., 1982, tables 2–5.

17 tapered off by 16.4 percent (119,577). Meanwhile, working-age adults (that is, those aged 18 to 64) increased their proportions by 15.3 percent (260,594) and those aged 65 or older, by 31.9 percent (54,808).[2]

By jurisdiction, the age structure is differentiated, however. A very consistent pattern is apparent in the Washington area. In the District of Columbia there was a sharp drop in the share of young people under age 18, accompanied by a smaller decline among working-age adults and a very slight gain among the elderly. In the older inner suburban communities of Arlington and Alexandria, there were similarly large proportional decreases among young people and similarly marginal changes among working-age adults. But these jurisdictions were unlike the District in that they had notable gains in their percentages of elderly citizens. Montgomery and Prince George's counties, encircling the District on its Maryland perimeter, also experienced significant proportional declines among young people but had countervailing increases among their shares of working-age adults and even larger gains among the elderly. In Fairfax County, the most rapidly urbanizing inner-tier jurisdiction during the 1970s, the percentage decline among young people was marginal. But there were even larger proportional gains among working-age adults and the elderly than in Montgomery and Prince George's counties. Finally, the second-tier counties showed substantial population growth among all three age cohorts.[3]

The pattern of age-structure shifts, then, is fairly consistent in the Washington metropolis. In every community the elderly have increased their representation, although the sharpest gains have been outside the older core communities of Washington, Arlington, and Alexandria. On the other hand, these three jurisdictions have had the greatest proportional declines among young people, followed by significant, though less substantial, reductions in the maturing suburban counties of Montgomery and Prince George's. The more recently suburbanizing Fairfax County is perhaps pivotal in age-structure circumstances because its pattern falls between that of the maturing counties and the rapidly growing second-tier counties. Hence, it has shown virtually no change in its population of young people but continues to have larger increases among adult and elderly residents. The second-tier counties, on the other hand, have had growth in all three age cohorts.

The general profile of age-structure shifts in the Washington metropolitan region during the past decade indicates that the greater a community's age, the greater the propensity toward increasing dominance by an older population. And, of course, the corollary is that as a community ages, the kinds of issues that tend to predominate in the public realm reflect the concerns of an older population. Yet recent evidence has shown that the aging trend so preeminent during the early 1970s may have been moderating somewhat during the late 1970s and 1980s in the city of Washington. There, an increase of 15 percent occurred in the total number of births between 1980 and 1981. This shift was part of a reversal of declining birth trends that had been underway throughout much of the 1970s. However, among women over age 30 the birth rate was rising most rapidly. Between 1975 and 1981 it rose by 40 percent in this age group.[4] Thus, a growing number of women nearing the end of their reproductive years who have a desire to have children may help to moderate the aging pattern, at least in the central city. (Birth rates in the District will be explored further in Chapter 6.)

Shrinking Household Size

A second demographic condition in the Washington metropolitan area was declining household size. Again paralleling national trends, the Washington metropolis witnessed a shrinking of average household size from 3.09 persons in 1970 to 2.67 ten years later. Thus, in only ten years the average household was diminished in size by almost 14 percent. The area experienced a 63 percent increase in one-person households and a 31 percent gain in two-person households. Households made up of three or four persons increased by 19 percent. Notably, it was households made up of five or more persons that declined in number (−24 percent).[5] Simply put, the smaller the household size, the greater the increase in its relative frequency.

Among jurisdictions there were unmistakable variations. While all jurisdictions gained one-person households, the District of Columbia was the only one to lose two-person households. Although the loss rate, 6 percent, was modest, it perhaps signified the greater desirability of suburban living even for couples without children. The rate of increase in two-person households ranged from zero percent in Arlington County to over 100 percent in Fairfax and Prince William counties.[6]

In the category of three- or four-person households, the District, Arlington, and Alexandria all had losses in the 10 to 20 percent range. Meanwhile, Montgomery and Prince George's counties gained 27 and 11 percent, respectively. Fairfax County, not as completely suburbanized, realized an increase of 49 percent in its number of households made up of three or four persons. The outlying second-tier jurisdictions of Loudoun and Prince William counties, the most recently suburbanizing, each experienced almost a doubling of its number of these households. Finally, only Loudoun and Prince William counties had increases in households of five or more persons, and these gains were negligible. All the remaining jurisdictions had net losses of the larger households.[7]

In the case of household size, the general rule in the Washington metropolitan area during the 1970s was that the older and more densely settled the community, the more appealing it was to single people and small households. Conversely, the younger and more sparsely settled the community, the more attractive it was to conventional family-sized households. Larger households, characteristic of extended-family living arrangements, were becoming much scarcer throughout most of the metropolitan area.

One major factor related to the increasing incidence of smaller households was the drastic rise in divorces and separations both nationally and locally during the past decade. The number of divorced and separated people in the Washington metropolitan area grew by 79 percent in the past decade, while the number of family households with children and only one parent present increased by 90 percent.[8]

*Socioeconomic Status: Washington
and Other Large SMSAs*

Along with an aging population and declining household size, the national
capital metropolitan area has an overall level of socioeconomic status that
is uncommon by national standards. For example, it has a relatively highly
educated population. In 1980 about one-third of the people aged 25 and
older in the SMSA had a four-year-college degree. By comparison, only
16 percent of such people nationwide had equivalent credentials. Even in
the city of Washington itself, almost 28 percent of those 25 and older had a
college education. This was a slight increase over the 1970 level of 23
percent.[9]

A high level of educational achievement combined with a large white-
collar labor force have conspired to raise income levels to among the
highest in the nation. In 1979 the area median household income of
$23,344 was 39 percent higher than that of the nation as a whole ($16,830).
Among major metropolitan areas with populations of 2 million or more,
the capital area ranked first in income. Minneapolis–Saint Paul, ranking
second highest, had a $20,890 median household income. The remaining
12 SMSAs ranged from Houston's $20,587 to New York's $15,613.[10] Thus,
not only is the Washington metropolis first in median income but it is
so by the considerable margin of more than $2,400 over second-place
Minneapolis–Saint Paul.

Similarly, a comparison of 1979 per capita incomes in large metropolitan areas reveals that Washington's is the highest. At $10,223, the national
capital metropolitan area exceeds second-place San Francisco–Oakland's
$9,815 income. The remaining SMSAs ranged from Houston's $8,999 to
Baltimore's $7,501. In rate of growth in median income between 1969 and
1979, Washington's metropolitan area was exceeded only by the metropolitan areas of Houston and Pittsburgh. Thus, while Houston's median income rose by 135 percent and Pittsburgh's by 125 percent, the Washington
metropolitan area's expanded by 113 percent, about the same growth rate
as in San Francisco–Oakland and Minneapolis–Saint Paul.[11]

Among Washington's suburban communities, Fairfax and Montgomery
counties had household incomes that ranked them fifth ($30,011) and sixth
($28,987), respectively, in comparison with over 3,000 counties, boroughs,
and independent cities in the United States. Two other Washington-area
jurisdictions—Prince William County and Fairfax City—ranked among
the highest 25 in the nation in this comparison.[12] Similarly, in measures of

per capita income in 1979, 5 Washington-area cities or counties ranked among the upper 11 jurisdictions of the nation. These were Falls Church and Alexandria and Arlington, Fairfax, and Montgomery counties.[13]

Nevertheless, as local observers often hasten to point out, even though Washington-area incomes are relatively high, so is the cost of living. In 1960 the Consumer Price Index (CPI) for urban consumers in the Washington SMSA ranked slightly below the average CPI (88.7) in a study of 85 metropolitan areas nationally. By 1970, however, the capital metropolitan area exceeded the national CPI and has generally remained higher ever since. For example, in 1978 its CPI was 197, compared with the national metropolitan-area average of 195.4.[14]

One major expenditure for Washington-area households is housing, a commodity that rode the inflationary cycles of the past decade. Between 1970 and 1974, for example, the median value of a single-family house in the SMSA rose approximately 74 percent, while the median income of homeowners increased by 43 percent. Nationally, single-family homes rose 59 percent in value, while median incomes increased by 32 percent.[15] Throughout the 1970s this pattern of housing expenses consuming a larger and larger share of income continued to place limits on real purchasing power. Therefore, overall living costs in the capital have outpaced those in most other parts of the nation.

*Socioeconomic Status: Variation within
the Washington SMSA*

In spite of the relatively high socioeconomic status of Washington's metropolitan population nationally, communities within the metropolitan area of Washington have varied considerably in terms such as income. The District of Columbia, for example, had a 1979 per capita personal income of $12,050; yet lower than the District was Prince George's County, with a comparable figure of $10,400. Highest in the area was Arlington County at $17,690. Montgomery County, with a per capita personal income of $15,641 and Alexandria, at $15,955, trailed considerably. In Fairfax County the comparable figure was $13,403.[16] Thus, it is clear that the District and Prince George's County had substantially lower income levels than the remaining jurisdictions. But even at this level the range of variation among population subgroups such as racial minorities is masked. (Chapter 7 explores this theme in some detail.)

One indication of this variation is the status of poor families. The District of Columbia continues to have the largest share of families in the

Table 2.3   Families with incomes below the poverty level
in the Washington metropolitan area, 1969 and 1979

	1969		1979	
Jurisdiction	Number of families	Percentage of jurisdiction	Number of families	Percentage of jurisdiction
Washington SMSA	41,949	NA	44,350	NA
District of Columbia	20,787	12.7	20,507	15.1
Virginia				
Arlington	1,687	3.7	1,656	4.5
Alexandria	1,836	6.4	1,651	6.7
Fairfax	4,000	3.5	4,824	3.0
Loudoun	873	9.6	750	4.8
Prince William	1,461	5.6	1,922	4.1
Maryland				
Montgomery	4,011	3.0	4,661	3.0
Prince George's	7,031	4.3	8,137	4.8

Source: Ronald Kessler, "Number of Poor Families Down in D.C., Up in Suburbs," *Washington Post*, February 9, 1984, p. C4.
NA = not available.

SMSA with incomes at or below the federally set poverty line (see Table 2.3); in 1969 there were almost 20,800 such families. But ten years later the number was almost unchanged (20,500), even though the city's overall population declined by about 16 percent. Therefore, by 1979 the poor made up an even larger share of Washington's population (15.1 percent) than they had ten years earlier (12.7 percent).[17]

In the suburbs there was a slight increase in poverty over the same period, from approximately 21,200 families in 1969 to 23,800 in 1979, a gain of about 13 percent. By the end of the last decade, therefore, the number of poverty-level families living in the District of Columbia was only slightly smaller than the number living throughout the *entire remainder* of the metropolitan area.[18]

One factor that accounts for poverty increases throughout the SMSA is the large rise in divorce and separation. The proportion of the total population aged 15 years and older who were divorced in 1970 was slightly above 3 percent; by 1980 the figure had doubled to 6.4 percent.[19] The fragmentation of many families into two or more households of single adults or single parents with children (especially in the case of unemployed females) led to an increase in the number of poverty-level families.

Shifting Racial Migration Patterns

Just as there are wide disparities in demographic circumstances between city and suburb, so also are there varying patterns of racial settlement. Recent evidence has suggested that the postwar pattern of racial migration may be changing in the national capital metropolitan area.

Historical Antecedents

In 1950 about 35 percent of the District's population was black, while in the suburbs the proportion was approximately 9 percent. By 1960 54 percent of the city and 7 percent of the suburbs were black. Only one suburban jurisdiction, Alexandria, had as much as a 12 percent black population. The remaining communities ranged between 2 and 9 percent black.[20] After World War II the city's white population began to decline. From 510,000 in 1950, it had dropped to 345,000 by 1960. The black population, on the other hand, had been rising steadily ever since 1920. Between 1920 and 1960 it rose almost fourfold, from 110,000 to 412,000.[21]

Although both patterns have had their metropolitan counterparts across the nation, there are now signs that the city of Washington has been experiencing a partial reversal. In short, it appears that whites have been moving into the District at about the same rate as those moving out. But there is clear evidence that blacks have been moving out of the city in numbers far in excess of those moving in.

During the period 1965–1970 net white migration amounted to the departure of more than 51,000 whites from Washington, but from 1975 to 1980 this tidal wave had ebbed to the point where about 500 more whites had moved into the city than had moved out. Conversely, while net out-migration of blacks during 1965–1970 reached 8,600, by 1975–1980 it had soared to over 55,000. Overall, the city's net out-migration had slowed slightly from almost 59,800 during the late 1960s to more than 55,400 in the late 1970s.[22]

While it is too early to determine whether Washington has since reached a long-term, stable state in its white migration pattern, it is clear that blacks are now able to choose between urban and suburban living to a much greater degree than was true in the 1950s and 1960s. Moreover, another encouraging sign for Washington's future emerged very recently. The U.S. Census Bureau estimated that the District's total population held steady at 623,000 in 1983 and 1984; this followed annual declines since 1967.[23] Whether the city has "bottomed out" in its loss of predominantly middle-class families is too early to tell. If so, however, it is a positive signal that perhaps some of the worst reactions to urban life in the Washington area have passed. (Chapter 7 traces suburban racial conditions in greater detail.)

From "Company Town" to Advanced-Services Economy

Unlike most major metropolitan areas in the United States, the Washington SMSA has not been viewed historically as an industrially based metropolis. The presence of the federal government, of course, has given a strong public-sector identity to the economy. Consequently, the capital city has been viewed by many observers as a "company town"—the "company" being the federal government. The conventional wisdom held that everybody, or nearly everybody, worked for the federal government. In fact, the federal government has been the largest employer of Washington's labor force for many years. But even during the early years of this century, Washington had a strong and relatively prosperous local business community. Unlike most industrial cities, though, Washington's manufacturing sector exported relatively few products to domestic or international markets. In this role it was vastly overshadowed by Baltimore, only an hour's drive to the northeast. Thus, business had a distinctly local cast, and Washington's commercial and industrial sectors tended to provide goods and services largely to the city's own immediate region.

To be sure, the public sector of Washington's economy dominated local employment and income dynamics. Especially during the New Deal, World War II, and Great Society eras, federal employment rose substantially. But white-collar employment in the private sector has risen drastically as well. In recent years the area's economy has produced a more diverse mixture of goods and services, and the relationship between public and private employment has shifted somewhat. This section traces recent employment trends in the Washington area.

Federal Employment

Since the late 1950s federal government employment has risen fairly steadily. In fact, the total number of federal employees in the national capital metropolitan area rose from 285,000 to 419,000 between 1950 and 1980, a gain of 47 percent. While military employment has been a major influence on the Washington economy during wartime, it has had only a moderate effect on long-term trends. The net increase in military personnel from 1950 to 1980 was less than 2,000 workers (3 percent).[24] In fact, the military work force, peaking in the Vietnam War era, began a long decline in 1970 and levelled out at slightly less than 58,000 employees in 1980. The largest share of employment gains in the three decades since 1950 has been confined to civilian employment, which increased by 133,000 workers (58 percent). Most of the civilian federal employment was confined to the executive branch, which constituted about 89 percent of all nonmilitary employment in the national capital area in 1980.[25]

Geographically, the largest share of federal employment in the metropolitan area continues to be located in the city of Washington. In 1980, 58 percent of the metropolitan federal civilian labor force (or 243,000 workers) was carrying out its duties in the central city. During the 1960s a deliberate effort by the federal government to decentralize employment (in response to the threat of nuclear attack) brought about a rapid rise in suburban employment trends. Thus, there was a 90 percent increase in federal employment in Maryland and a 52 percent increase in Virginia between 1960 and 1970, but only a 12 percent gain in the capital. Nevertheless, during the 1970s this pattern abated; federal civilian employment in Maryland rose by only 6 percent, and that in Virginia actually declined by 13 percent.[26]

Nonfederal Employment

Slightly more than one-third (36 percent) of the Washington labor force was made up of government employees by 1980. Of this figure, the federal government composed the largest share of public-sector employment (26 percent). Employment at other levels of government made up the remaining 10 percent. Approximately two-thirds of the Washington-area employment base was constituted by private-sector jobs.[27]

Less than one-fourth of the local economy was based on manufacturing, construction, transportation, and wholesale and retail employment—subsectors that are more strongly represented in most major employment markets in the United States. The largest single subsector of manufacturing employment, for example, was printing and publishing—no surprise to those who witness the tidal waves of newsletters, reports, magazines, books, and maps produced each year in the capital. Yet printing and publishing made up slightly more than 1 percent of total local employment in the capital metropolitan area in 1980.[28] A larger share of local employment in industries with traditionally heavy concentrations of blue-collar workers exists in construction and transportation. But only about 4 percent of local employment was composed by construction and 2 percent by transportation in 1980.[29]

Even the wholesale trades, a traditionally labor-intensive area for unskilled and semiskilled workers, made up slightly less than 3 percent of local employment. A larger employment sector was retail trades. Including employers such as food stores, auto dealers, gas stations, eating and drinking establishments, furniture stores, and building equipment and hardware outlets, retail trades constituted almost 14 percent of all local employment in 1980.[30]

By 1980 the Washington metropolitan area's employment base had reached the point where one-fourth of all workers were employed in private-sector services.[31] For the most part, these jobs encompassed what has come to be known as the advanced-services sector.[32] Included are business, health, educational, legal, and social services, as well as membership organizations such as professional societies and trade associations.

Evidence of the relative strength of the advanced services in the national capital metropolitan area is provided in a recent study comparing the ten SMSAs in the United States with the highest share of their respective labor forces in executive, professional, and technical occupations in 1980. Washington was found to rank first. Forty percent of its SMSA labor force worked in these fields. There were several occupations that were at least twice as likely to be found in the Washington metropolitan area as in the nation as a whole. These included several categories of scientists, as well as engineers, management analysts, computer professionals, lawyers, statistical workers, personnel and labor relations workers, authors, editors and reporters, economists, architects, urban planners, and public administrators.[33]

Not only has the Washington metropolitan area become a center for occupations such as these but it has also become the locus of substantial corporate and industrial interests. To be sure, it is not a major area for corporate headquarters as is New York City. But it has vastly increased its share of trade association headquarters. For example, it was estimated that in the early 1970s New York had 31 percent of all trade associations in the nation and Washington had 21 percent. By the early 1980s, however, 21 percent were located in New York and 28 percent in the nation's capital. Today there are approximately 1,700 trade associations in the Washington metropolitan area.[34]

Recent Employment Trends

The preceding discussion has described a long-term trend toward comparatively vigorous expansion in advanced services and civilian government jobs in the Washington employment market. Nonetheless, this robust pattern has not been uniform throughout the postwar decades. Indeed, whereas overall employment in the Washington metropolitan area grew at *two and a half times* the national rate from 1967 to 1977, it declined to a rate only slightly faster than the nation's in the period from 1977 to 1981. In 1982, as was the case with most urban economies in the nation, the Washington metropolitan area suffered. The combined effects of the recession and the Reagan administration reduction in federal employment resulted in a net loss of 10,400 jobs. However, during 1983, 23,300 jobs were added to the employment base, 93 percent of which were in the private sector.[35]

Doubtless, the Washington metropolitan area economy gives many observers the impression that unemployment is relatively low. But the problem of unemployment is linked not to the rather robust growth in employment in the advanced services but, instead, to the loss of jobs in unskilled and semiskilled blue-collar fields or to lagging growth in skilled trades and lower-level clerical and technical occupations. In effect, the mismatch between the skill levels of Washington's unemployed population (largely low-and moderate-income) and the needs of government and advanced-services employers has led to a tragic situation with distinct geographical dimensions.

Unemployment and the Metropolitan Job Base

When the District of Columbia's unemployment rate (8.9 percent in June 1984) is compared with that of many older industrial cities of the "frostbelt" region, it appears relatively modest. Never having had a large export manufacturing base, the city has never become highly dependent on such employers. Yet its blue-collar population, most of which is black, has found work in a variety of unskilled and semiskilled occupations, such as busing and waiting on tables, gardening, working as domestics and porters, driving trucks and taxis, and doing public transit, warehouse, or construction work. Others have found skilled work in the building and repair trades. In more recent years many have found work with local and federal government agencies as sanitation workers, building superintendents, security guards, and postal service employees. Unlike blue-collar employees in most industrial cities, those in Washington have worked largely in businesses serving primarily a local and regional market. Few goods have been exported to other regional markets in the nation or abroad.

But while government and advanced-services jobs continue to rise in prevalence, those appropriate to the skills of school dropouts, and even to the skills of many high school graduates, have not kept pace with demand. Thus, though low by some standards, the District's unemployment rate is still a prime local public policy issue. Since 1970 the city's rate has exceeded the national rate in 10 out of 14 years.[36] In June of 1984, while the city's rate was 8.9 percent, the national rate was 7.1 percent.[37]

The irony, however, is within the capital metropolitan region itself, where suburban communities had unemployment rates ranging from 2.9 to 4.1 percent in June 1984. Although the city's unemployment has declined from its high of 12.8 percent during the 1982–1983 recession, it continues at this writing to be at least twice the suburban rate.[38] One result is that there are numerous jobs for young and relatively unskilled people in some parts of Washington's metropolitan area that go unfilled. Employers in Montgomery and Fairfax counties have complained that they have had few applicants for clerical jobs, for example, from workers who live in the District.[39] Yet in the District only jobs requiring advanced education or training are plentiful. In part, the problem of unfilled suburban jobs is due to the decline in numbers of teenagers and young adults discussed above. Yet even though there is a current surplus of jobs in the capital's suburbs, unemployment in the central city continues to plague the District government.

When Washington's new Metro rail transit system was first opened in 1976, many urban planners and public officials had placed great faith in it as a means of bolstering the area's economy. It was thought that new investment and development would occur in many station locations and that the system would make it easier for Washington's chronically unemployed to commute to new job opportunities in the metropolitan area. One recent study has shown, though, that employment growth in commercial neighborhoods around Metro stations has lagged behind overall metropolitan employment growth. In fact, between 1976 and 1980 station-area job growth rose only 2.9 percent in the central city but ranged from 7.4 to 30.5 percent in suburban jurisdictions.[40] Not only had Washington's employment gains not kept pace but it was found that the greatest increases in accessibility to employment were realized in inner-tier suburban communities; only slight gains in accessibility accrued to residents in the central area of Washington.[41] Unless this pattern has improved since 1980, the most recent date for which accessibility data are available, it appears that the Metro system has had little effect on Washington's central-city unemployment rate.

Suburban/Central-City Population and Employment

If one were to look no further than the previous discussion, it would not be unreasonable to conclude that, comparatively speaking, the national capital metropolitan area is dominated by middle- and upper-class opportunities. It boasts one of the healthiest metropolitan economies, with a level of income and occupational standards that would be difficult to match almost anywhere else. Smaller families and more two-worker households have boosted economic opportunities for many urban and suburban households. The federal government has provided a substantial buffer against the pitch and yaw of national economic trends, and private-sector job growth has served to further stabilize the economy.

The Washington metropolitan area's relatively large middle-class has been in the forefront of the evolving pattern of reversals in metropolitan racial migration dynamics. As more college-educated people have moved to the capital region—in part a legacy of the baby boom "bulge" in the national population—patterns that held sway for 20 years or more have begun to show signs of change. It would be difficult to conclude from these observations that, overall, people in the Washington metropolitan area are *not* better off today than they were two or three decades ago. Yet, as noted, there are still many people, urban residents in particular, who suffer from poverty and unemployment. In the Washington metropolitan area, as in most major metropolitan areas of the country, the disparities between classes often take on racial dimensions.

In short, the national capital metropolitan area has progressed in directions that comport with goals often cited by those in the Civil Rights and War on Poverty movements of the 1950s and 1960s. As subsequent portions of this book will show, opportunities for minorities to live in suburban communities have increased. The willingness of middle-class whites to live in the central city has risen. Parts of the downtown and many neighborhoods—beset with disinvestment, riots, and physical decline in the 1960s—have undergone substantial revitalization. Moreover, black politicians have risen to power in the central city and some suburban governments.

As mentioned in Chapter 1, the remainder of this book is divided into three parts. The purpose of these sections is to describe and analyze shifting patterns of socioeconomic and racial restructuring as they have occurred in Washington's inner core and its surrounding suburbs. Part One, which follows, will explore the economic, social, and physical dimensions of urban decline and revitalization in Washington. It will also enrich the previous profile on metropolitan demographic and employment patterns, elaborating on the disparities between the "haves" and "have nots" in the city of Washington.

Part One

Deterioration and Revitalization in the Central City

3

The Decline and Rise of the
Central Business District

Like so many metropolitan downtowns during the mid-twentieth century, the national capital's downtown began to experience serious signs of decline at least as early as the post-World War II era. Except for the federal mall area, which includes the White House, the Capitol and several galleries, museums, and government office buildings, the downtown of the central city (see Map 3.1) was composed mostly of myriad post-bellum commercial buildings and a collection of pre-World War II office and retail structures. Little new construction was occurring in this area. Indeed, in the entire decade of the 1950s only seven private buildings were constructed in the downtown.[1]

Because the height of buildings in the capital has been controlled by Congress since 1899, the downtown was marked by an absence of the skyscrapers so characteristic of most large urban centers in the United States. Also, the grid system of streets, a monotonous trademark of most American cities, was relieved by the discipline of Pierre Charles L'Enfant's eighteenth-century plan for the capital city. More or less respected by subsequent plans, L'Enfant's street grid was overlaid with a baroque tracery of diagonal streets, several of which intersected at focal points such as Dupont, Sheridan, Scott, and Washington circles. The pattern of grid and diagonal has given a distinctive identity to the District of Columbia's downtown. While the grid provides for ready circulation, access, and land subdivision, diagonal streets such as Pennsylvania, New York, and Massachusetts avenues delineate downtown boundaries and lend a sense of dramatic perspective to the area.

Retail Area Decline

Even with height restrictions and monumental street patterns, the effects of neglect and disinvestment on the downtown overwhelmed these aes-

Map 3.1   Washington's old and new downtowns
Source: Prepared by Dennis E. Gale.

thetic and functional attributes. The retail area, located to the north and
south of F Street, reflected both the effects of metropolitan growth and the
racial divisions that were the legacy of *de jure* and *de facto* segregation.
With the rapid expansion of the Maryland and Virginia suburbs during
the 1950s and 1960s, Washington experienced the loss of many businesses,
primarily as a result of poor sales. Some businesses were simply liquidated,
and others were relocated to other parts of the city or to the suburbs. As
the downtown's position as the regional center of retail sales succumbed to
the newly arising suburban shopping malls, downtown businesses such as
department stores diverted expansion to those more promising outlying
locations. Thus, neither retail employment nor sales were increasing as
rapidly in the downtown as in the suburban shopping enclaves. This dy-

namic imposed a drain on Washington's retail corridor, contributing to economic stagnation and physical decline.

More or less concurrent with these economic shifts was the rapid in-migration of black households to the city of Washington. For example, in 1950 blacks composed 35 percent of the city's population; by 1960 they made up 54 percent. As a result, the downtown received growing patronage from blacks.[2] With the success of civil rights efforts in the 1950s and 1960s, restaurants and retail stores gradually ended racially restrictive practices and increased the number of blacks on employment rolls.[3]

Suburban growth patterns and changes in the city's racial profile were accompanied by a third trend. The historical location of most government office buildings in the capital was along Pennsylvania Avenue and adjacent blocks. Private office development had occurred along the avenue, as well as in the blocks to the north, in the late nineteenth and early twentieth centuries. This pattern included the F Street retail spine and some of the blocks to the north of it. As in the conventional American urban form, retail and office land uses were mixed or in close proximity to each other, the assumption being that they were mutually reinforcing. But in post–World War II Washington, a different course evolved. Office development was no longer occurring in the city's original downtown; instead, it began to take place largely in another location several blocks to the north and west. Consequently, over the past quarter-decade, a new downtown has emerged in an area encompassed more or less by 15th Street on the east, Massachusetts Avenue on the north, New Hampshire Avenue on the west, and Pennsylvania Avenue on the south (see Map 3.1).[4] Together, the old and new downtowns compose most of Washington's contemporary central business district (CBD).

The Dichotomous Downtown Emerges

Formerly a section of northwest Washington composed of a mix of residences and neighborhood shopping facilities, the area encompassed by the new downtown declined by approximately 550 dwelling units and 1,400 inhabitants between 1960 and 1970.[5] The 16th Street and Connecticut Avenue corridors north of the White House had become the center of over 30,000 office jobs as early as 1962. However, during the 1960s, even prior to the riots of 1968, numerous additional office buildings were constructed, especially west of the Connecticut Avenue shopping and office corridor.[6]

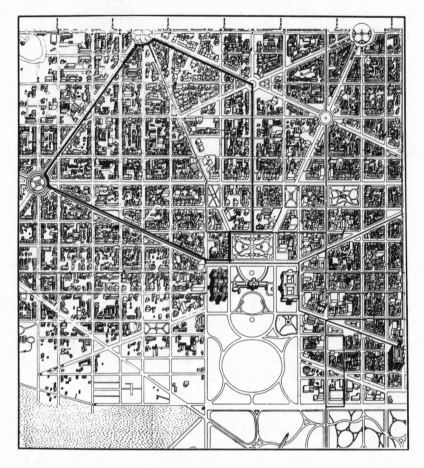

Map 3.2 Central Washington, 1903, before new downtown
Source: From a map prepared by Joseph Passonneau and Partners, Washington, D.C. Partially financed by the National Endowment for the Arts.

Several more were located along K Street, a strip whose name became synonymous with bland, unimaginative architecture in the Washington city planning lexicon. Maps 3.2 and 3.3 illustrate how profoundly the new downtown's development pattern has shifted, from low density commercial and residential to high density office uses.

The reasons that developers sought to disengage the office function of the city's old downtown from its traditional retail function were complicated. Reputedly, the lower cost and easier consolidation of land parcels in the new downtown area was one factor. The shabby appearance of many

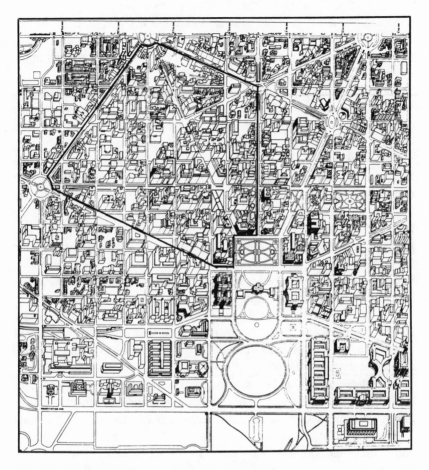

Map 3.3 Central Washington, 1973, with new downtown
Source: From a map prepared by Joseph Passonneau and Partners, Washington, D.C. Partially financed by the National Endowment for the Arts.

old downtown properties and businesses was another. In addition, *A Plan for the Year 2000*, released in 1961 by the National Capital Park and Planning Commission (now the National Capital Planning Commission) and the National Capital Regional Planning Council, pointed out that the new downtown was "closer to high-income residential areas" than the old downtown.[7] This implied that new office buildings required nearby housing for their white-collar workers. Yet most office workers in the area were commuting from suburban locations (and still are). It may also have suggested that the high-income residential areas would generate pedestrian shopping traffic for ground-floor retail establishments in office buildings. But retail business along upper Connecticut Avenue (to the north) and in Georgetown (to the west) was already superior to any incorporated in the early new downtown office development plans.

Today it is difficult to escape the impression that the primary motivating force for diverting new office construction to the area north and west of the White House was not only to escape the deterioration of the old downtown but also to avoid the black shoppers and pedestrians who were beginning to predominate there. Fear among real estate business people and investors that new offices in the old downtown could not be leased at desired rates of financial return certainly inhibited construction there. Fear of crime was influential too. But the "high-income residential areas" referred to in the plan were the white neighborhoods of Georgetown, the embassy area, and the upper northwest. Proximity to these sections and the buffer provided by the White House on the south created a location for the new downtown to grow and prosper relatively "safe" from what were considered racial and physical deterrents of the old downtown.

A Plan for the Year 2000, although ignoring the obvious racial rationale for the emergence of the new downtown, pointed out that diversion of offices away from the old retail center was "undesirable." The plan correctly noted that daytime office workers could have helped to upgrade retail sales in the old downtown, had office construction occurred there. It called for the integration of future office development with the retail function in the old downtown.[8] Twenty years later another planning document echoed this recommendation, stating, "It is necessary to focus the market for office and retail expansion into Downtown rather than allowing such activity to spread."[9]

Nonetheless, a generation of potential retail patronage for the old downtown was lost as private office employment mushroomed in the new downtown. For example, between 1962 and 1967 Washington's entire CBD, including the federal mall area, increased its employment by 17 percent. Yet the new downtown (roughly the western portion of the CBD) experienced a gain of 41 percent or almost 20,000 jobs. Furthermore, from 1967 to 1973 employment in the CBD and federal enclave grew again by 17 percent, while employment in the new downtown rose by 36 percent or nearly 25,000 jobs.[10] The large majority of new jobs in the 1962–1973 period were in office-related work. Therefore, the rate of growth in office activity in the new downtown was proceeding at more than twice the rate of that in the CBD–federal enclave of which it is a part.

Doubtless, the imbalance in growth between the two sections of Wash-

Map 3.4   Consolidation of Washington's central business district
Source: Prepared by Dennis E. Gale.

ington's dichotomous downtown was further exacerbated by the 1968 riots, which occurred primarily in deteriorating neighborhoods to the north and east. Spreading to small parts of the old downtown, the burning, looting, and vandalism had a pronounced effect on existing businesses, as well as on potential investment activity. Meanwhile, construction continued apace in the new downtown.

The Pattern Finally Shifts

Since the mid-1970s, as space for further office development has diminished in the new downtown, earlier inhibitions among developers about the section of the city's CBD *east* of 15th Street NW have declined. Part of the attraction was the opening of the McPherson Square Station on Metro rail's Red Line. Although the Metro's effect on job development appears questionable (as pointed out in Chapter 2), there is little doubt that it has had a profound effect on real estate development in the CBD. Recognizing a new accessibility to the area, developers began tearing down old hotels and apartment and office buildings, constructing larger office structures in their places. Several were located along the southern crescent of Thomas Circle and on the Vermont Avenue axis connecting the circle to K Street to the south. The effect of this development pattern has been to spread the new downtown eastward into an area encompassed by Massachusetts and New York avenues. This area abuts the northwestern edge of the old downtown (see Map 3.4).

Simultaneously, the old downtown of Washington has begun to experience new construction and renovation in several sections. A well-intentioned effort was the District's creation of a pedestrian median along F Street to enhance the visual appeal of the retail spine. More effective, however, was the opening of the Metro subway system in 1976, helping to spur investor confidence in real estate near stations along the Red Line. The Metro Center station, a major transfer point between three lines, is located in the heart of the old downtown. Furthermore, the extensive redevelopment and renovation performed along Pennsylvania Avenue (the southern perimeter of the old downtown) under the auspices of the federally sanctioned Pennsylvania Avenue Development Corporation (PADC) has determined the character of revitalization there. Under the PADC plan, Pershing Park and Western Plaza were constructed as public spaces to reinforce the monumental legacy of Pennsylvania Avenue. The National Theater was renovated, and a large interior mall, the Shops at National Place, was built as well. Along the northern edge of the old downtown, on New York Avenue, the District's newly opened convention center is another feature encouraging investor confidence. Opponents of this highly controversial project feared it would become a net drain on the city fisc. At this point it is too early to tell whether their worries were justified.

Thus far, most of the reinvestment activity has occurred in the western half of the old downtown, the part located closest to the prestigious White House, Treasury, and Federal Triangle section. As of May 1982, 7 new office buildings had been completed in the old downtown area, and 16 more were planned or under construction.[11] Among these were the National League of Cities building, the National Press Club, Metropolitan Square, and several structures on the Metro Center renewal site.

The city's three major department stores, too, have reinvested in the old downtown. Hecht's built a new facility, and Woodward and Lothrop's and Garfinkel's have performed multimillion dollar renovations of their stores. As early as July 1978 a *Washington Post* headline proclaimed, "Downtown D.C. on the Verge of Spectacular Rebirth," and eight years later a headline declared, "Downtown Is Back." [12]

The construction of new hotels and the renovation and expansion of existing hotels have embodied another development trend since the late 1970s. Prior to this, the Washington Hilton, built in the early 1970s, was located well outside the old downtown. One of the few hotels to be constructed in the years after the riots, it was intended to cater primarily to the office industry located in the new downtown. However, it was the new Hyatt Regency Hotel, opened in 1976, that helped to remove the stigma associated with downtown locations.[13] Located near a new Metro station only a few blocks northwest of Capitol Hill, it was built in an otherwise run-down section of the eastern edge of the old downtown. It represented a critical turning point in developer attitudes about the old downtown. In the years that have followed, several established hotels in the core of Washington have renovated or expanded their facilities. Symbolically important, for example, was the decision to renovate the vacant Willard Hotel, a historic landmark located across the street from the District's city hall. It was closed in 1968, the year of Washington's urban riots. So drastically has the development climate changed since the post-riot period that by 1982 at least 13 new hotels had been proposed or were under construction in the old downtown.[14] In 1980 there were 3,250 hotel rooms in the old downtown area; since then, new Marriott and Vista International hotels have been built, and renovations are underway at other hotels. A 1984 *Washington Post* article reported that approximately 5,400 hotel rooms were expected to be added by 1986.[15]

Historic Preservation Finds a Constituency

As the national capital, Washington possesses a historic and symbolic identity like that of capitals throughout much of the world. It might be expected, therefore, that support for the preservation of historical buildings and spaces would be widespread in the city. Indeed, there has been a long list of officially designated landmark buildings in the District of Columbia for over 15 years. But most of the properties for which the strongest protection was provided were public buildings or spaces belonging to the federal or District governments or institutional structures owned by churches and philanthropic organizations.[16] The least potent sanctions were designated for a large list of landmarks that were mostly in private residential, office, or commercial use. Many of these did not have the historic identity that comes from occupancy by a respected diplomatic or cultural organization. Many were simply older buildings that, for the most part, had attained a certain visual appeal because of their architecture and the affectionate familiarity they had bred in generations of Washingtonians.

Perhaps it was the Civil Rights Movement of the 1950s and 1960s that provided the template for action, motivating many middle-class residents of the city to take up the cause of historic preservation with tactics that were more aggressive than those typical of previous years. Certainly, earlier neighborhood-level activism in historical Georgetown had shown that preservation had a distinguished constituency there. No doubt, the city's unofficial preservation action group, Don't Tear It Down, was the single dominating force in the ascendency of the preservation ethic. Formed in the early 1970s, its membership initially coalesced around the threatened demolition of a federal building known locally as the "Old Post Office." The struggle to save the Old Post Office (located on Pennsylvania Avenue on the southern edge of the old downtown) ultimately resulted in a victory for the fledgling preservation action group. The structure was restored and adapted for office, retail, and cultural purposes. Opened only recently, it has become the flagship project in the Pennsylvania Avenue Development Plan, drawing new crowds to the downtown on evenings and weekends. Since that effort, the organized preservation movement in Washington has fought many battles over individual landmark buildings, most of which were located in or near the CBD. Clearly, more struggles have resulted in success than in failure. For example, the PADC plan includes restoration of the old *Evening Star* building, a row of nineteenth-century commercial buildings on 7th Street NW, the National Bank of Washington, and other structures. And with the new saliency of historic preservation, broader rationales have been advanced to justify such efforts. As a result, many developers, as well as federal and local government officials, are less likely to scoff at the local significance of an older building. For example, buildings designed by locally prominent architects or those of importance to local, rather than national, history are often more vigorously (and successfully) defended than before. Victorian-era structures and those designed in the art deco style, even though not as old as Washington's earlier-period buildings, are no longer routinely relegated to the ravages of the wrecking ball.

One of the surest indicators of the saliency of historic preservation in

Washington's CBD is the frequency with which it is now discussed in local government planning, as well as in business circles. Little more than an afterthought in the comprehensive plans of the 1960s, it has been much more extensively discussed in plans and proposals of the late 1970s and 1980s. For example, an entire volume of the seven-volume Comprehensive Plan recently adopted by the District of Columbia government was devoted to historic preservation. Another volume on Washington's downtown included several sections on preservation. In addition, the District's law providing for a delay-of-demolition order for certain categories of older buildings is regarded as one of the most stringent in the nation.

The Historic Preservation Ethic

With the rise of the historic preservation ethic in Washington, land-use controversies were no longer limited to conflict and cooperation between investors, developers, and real estate agents on the one hand and zoning, planning, and design review agencies on the other. Increasingly, in several of the inner-ring neighborhoods and in the central business district, historic preservationists entered these relationships. In most cases, they took neither the business nor the government side but rather raised a comparatively new set of issues for which they became the primary spokespersons. Through landmark building designations, stay-of-demolition orders, demonstrations, and lengthy court litigation, they argued for the protection and restoration of the city's architectural legacy. Although they suffered setbacks, their record of successes is impressive.

Most important, the intervention of the historic preservation ethic has complicated numerous land-use decisions in the core. Now such issues are no longer uniformly discussed in terms of private property rights and the public interest. No longer are new development proposals discussed solely in terms of blight clearance, higher tax revenues, and new employment. But neither are they so often considered in terms of the need for subsidized housing, youth recreation facilities, or neighborhood shopping outlets. The preservationists introduced a new set of terms, which for the most part represent the interests of middle- and upper-class, white residents of Washington. Few blacks have taken an active role in historic preservation campaigns, even those in Washington's relatively large black middle-class population.

As a result, many land-use controversies in the core are now more commonly resolved through compromise between business, government, and preservation interests. Those who rent their places of business or homes are least likely to benefit from this new process. Thus, small businesses in the downtown and in neighborhood retail corridors—often with minority proprietors and employees—are most likely to be the victims of the new land-use decision-making process in Washington. Housing tenants, especially minorities with low and moderate incomes, are also likely to be victims. Female-headed households with children and households with elderly members on fixed incomes commonly fall into this category.

Although tenant associations for housing and, more recently, for small shops in the old downtown, have attempted to gain a foothold in some land-use issues, their influence has been limited. As of 1985, the revitalization of Washington's core has worked overwhelmingly to the benefit of white, middle- and upper-class interests. Both rent-control and condominium-conversion legislation in the city were more protective of housing-tenant interests during the mid-1970s. In more recent years, though, these measures have been rewritten such that they are more favorable than before to the interests of landlords and developers. As such, tenants have lost ground in Washington's rental-housing policies.

Historic preservationists, too, have shifted their strategies in land-use controversies in the central business district. A monumental conflict arose over the preservation of the Rhodes Tavern, one of the city's oldest commercial structures, located across the street from the federal Treasury building. Serving as the temporary seat of government during the War of 1812, the tavern had been radically altered in a variety of commercial uses during the ensuing years. The new developer of the site had offered to move the structure to a new location and had preserved several other buildings nearby. But the ranks of preservationists were split over the preservation of the tavern. For several years members of a splinter group fought ingeniously to save the tavern, while the city's main preservation coalition refused to endorse their efforts. In mid-1984 the Rhodes Tavern was demolished.

This episode provided evidence that developers and mainstream preservationists in Washington had moved away from confrontation over individual properties in the CBD and in some neighborhoods. And other indications point in the same direction. For example, the development-prone Board of Trade prepared a downtown plan in 1981 calling for a comprehensive survey of historic buildings.[17] Furthermore, even as the Rhodes Tavern controversy was unfolding, preservationists were recommending historic district status for two sections of the old downtown, thereby delimiting the turf over which they would struggle most strenuously and, by default, indicating the areas that were of lesser concern. Rather than wait for developers to seek permission to demolish a building before deciding whether to confront them (as they did in the case of the Rhodes Tavern), preservationists now show a greater willingness to cooperate, by indicating their priorities publicly and in advance of such development initiatives. Downtown Partners, a group of developers and landowners, has voiced support for the historic district designation but has sought to scale down the boundaries of one of the districts in order to exclude certain properties. The District of Columbia government's economic development division favors almost any request by businesses in its effort to redevelop the old downtown, while its historic preservation office shows little inclination to endorse any changes in the district boundaries.[18]

Thus, even though land-use issues in the old downtown continue to display tensions between preservation and development forces, the emphasis appears to be shifting to proactive rather than reactive interaction. Both sides seem to favor a strategic, long-range approach to the downtown rather than the tactical, confrontational stance that arose around issues such as the Rhodes Tavern. Most important, however, is the fact that land-use conflicts in the city's core have increasingly become the province of middle- and upper-class participants.

The loosely knit coalitions of minorities and middle-class people that arose during the War on Poverty era and cohered with declining strength until the late 1970s have diminished considerably. Increasingly, then, land-use conflicts in Washington's core have been resolved through trade-offs between aesthetic, cultural, and historical values on the one hand and business and economic values on the other. Social values no longer have the priority or salience they once enjoyed.

Thus, it is apparent that there is now a generally effective coalition of Washingtonians that has successfully integrated historic preservation into the complicated structure of the city's political and economic life. Still, the District Government's comprehensive city planning process begs for elaboration. For it is municipal planning that is supposed to ensure that a balance is achieved between competing interests in the physical, economic, and social development of the nation's capital.

Comprehensive Planning and the Old Downtown

After a lengthy period of neglect and deterioration during the 1950s and 1960s, Washington's old downtown has begun to experience economic and physical revitalization. To be sure, the casual observer would find little difficulty in spotting many run-down structures there. Some businesses are obviously faltering. Unsightly public spaces and parking lots abound. Yet the sheer volume of new investments and planning activities indicate that sufficient momentum has probably been generated to propel much of the old downtown into a new era.

Several properties along Pennsylvania Avenue have been either redeveloped or rehabilitated, and several more are programmed for improvement in the next few years. Pershing Park and Western Plaza, major capital improvements, now lend a monumental air to the southwestern corner of the downtown. Metropolitan Square, a large office complex grafted onto several historic facades, graces the western edge of this area. Newly renovated or redeveloped office, hotel, and public buildings reflect further confidence in the area. The new Metro subway and the bus system connect the old retail area to numerous sections of the metropolitan area. On the northern perimeter, the new convention center, a $99 million investment, draws tourism to the city.

Paralleling these developments has been the formulation of a Comprehensive Plan, the first to be adopted by the District government under home rule.[19] Through an agonizingly slow process, the plan has been under preparation since the mid-1970s and at this writing remains "in process." To its credit, the planning process has involved extensive citizen participation. Nevertheless, it has been widely criticized as indeterminate. The original draft was not a conventional plan but a policies plan. This document bristled with pronouncements about goals, strategies, and directions but contained almost nothing about their precise locational applications. Many citizens complained and the District added a vaguely constructed map showing broad categories of land use, but the map was deemed a "guide" to policy rather than a literal interpretation of policy locational applications. Criticisms then were raised about the accuracy of the map, and several observers charged that it ignored existing uses on many individual parcels of land. Before the Comprehensive Plan was adopted in its entirety by the city council, approximately 240 amendments were made to the map, and innumerable changes were made in the text.

Other critics raised the issue of compatibility between the plan and the city's existing zoning code, which, as in most cities, has regulatory authority under the police power. City officials resist empowering the plan with the sanctions necessary to render it the final authority on land use and development matters. As it currently stands, the Comprehensive Plan appears to be viewed by city officials as a nonbinding document to be *consulted* (but not necessarily heeded) in making decisions about the city's growth and preservation, especially in the downtown. Yet the city's Home Rule Act of 1973 requires that the zoning code and zoning map not be inconsistent with the plan. Not wanting to face the political ramifications of extensive re-zoning in the city, local officials procrastinated for several years in explaining how this requirement would be carried out. Finally, it was announced that after the Comprehensive Plan was adopted, "Small Area Plans" would be prepared by the District, working closely with neighborhood groups. From these elements of the Comprehensive Plan, it was announced, would come the information needed to bring the plan and the zoning ordinance and map in conformance with one another.

The District's zoning machinery, concerned with an incremental view of changes and continuities in small areas, cannot provide the comprehensive, coordinated perspective necessary to ensure a reasonably consistent pattern of development and preservation throughout the city. Zoning is conservative by nature and short-term in its perspective of the future. The zoning map is based largely on existing land-use patterns in the city, even though many zoning designations may no longer adequately reflect the purposes for which they were originally zoned. Zoning is designed to react to land-use proposals as they arise, its primary purpose being to protect property values; a viable plan is supposed to present a vision of the future concerned primarily with the overall public welfare. To erase inconsistencies between zoning and planning is not an easy task. But in a city that is home to over 600,000 people and one of the most important national capitals in the world, it is absolutely essential to minimize the number of land-use policies that work at cross-purposes.

The comprehensive planning process has served for years as the focus of public debate for several interests in the city. Members of neighborhood groups, preservationists, merchants, corporate business people, real estate entrepreneurs, institutional administrators, and others sought to indemnify their individual interests through the plan. The technical documentation and research that has gone into this document is unparalleled in Washington's planning history. Its breadth was expressed in well over 500 pages of text. The range of community residents and business people serving on advisory committees and participating in public meetings was impressive. Still, part of the blame for the exceedingly lengthy period of preparation is not the fault of city officials. Because this is the first comprehensive planning process Washington citizens have experienced under home rule, many are not familiar with the nature or purpose of these documents. Throughout the controversy, many neighborhood groups have repeatedly insisted that the plan be constructed so as to *embalm* individual neighborhoods, with no possibilities for future redevelopment or land-use changes. Inherent in their expectations was a plan that reads like a glorified zoning map, showing parcel-by-parcel existing land-use designations preserved for infinity. The District has taken the view, rightfully so, that planning is for future generations, as well as for current citizens, and must provide for enough flexibility to anticipate future housing, recreational, shopping, employment, transportation, and cultural needs.

As for the old downtown, the Comprehensive Plan is conspicuous *inter alia* for its strong emphasis on redevelopment and, to a lesser extent, historic preservation; existing small businesses are largely ignored. For independent merchants, the Comprehensive Plan offers little, if any, hope of reaching an affordable accommodation between their interests and the larger economic concerns of bankers, developers, government administrators, preservationists, and others. The lessons of the convention center, a gargantuan facility consuming two city blocks, are still fresh in their minds. When property was acquired for the center, several merchants lost their leases. The redevelopment area included 88 households and 56 businesses.[20] Merchants on surrounding blocks saw their rents rise onerously. Shoe repair shops, carryout food services, dry cleaners, cafeterias, newsstands, hardware stores, and similar small businesses throughout much of the remainder of the old downtown now operate with uncertainty. Some face lease termination; others have felt the effects of rising property-tax assessments as a result of reinvestment. As real estate investors and developers bid up the sales prices of existing properties and improve others with multimillion dollar redevelopment projects, the value of real estate in the downtown has risen. For some, this has resulted in significantly increased rents, as landlords have sought to cover their costs and exploit new economic opportunities.[21]

Ironically, even the downtown's "erogenous zone" has been affected by the increasing competition for urban space. A section of 14th Street has long been the locus of burlesque houses, massage parlors, adult bookstores, and related sex-based businesses. As in many cities, officials have looked the other way as these businesses catered to tourists and crowds from the city and the suburbs. Since perhaps, 1978, as real estate and other interests have sought to enhance the market for redevelopment in the old downtown, seven sex-oriented businesses have been closed. Some have had their liquor licenses suspended or revoked. Others have lost their leases. One business converted to a restaurant, allegedly because of the pressure.[22] The real power of downtown economic interests is measured in events such as these.

As competition for property in the CBD has increased, other types of businesses have felt the pressure. For example, traditional enterprises such as movie theaters and gas stations—dwindling in numbers even prior to the recent surge of reinvestment in the old downtown—have suffered the loss of leases, rising rents, or climbing property-tax liabilities. One study found that only 15 service stations now operate in the entire CBD, a number perhaps one-third that of five years ago.[23] Similarly, in 1960 there were 54 movie theaters in Washington, but by 1975 the number had shrunk to 30. Today there are 25 such businesses, 18 of which are located in the new downtown or the predominantly white neighborhoods of northwest Washington.[24]

While there were almost 100 supermarkets operated by major food chains in the late 1960s, the city now has only 37.[25] Sholl's Cafeteria, an inexpensive, almost legendary eatery for a generation of tourists and residents, recently relocated to Alexandria, displaced by redevelopment of its location in the old downtown. A sister cafeteria in the new downtown had been similarly displaced by redevelopment five years earlier.[26]

The surge of reinvestment in the old downtown notwithstanding, public attitudes about shopping there suggest that business-sector confidence exceeds that of consumers. A 1983 survey of residents in the District and inner-tier jurisdictions and of shoppers in the District's old downtown provides the evidence.[27] It found that even as most respondents were supportive of downtown revitalization, 69 percent said that they expected to continue shopping in the suburbs; among District residents, about one-half preferred suburban shopping. About 90 percent of those polled said that better parking arrangements and police patrolling would encourage them to shop more frequently in the downtown.

A more recent study, conducted in December 1984, pointed out that when suburbanites went shopping, to the movies, or to a restaurant, they were likely to go into the District less than 20 percent of the time.[28] Museums, historical monuments, and live theater, however, were able to draw them in more frequently. Thus, the city, and especially the CBD, has lost much of its competitive edge in routine kinds of consumer goods and services. It is largely toward those attributes which are unique to the city —cultural and historical institutions such as the Smithsonian Institution, the Kennedy Center, and the monuments—that suburban attraction is strongest.

While the old downtown may still have the opportunity to attract a significant share of District residents for routine retail shopping needs, its primary identity will probably shift to that of an office center and a night-time entertainment area. It is simply too costly and inconvenient to draw large numbers of consumers for general household shopping. But it can cater to the convenience shopping needs of weekday office workers, as well as to the needs of evening cultural enthusiasts and amusement seekers.

The central business district of Washington has progressed from a threatening period of deterioration and stagnation in the old downtown to a course that now suggests that substantial portions will be revitalized by the year 2000, if not sooner. Although there is nothing unusual about declining business districts in American cities, the sort of revival that has occurred in Washington's CBD is less common. Similar cycles have, however, been documented in a few other cities, such as Denver and San Francisco.[29]

Although the numerous development projects completed, underway, or proposed for the old and new downtowns have unfolded in tandem with the city's comprehensive planning process, there is little evidence that the District government has done more than react to events as they occur. Typically, Washington's local government is predisposed to accommodate, rather than guide, the thrust of real estate activity. This helps to explain both the creation of the new downtown during the postwar decades and the decline of the old one. It also undergirds explanations for the recent signs of reinvestment in the old downtown.

Massive public investment projects such as the convention center, the Metro rail transit system, and the Pennsylvania Avenue redevelopment program point out the apparent willingness of public authorities to exercise their powers of public spending to affect land use in the old downtown. But so far the District government has been reluctant to take a forceful, proactive stance to direct land use and development activity there through the Comprehensive Plan. Relying instead on the zoning ordinance, it has too often reacted to development initiatives as they arise. With no coordinated vision for the future, no firm direction in mind, and a disjointed set of land-use controls, the District will probably surprise no one if it shows little effort to balance interests in the old downtown or in the CBD in its entirety. Paradoxically, this situation appears to result not from the lack of a talented or able District planning staff but rather from the mayor's preference, like that of most mayors, to keep his options open as long as possible. Rather than commit the city to a clear direction for the future, rather than set explicit priorities among competing land uses and social purposes, he has opted for a nearly formless planning process, which allows arbitrary and inconsistent decision making.

Central Business District Decline and Revitalization

For any observer who takes "the long view" of planning and development in the capital's central business district, a compelling irony becomes evident. In the short space of 20 years, the city has gone from a period during which office and retail reinvestment was consciously diverted away from the old downtown to a situation in which economic interests and historic preservation groups actively vie for influence there. The result is that Washington's CBD encompasses two downtowns—one, the historical retail center and the other, a modern office concentration. Even today the differences between the two areas transcend the distance. (A scant half-dozen blocks separate them.) At any time of night or day, the new downtown is dominated by white, middle-class people. Relatively few black faces appear there. Yet in the old downtown blacks are still in the majority, both as shoppers and as employees in the department stores and retail shops. Clearly, each race claimed turf for itself in Washington's CBD during the postwar decades. In recent years, however, economic interests in Washington have rediscovered the old downtown. Now they compete actively with historic preservation interests to reclaim sections of the retail area primarily for new office and hotel construction.

Caught between these forces are many small businesses, several of which are minority-owned and/or-staffed. Rents for retail space in the new "upscale" development projects are prohibitive for most of them. Meanwhile, the District government, with potentially one of the most powerful urban-planning mandates in the nation, has shown little inclination to exercise a true leadership role in the old downtown. On the eve of a possible period of reunification of office, hotel, and retail activity there, many of the small businesses, which clung faithfully and tenaciously to the hope of downtown revival, face a thankless future. The goods and services they have provided for a generation of Washingtonians (especially minorities)—even when the downtown's death knell was being sounded after the 1968 riots—may soon be replaced by the goods and services of gourmet food shops, boutiques, and other "upmarket" retail concerns.

Paradoxically, this kind of upward socioeconomic transition—some would call it gentrification—is not unique to Washington's old downtown. As Chapter 4 will point out, the old port community of Georgetown, a section of Washington since the late 1800s, underwent a similar revival of its commercial section beginning in the 1950s. Moreover, revival of some of the *residential* neighborhoods surrounding the CBD has also predated current trends in the old downtown. In fact, later sections will point out that much of the entire core of the city of Washington, including its CBD and inner-ring neighborhoods, is undergoing a revitalization the roots of which can be traced back as early as the 1920s.

4

The Degeneration and Regeneration
of the Inner Neighborhoods

The kind of physical and economic decline that affected parts of Washington's central business district, especially its old downtown, had a precedent elsewhere in the capital city. So, too, has its relatively recent revitalization. In fact, the pattern of degeneration and regeneration has characterized parts of the core of the city for several decades. The earliest experience with this dynamic, however, belongs to the Georgetown community. Referred to as a neighborhood in the city of Washington by most people, it is in fact a collection of neighborhoods more or less corresponding geographically to the late-nineteenth-century port community of that name. Now the oldest historic district in Washington, Georgetown is the proper departure point for a discussion of neighborhood revitalization in the nation's capital.

The Georgetown Model

Throughout the nineteenth century Georgetown's economy ebbed and flowed but gradually lost vitality to the burgeoning capital city of Washington and to superior port communities such as Alexandria and Annapolis.[1] The little town's *fin de siècle* identity had assumed the proportions of a faded, but genteel, southern community. In comparison with Washington to its east, it appeared rather dated and lacking in dynamism. Washington's myriad newcomers found greater opportunities for economic and social advancement in the newly built Victorian-era neighborhoods of Dupont Circle and Logan Circle, as well as in suburban towns such as Cleveland Park, Takoma Park, and Chevy Chase. By the end of the century, Georgetown had even lost its separate legal status as an incorporated community and was enfolded in the urbanized mass of the District of Columbia. It had become just another group of neighborhoods without its own government and with responsibilities to a distant bureaucracy in downtown Washington.

By the time that Washington's predominantly post-bellum building stock had become the locus of the city's economic, social, and political life, many parts of eighteenth- and nineteenth-century Georgetown were already considered obsolete for contemporary purposes. Patches of slums had emerged, especially in some of Georgetown's alley-dwelling enclaves, and several old mansions had been subdivided into rooming houses. Deteriorated and underused mills, warehouses, manufactories, stables, and other structures contributed to the image of decline.

It is not so surprising, then, that Georgetown would become the site of Washington's first efforts in renewal of a residential area (see Map 4.1). There were early signs of reinvestment in individual old houses in the eastern section of the community (north of M Street and east of Wisconsin Avenue) in the years following World War I. By 1924 residents there had successfully lobbied Congress for zoning changes to prohibit high-rise buildings in their neighborhood. They published a booklet extolling Georgetown's historical and "quaint" character in the same year. By 1926 a neighborhood association was established to enhance the quality of residential life in Georgetown. With the advent of the New Deal, however, thousands of newcomers poured into Washington, and many, desperate for housing, settled in Georgetown. Many were relatively young, college-educated easterners pursuing white-collar careers. Their presence in Georgetown lent an image of youthfulness, and a social cachet was attached to residence in the former port community. During the period between the First and Second World Wars, several hundred older dwellings were restored, gardens were replanted, house and garden tours publicized the community's historical identity, and newspapers and magazines published articles about Georgetown's "revival." Another tidal wave of newcomers arrived during World War II, placing further demand for shelter on Georgetown, as well as on other areas of the city. In 1950 residents succeeded in convincing Congress to designate the first historical district established in the national capital. The district encompassed the residential portion of Georgetown above M Street. By that time, only a handful of communities in the United States had had historic districts designated, all by state and local government authority.

With the termination of wartime materials rationing, restoration and rehabilitation, now under Georgetown's historic district controls, accelerated during the 1950s and 1960s. Nevertheless, renewal of the commercial sector, located primarily along its major intersecting corridors, Wisconsin

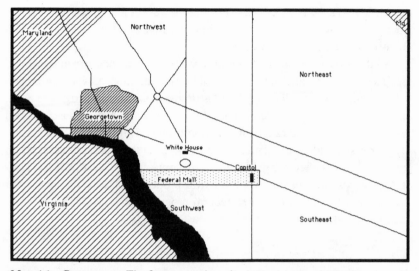

Map 4.1   Georgetown: The first generation of neighborhood revitalization
Source: Prepared by Dennis E. Gale.

Avenue and M Street, lagged far behind the pace of residential renovation. Gradually, antique shops, restaurants, wine and cheese shops, boutiques, cafes, pubs, craft shops, and the like replaced family businesses such as grocery stores, bakeries, barber shops, beauty shops, millinery shops, tailor shops, diners, hardware stores, jewelery stores, and book shops.

Except for a few small residential enclaves, the final chapter in Georgetown's revival—the refurbishing of its largely obsolete industrial and heavy commercial waterfront south of M Street—resisted initiative until the 1970s. Demand for residential space in Georgetown had risen to the point that even modest row housing and alley dwellings, originally built for waterfront workers, were being renovated as early as the 1950s. The federal government designated the nineteenth-century Chesapeake and Ohio Canal, in the heart of the waterfront area, a national park, further enhancing Georgetown's attraction. Yet it was not until major zoning decisions were resolved during the 1970s that large-scale redevelopment and renovation invaded the waterfront section. The Georgetown Citizens' Association (and its predecessors) had successfully fought for several years to prevent development and foster preservation of the area. During the early 1960s it voted down the establishment of a federal urban renewal project, which sought to bring a mixture of preservation and redevelopment to the waterfront. It was rumored that some members feared that government intervention would bring public housing and poor blacks to live in Georgetown. Mindful of the city's first urban renewal project (discussed below), located in southwest Washington, they had little trust in what was then a relatively untried federal program.

As the 1980s unfold, the community's waterfront has become infested with several office and apartment buildings, condominiums, and a honeycomb of new ground-floor retail shops. Redevelopment of a large site along the riverfront, now completed, has added a quay and a large plaza, as well as "upscale" offices, a hotel, and condominiums. But the level of medium- to high-rise building construction brought about through zoning litigation and relatively ineffective public planning controls far exceeds the level originally envisioned in the urban renewal proposals of 20 years ago. As it turned out, the much-maligned federal program may have been the community's "last best hope."

The Second Generation

Perhaps even more important than its own physical renewal, Georgetown's privately financed revitalization experience achieved another purpose. It demonstrated to some Washingtonians that even when a neighborhood ages and begins to show signs of deterioration, it may be possible to stimulate a resurgence of vitality. Even more important, the Georgetown historic preservation movement, at least in the residential area north of M Street, showed that it was not necessary that government programs and funding à la Urban Renewal Program be involved. It was now apparent that in at least one case in Washington, it was possible to direct a neighborhood away from the path of decline and decay without public eminent domain and condemnation proceedings, massive clearance, and redevelopment. While Georgetown's was the first large-scale, privately financed neighborhood restoration experience in Washington, similar historically based revivals had occurred at about the same time on Beacon Hill in Boston; in New Orleans; in Charleston, South Carolina; and in Alexandria, Virginia.

Still, it would be overstating the Georgetown experience to suggest that confidence in private, neighborhood-based historic preservation movements was widespread—even after Georgetown's restoration was indemnified by congressional designation of the community's historic district in 1950. The prevailing attitude, it seems, was that reliance on purely private-market forces to revive Washington's second generation of declining neighborhoods was misguided, if not doomed to failure. As in most older communities in the United States, especially those with rapidly growing

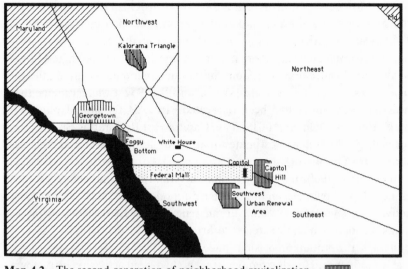

Map 4.2   The second generation of neighborhood revitalization
Source: Prepared by Dennis E. Gale.

poor and minority populations, business people in Washington were skeptical about the profitability of inner-city reinvestment. Neither neighborhood nor downtown revitalization was thought likely to occur unless heavy public subsidies were provided and regulatory and planning controls were imposed. In short, many business people and public officials agreed that federal urban renewal was necessary. Of the Georgetown precedent, one prominent city planner observed in 1946, "Georgetown, far from becoming a blighted area, has shown a remarkable renaissance in the last two decades. This same rejuvenation cannot be applied generally to other portions of the city. Only a few blocks of Georgetown and Alexandria have this historic, sentimental and aesthetic interest."[2] In spite of the prevailing skepticism about privately initiated neighborhood revitalization in Washington, citizens in three other neighborhoods of Washington decided that perhaps the Georgetown approach could arrest decline and promote reinvestment in their areas. By the late 1940s Capitol Hill, Foggy Bottom, and Kalorama Triangle were all showing signs of decay similar to that of Georgetown in 1900. Widely dispersed, they each began to experience the renovation and restoration of individual town houses in a few concentrated city blocks during the ten years following World War II (see Map 4.2).

Capitol Hill was the second neighborhood in Washington to undergo revitalization. A former president of a Georgetown citizens' association and assistant principal at a junior high school on Capitol Hill, she campaigned to interest homeowners and business people in efforts to renovate building facades and clean yards.[3] Business people sponsored a contest in 1950 awarding prizes to homeowners who painted the exteriors of their houses. About 150 houses were painted, according to one estimate.[4] Much of the early restoration was done in patches scattered in the first eight blocks of Capitol Hill's southeast quadrant. By 1952 it was estimated that nearly 200 dwellings had been renovated.[5] In 1951 the first Capitol Hill house tour was held, and in 1955 the Capitol Hill Restoration Society was formed. By 1960 it was estimated that about 1,000 houses had been restored on Capitol Hill.[6]

In the early 1950s the Foggy Bottom neighborhood, immediately southeast of Georgetown, began to experience a modest amount of reinvestment activity. In spite of a pending urban renewal project designation in the neighborhood, which threatened to bring about the demolition of several buildings, restoration proceeded apace. Again, the Georgetown experience was an influence. Housing remodelers who had been active in Georgetown were continuing such work in Foggy Bottom.[7] In fact, one observer contrasted Foggy Bottom with Capitol Hill, Georgetown, and Kalorama Triangle. He said that in the other neighborhoods restoration work was first undertaken by individual home buyers. These amateurs did much of the renovation work themselves or supervised others. Only later did commercial renovators begin to carry out their trade. But in Foggy Bottom, renovation was initiated by commercial renovators deliberately hoping to provoke a reinvestment movement such as that in Georgetown.[8] By 1956 it was estimated that about 110 buildings—approximately 25 percent of the neighborhood's building stock—had been renovated.[9]

The Kalorama Triangle area, located along Connecticut Avenue north of the central business district, began to experience reinvestment slightly later than Foggy Bottom.[10] By the mid-1950s young couples and families were moving into the neighborhood in small numbers and renovating town houses, most of which had been built in the early twentieth century. An area with numerous embassies and chanceries in its western section, Kalorama had begun to harbor blight and deterioration in concentrated areas in the eastern section near Connecticut Avenue. As on Capitol Hill, its residents founded a restoration society in the 1950s to encourage reinvestment activity in keeping with the architectural and historical heritage of the neighborhood.

While there were still many in Washington who were doubtful about the Georgetown approach to neighborhood revitalization, it was clear to others that private investment guided by historical preservation principles and a strong neighborhood association could revive many older residential areas. Thus, the die had already been cast in Washington when the advent of gentrification gave national and international recognition to this form of regeneration during the 1970s. By 1970 Washington had had 45 years of experience with privately financed neighborhood revitalization. But it was not until the 1970s that the influx of thousands of young adults, products of the baby-boom generation of the post–World War II era, occurred. Similar to the New Deal hordes in Georgetown a generation earlier, these people created a demand for inner-city housing, which could not be met without increasing the supply of middle-income units. The high cost of new construction and the limited availability of land in close-in locations rendered renovation of the existing housing stock along Georgetown lines a distinct business opportunity.

Public Intervention in Neighborhoods

Privately financed housing rehabilitation and restoration in Washington had already been undertaken in at least four neighborhoods by the time that the federal and District governments began to transform the city's first urban renewal area (see Map 4.2). Under the federal program a large section of the southwest quadrant of the city had been designated for massive demolition, clearance, and redevelopment in the early 1950s. It was plagued by dense poverty, crime, and private disinvestment. Many structures were of wood-frame construction and were in very poor condition. About 23,000 people, mostly black and poor, lived there in 1950. More than two-thirds of the homes had no central heating, and 43 percent had no indoor toilets. Twenty-one percent had no electricity.[11] On the eastern perimeter of the urban renewal area was a large public housing project with several thousand residents, almost all of whom were black.

With the advent of demolition, most families were relocated to other parts of the city, and new apartment towers, town houses, offices, and retail buildings replaced their former neighborhood.[12] Population declined by almost 10,000 people in the southwest urban renewal area. The large majority of new residents were white. Several federal government agencies built office structures in the northern section, and a theater, schools, churches, a branch of the free library, and several parks were added. Bordered on the west by the Washington Channel, the neighborhood's waterfront was improved with restaurants, a hotel, a marina, and a waterfront esplanade.

Massive amounts of public monies were spent to acquire property, clear land, relocate incumbent households, upgrade public services and facilities, and redevelop each site. Many of the most highly regarded principles of planning and design in the postwar decades were adhered to in creating a new southwest. The historical gridiron street pattern was converted to a suburbanesque web of cul de sacs; pedestrian walkways were separated from street rights-of-way in many places; buildings were massed on large parcels of property, leaving more land for open space; close juxtaposition of radically different building heights and densities was meant to provide visual appeal; and a modern suburban shopping center was located in the neighborhood.

Today the last properties to be redeveloped in the southwest are near completion. Ironically, even with extensive public intervention, the population characteristics of the southwest are very similar to those in neighborhoods that experienced the earliest private revitalization. Largely white and middle- to upper-middle-class, people in the southwest—as well as in Georgetown, Foggy Bottom, inner Capitol Hill, and Kalorama Triangle— are white-collar workers, typically with advanced education. There is little evidence of the poor and working-class minority families who populated these areas during the 1950s and 1960s. To be sure, the physical fabric of the southwest is entirely unlike that of the other neighborhoods. It now resembles nothing so much as a swath of suburbia infected with shopping mallaria. To wander through the southwest today is to be entirely exiled from the identifying legibility of Washington's inner town- house neighborhoods. A token landmark building exists here and there, but to the eye, the neighborhood appears to have materialized only yesterday. Cheek by jowl with the affluence of the new southwest is the Greenleaf public housing project, its children enviously eyeing the swimming pools and comfortable homes of their well-heeled neighbors. These sharp race and class distinctions have created tensions, which persist to the present day.

The southwest was the first and only full-scale clearance-and-redevelopment effort at neighborhood revitalization in Washington under the federal Urban Renewal Program. Efforts were made to designate other neighborhoods, including the Georgetown waterfront and the Foggy Bottom neighborhood around George Washington University. But the southwest experience with massive clearance and household relocation and, for some, the threat of new public housing projects, conspired to bring opposition to further such efforts.

By the late 1960s federal strategy had been revised, and the emphasis was placed on rehabilitation of existing structures, with spot clearance and

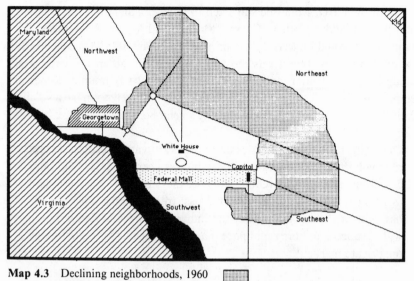

Map 4.3   Declining neighborhoods, 1960
Source: Prepared by Dennis E. Gale.

redevelopment only where absolutely necessary. Nevertheless, throughout the 1950s and much of the 1960s, notions persisted among developers, investors, and city and federal planners that the only way to revitalize a deteriorating inner residential area was through a kind of scorched-earth policy of clearance and redevelopment. For example, both the Comprehensive Plan of 1950[13] and the successor, *A Plan for the Year 2000* (1961),[14] indicated that substantial decay was occurring in the ring of neighborhoods to the north, northeast and east of the central business district (see Map 4.3). While Georgetown, Kalorama Triangle, and Foggy Bottom had less evidence of neighborhood decline, substandard dwellings in Dupont Circle, Shaw, Logan Circle, and Capitol Hill ranged from 16 to more than 30 percent of the housing stock in those neighborhoods.[15] Furthermore, the highest residential population densities in the city were concentrated in the latter group of neighborhoods. The plan prescribed higher-density housing for these sections, in effect encircling much of the CBD with apartment buildings and destroying the town-house character.[16]

With the federal government's revision of urban renewal policies in the late 1960s, planners in the District's Office of Community Renewal propounded a different scheme. Stung by the enormous costs, delays, human suffering, and political liabilities of the southwest project, they proposed different policies for each neighborhood, depending on the extent of deterioration.[17] For example, Dupont Circle and Columbia Heights, to the north of the CBD, would be subjected to redevelopment in some sections and rehabilitation in others. Adams Morgan and Mount Pleasant, on the other hand, would undergo "predominantly rehabilitation." Conspicuously excluded from treatment was most of Capitol Hill, an area already well along the gentrification pathway. Yet the Office of Community Renewal emphasized that this form of revitalization was not likely to make a significant dent in the overall decay of the city's neighborhood structure:

> One of the major program considerations is an evaluation of the extent to which the private market will expand into certain areas with poor conditions and thereby reduce some of these needs [for government assistance]. However, assuming that past trends are the most reliable basis for predicting the future, the indications are that deterioration will advance at a more rapid pace than any prospects for reduction by the private market.[18]

Hindsight, however unfair, reveals how badly the Office of Community Renewal planners misjudged the future demand for living space in several of Washington's inner neighborhoods. But it also points out how little confidence they (and many other observers) had in the likelihood that private enterprise would transform these areas without major government assistance. As the next section will show, these negative prognostications were uttered virtually on the eve of a third generation of neighborhood revitalization. Furthermore, Chapter 5 will analyze several demographic trends occurring in third generation neighborhoods.

The Third Generation

During the late 1960s and 1970s, private reinvestment continued to spread throughout Georgetown, Capitol Hill, and Foggy Bottom. But it reached several other neighborhoods as well. Areas such as Adams Morgan, adjacent to the Kalorama Triangle section, began to attract young postcollege adults. Dupont Circle, Logan Circle, LeDroit Park, Mount Pleasant, Columbia Heights, and the Shaw area were also affected (see Map 4.4). While most revitalization activity was concentrated in the core of Washington, older suburban communities such as Alexandria, Virginia, and Takoma Park, Maryland, had historical districts, and active restoration was underway. By the late 1970s it was apparent that gentrification, as this phenomenon had come to be known, was not limited to a few cities such as

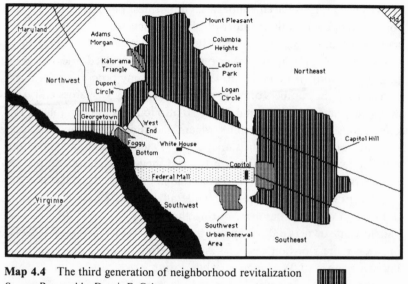

Map 4.4 The third generation of neighborhood revitalization
Source: Prepared by Dennis E. Gale.

Washington, Boston, New Orleans, and Philadelphia. National studies found evidence of neighborhood revitalization in many communities but especially in those in the eastern, midwestern, and southeastern states.[19] Even in Canada, Europe, and Australia, there were cities experiencing comparable revitalization dynamics.[20] In each case the trend was led by young, mostly white, middle-income people. Relatively few had children, and most worked in professional, technical, managerial, governmental, or artistic occupations.[21]

Population characteristics of Washington's gentrifying neighborhoods generally coincided with national trends.[22] Surveys of new home buyers in Mount Pleasant (1976) and Capitol Hill (1977) found that no more than one-fifth of each sample had moved in from suburban communities; the large majority had been residents of Washington for a year or more when they purchased their homes. Thus, there was no evidence that gentrification was attracting significant numbers of people "back to the city."[23] Nevertheless, a more recent study of the Dupont Circle neighborhood suggested that many gentrifiers, while existing city residents, had migrated earlier to Washington from other parts of the nation.[24] In short, by acting as attractive residential settings for large numbers of relative newcomers to the metropolitan area, gentrifying communities may serve the city particularly well in offsetting losses of middle-class households to out-migration.

Still, gentrification in Washington, as in many cities, has been charged with causing the displacement of racial minorities. For example, one study found a reduction in the number of black households in the Adams Morgan area, where both blacks and Hispanics have been threatened by reinvestment.[25] Nevertheless, other research has uncovered a less clear-cut pattern. A study of Dupont Circle found declining proportions of blacks and gains in the numbers of other minorities (mostly Hispanics and Asian Americans) between 1970 and 1980.[26] It also found, however, that in 1970 proportions of black and white owners and renters of Dupont Circle's housing units were about the same; but by 1980 there was an almost fourfold rise in the share of whites who owned their own homes. Yet the proportion of black-renter-occupied units had not decreased significantly during this time either.[27] Therefore, while all Dupont Circle racial groups declined in absolute numbers during the decade of the 1970s, the large gain in white owners did not appear to correspond to a meaningful decline in black renters or homeowners. Another study pointed out that the revitalizing areas of Washington, while losing blacks and gaining whites during the 1970s, were also less racially segregated by 1980.[28]

The third generation of neighborhood revitalization in the District of Columbia has been further stimulated by the conversion of apartment buildings to condominiums and cooperatives. Many, perhaps most, such conversions have occurred in some of the revitalizing areas around the central business district.[29] Almost unheard of prior to the early 1970s, the apartment conversion phenomenon has affected many cities.[30] Nevertheless, it was estimated that by 1980 Washington had lost about 7 percent of its private rental stock to condominiums and cooperatives, one of the highest proportions in the United States.[31] Thus, apartment conversion and the renovation and reoccupancy of single-family housing units characteristic of gentrification have combined to raise the city's share of owner-occupied dwelling units. This outcome is generally considered a positive influence on neighborhood stability and property maintenance. But the cost, a decline in the supply of rental housing, has been a very high one for many low- and moderate-income households, often including the elderly and the young.

The process of gentrification in Washington has been remarkably similar from neighborhood to neighborhood. Typically, young singles and couples have purchased an older structure, which may have been subdivided earlier into apartments or rooms. Renovation is undertaken, and in most cases the building is converted to a single-family structure or to one with fewer units. Often, a single-family dwelling unit occupies the first and upper floors, and a separate apartment is added in the basement for rental purposes. Because the owners usually do a substantial amount of the renovation work themselves, they may realize substantial savings in construction costs. After a few years the completed property generally appreciates markedly in value. Some owners have refinanced their mortgage loan, borrowing on the security of the increased worth of their renovated homes. Then, many have acquired a second or third property in the same neighborhood for investment purposes, perhaps renovating it and selling or renting the finished structure.

Most observers seem to feel that individual owner-occupants and amateur investors are responsible for the first stages of revitalization in Washington. But there is little direct evidence to substantiate this. It is conceivable that in some cases professional investors and developers have participated in initiating reinvestment in neighborhoods adjacent to those actively undergoing revitalization.[32] It is clear that whoever initiates private-market revitalization, professional developers are almost invariably responsible for the bulk of the reinvestment in scattered new construction projects. Such "infill" projects have affected all of Washington's revitalizing neighborhoods.

All three generations of Washington's neighborhood revitalization experience have progressed almost entirely through private-market processes. With the exception of the southwest urban renewal project and a few scattered, publicly subsidized renovation and new construction-project areas, there has been comparatively little public intervention. Nonetheless, the District of Columbia government has designated historic districts in gentrifying areas such as Dupont Circle, Mount Pleasant, Capitol Hill, Logan Circle and LeDroit Park. By doing so, the public sector has extended special sanctions over property usage, which some observers argue has enhanced property values by lending prestige to the protected areas. Others have charged that such designations spur further renovation and reinvestment and hasten displacement of needy households. Nonetheless, there is no empirical evidence to substantiate these claims in Washington. It does appear, though, that the *timing* of historic district designation is critical. If it occurs early in a neighborhood's reinvestment cycle, it may send signals to investors that the area is ripe for exploitation. If, on the other hand, it occurs after several years of renovation activity, it seems unlikely that it would significantly catalyze the process.

Public intervention has also taken the form of governmental acquisition of property and renovation or construction of new facilities in revitalizing neighborhoods. For example, a federal grant subsidized the rehabilitation of the historical Eastern Market on Capitol Hill, a space that later accommodated artist studios and gourmet food shops. More recently, the District government completed construction of a large city office building in the former riot corridor of the Shaw neighborhood, an area of high crime and a major marketplace for drug dealers.[33] Located between the revitalizing Dupont Circle and Logan Circle areas, Shaw has shown evidence of residential gentrification for at least six years. In addition, other forms of private reinvestment have taken place: The Shaw area has become the locus of a budding theater district, with at least four new off-Broadway type theater companies opening.[34] The District government's construction of a city office building in the midst of this course of events indicates that municipal authorities have decided to hasten the reinvestment process through the capital budget. Moreover, police enforcement of loitering and antidrug laws and stepped-up building-code inspections have been employed in an effort to further the conversion of the Shaw area.

Although the level of public intervention in revitalizing neighborhoods is considerably less extensive than under the Urban Renewal Program or other federal plans, it cannot be said that gentrification has occurred entirely free of governmental influence. This is especially true of the third generation of revitalization. But now the public sector prefers to *respond to* private reinvestment once underway rather than *catalyze* it through eminent domain proceedings, massive public expenditures, and extensive police power regulation. Hence, the District government now typically awaits expression of resident preferences before proceeding with public gestures such as historic-district designation, re-zoning, building-code enforcement, and police-patrol reinforcement. With the exception of a few federally subsidized rehabilitation target areas, there have been no neighborhoods in the city in which the District government has recently exercised its own budgetary or legal authority in order to stimulate concentrated reinvestment.

Part of the explanation for this situation may lie in a recent report from the U.S. Department of Housing and Urban Development (HUD).[35] It found that the District government spent too much money to process federally subsidized home-rehabilitation loans. It cost an average of $11,300 to administer each of the 52 loans the District extended to low-income homeowners in 1985; this amounted to 51 cents for each federal dollar the District spent on the program. HUD guidelines recommend that processing costs not exceed 15 cents per federal dollar spent. Moreover, although federal guidelines require that at least 25 loan cases per full-time employee be processed each year, the District managed to complete an average of only 4 cases per employee.

This poor record followed a 1980 report card from HUD that cited myriad problems in the District government's housing rehabilitation program. Lackluster performance, moreover, has shown in other programs such as public housing. In March 1986 HUD organized a special task force to help the District address several problems in its public-housing program that had gone uncorrected after earlier HUD warnings. Hence, the District's own sorry achievements in subsidized housing suggest why it has not become a leader in neighborhood revitalization in the city.

Although much of Washington's neighborhood revitalization has taken place in the shadows, outside of public planning processes, more light can be shed on the subject through examination of U.S. decennial census data for 1970 and 1980. These statistics provide the first opportunity to probe in depth the period during which gentrification in Washington mushroomed. The relatively small areas encompassed by census tracts make it possible to combine several tracts to create a study area conforming approximately to the city's gentrifying areas. For insights into the conditions that have characterized neighborhood revitalization in the nation's capital, Chapter 5 explores several demographic variables.

5

Washington's Neighborhood Revival:
A Comparative Analysis, 1970–1980

As Chapter 4 showed the national capital has had an uncommonly long experience with private-market neighborhood revitalization or gentrification. Nevertheless, because the largest share of reinvestment activity occurred during the 1970s, it was not possible to gain a comprehensive longitudinal perspective of the demographic characteristics of gentrification from sources such as the 1970 U.S. decennial census. Since 1982, however, small-area statistics from the 1980 census have become available. Hence, this chapter will concentrate on the author's analysis of demographic and housing conditions in Washington's revitalizing neighborhoods. For this purpose, the census tracts corresponding to residential areas undergoing active revitalization during the 1970s have been aggregated into a single analytical unit termed "Revitalizing Areas" (see Study Area, Map 5.1). Included are tracts that were known to be undergoing gentrification during this period, as well as tracts in the residential part of the southwest urban renewal area. As discussed previously, the southwest underwent renewal through intensive public regulation and investment, while the gentrifying areas have been the subjects primarily of private-market forces. But in both cases substantial physical and social changes have resulted. The present analysis, then, will concentrate on measuring the nature and extent of these shifts.

For most variables under study, the 1970 and 1980 Revitalizing Area statistics will be compared. Second, the Revitalizing Areas will be compared with the remainder of the city, termed the "Remaining Areas," for the same period. These two measures will provide both a chronological and a geographical perspective, neither of which was available to researchers, planners, or public officials until recently. In particular, the latter measure provides an assessment of the overall nature of revitalization in Washington relative to the city's essentially nonrevitalizing areas. Methods of data collection and sources of data are described in the Appendix.

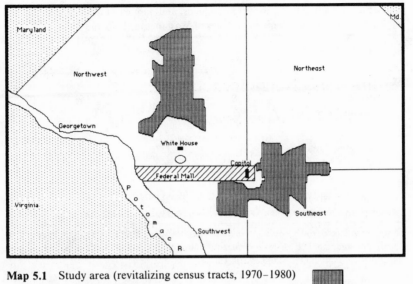

Map 5.1 Study area (revitalizing census tracts, 1970–1980)
Source: Prepared by Dennis E. Gale.

The variables to be explored are population, number of households, and number of families; educational achievement and occupation of residents; previous residential location of residents; number of dwelling units per structure type, and number of overcrowded housing units. The significance of each of these indicators will be explained.

Population, Households, and Families

Because previous research has shown that gentrifier households tend to be relatively small, with one or two occupants and few, if any, children,[1] we would expect that the population in Washington's Revitalizing Areas declined over the 1970s.[2] The in-migration of smaller households, coupled with the out-migration of the typically larger-sized incumbent households living in declining (or formerly declining) neighborhoods, should have resulted in a net population loss.

In fact, the Revitalizing Areas lost slightly over 27,000 persons, a decline of about 23 percent, during the 1970s (see Table 5.1). But when compared with the Remaining Areas of Washington, this figure takes on more importance. In these essentially nonrevitalizing areas, a loss of about 91,000 persons occurred. This change represented only about a 14 percent decline.

Table 5.1   Population, number of households, and number of families
in the Revitalizing and Remaining Areas of Washington, 1970 and 1980

Category	1970	1980	Net Change	Change as percentage
Population				
Revitalizing Areas	116,809	89,693	−27,116	−23.2
Remaining Areas	639,701	548,640	−91,061	−14.2
Households				
Revitalizing Areas	50,493	46,377	−4,116	−8.2
Remaining Areas	212,045	207,655	−4,390	−2.1
Families				
Revitalizing Areas	22,386	15,030	−7,356	−32.9
Remaining Areas	301,829	120,539	−181,290	−60.1

Source: Adapted from *Census of Population and Housing, 1970*, PHC (1), U.S. Bureau of the Census (Washington, D.C.: U.S. Government Printing Office), table P1 and *Census of Population and Housing, 1980*, STF 3A, tables 3, 9, 10.

Recalling that the entire city of Washington lost 121,000 persons, a loss of less than 16 percent (see Table 2.1), we realize that a relatively small area of the central city was experiencing net depopulation at a considerably faster rate than the remainder of the city (see Map 5.1).

Another measure of population change is the household. Households are defined by the U.S. Bureau of the Census as one or more persons occupying a housing unit. Households include related and unrelated individuals but do not include those living in group quarters such as dormitories, health-care institutions, penal facilities, and military barracks. Thus, both families and one or more single persons occupying a house, apartment, or mobile home would be considered households. Because many gentrifiers appear to live in nonfamily circumstances, while incumbent residents are more likely to live in families, we would expect household shifts to be less dramatic than family shifts in the Revitalizing Areas.[3]

Interestingly, the Revitalizing Areas lost almost the same *number* of households as the considerably larger remainder of the city—approximately 4,000 (see Table 5.1). But the *rate* of household decline in the Revitalizing Areas, about 8 percent, was almost four times that of the Remaining Areas of the city (about 2 percent). When these data are compared with those on family shifts, however, the pattern is reversed (see Table 5.1). The Revitalizing Areas were losing families at a slower rate (33 percent) than the Remaining Areas (60 percent). Thus, while the Revitalizing Areas were losing households at a faster rate than the Remaining

Areas, they were losing families at a slower rate. Of course, no observer can overlook the fact that both areas experienced a substantial loss of families. Nonetheless, the variations in the rates of change between households and families suggest that revitalization was not as closely associated with central-city family loss as were conditions in the rest of the city, but it was somewhat more closely associated with loss of nonfamily households. Thus, the most profound effects of revitalization may have been on single-person households and households composed of unrelated individuals, both types tending to be somewhat more mobile than families. These patterns have been found in very similar form in a recent comparative study of revitalizing neighborhoods in San Francisco, Denver, Cincinnati, Atlanta, and Washington.[4]

Educational Achievement

One important way the effects of revitalization can be measured is through socioeconomic indicators such as educational achievement. So far, empirical studies have found that members of most gentrifier households have attained relatively high levels of education, often possessing baccalaureate and graduate degrees; on the other hand, members of incumbent households tend to have attained considerably lower levels of education, rarely possessing more than a high school diploma.[5] Gentrification has been characterized, therefore, as a process that is marked by relatively rapid increases in a neighborhood's socioeconomic status as measured by education.

In the Revitalizing Areas of Washington, this characterization held true. For example, people aged 25 and older with less than a high school education (including those who never reached high school) made up 44 percent of the 1970 population of that age group; by 1980 they composed only 23 percent (see Table 5.2). While the 1970 proportion of such persons in the Remaining Areas was close to that of the Revitalizing Areas (43 percent), by 1980 it had dropped to 35 percent. Thus, persons with the lowest educational attainment were reduced by more than one-half in the Revitalizing Areas and by about one-fourth in the rest of the city.

Conversely, the proportion of people with the highest educational achievement, four or more years of college, rose from 24 percent of the 1970 population of the Revitalizing Areas to 47 percent in 1980. In short, the percentage almost doubled. Meanwhile, in the Remaining Areas the proportion shifted only slightly, from 21 to 24 percent during the decade.

Table 5.2   Educational achievement of people aged 25 and older in the
Revitalizing and Remaining Areas of Washington, 1970 and 1980

Years of schooling completed	1970		1980	
	Number	Percentage	Number	Percentage
Less than 4 years of high school				
Revitalizing Areas	31,317	43.8	14,140	23.0
Remaining Areas	158,403	42.8	117,137	34.7
4 years of high school				
Revitalizing Areas	15,193	21.2	10,840	17.6
Remaining Areas	95,574	25.8	90,977	27.0
1–3 years of college				
Revitalizing Areas	7,865	11.0	7,895	12.9
Remaining Areas	39,466	10.7	48,186	14.3
4 or more years of college				
Revitalizing Areas	17,191	24.0	28,574	46.5
Remaining Areas	76,698	20.7	80,904	24.0
Total				
Revitalizing Areas	71,566	100.0	61,449	100.0
Remaining Areas	370,141	100.0	337,204	100.0

Source: Adapted from *Census of Population and Housing, 1970*, PHC (1), U.S. Bureau of the
Census (Washington, D.C.: U.S. Government Printing Office), table P2 and *Census of Population
and Housing, 1980*, STF 3A, table 48.

Interestingly, the relative distribution of educational achievement in the
Revitalizing Areas in 1970 was much the same as that of the Remaining
Areas. In other words, residents in the areas soon to experience substantial
reinvestment activity and population turnover had about the same educational profile as residents in the nonrevitalizing parts of Washington. But
by 1980, although the distribution of educational achievement in the rest of
the city had shifted moderately in most categories, the shift in the revitalizing portions of Washington was nothing short of profound. (So decisive a picture was not drawn in a recent study of smaller revitalizing sectors
in five U.S. cities. Rather, there were similar gains among the highly educated but divergent patterns among less-educated people.)[6] To the extent
that education is a good measure of socioeconomic status or the ability to
succeed in life, it could not be said that people living in the future Revitalizing Areas of the city in 1970 were substantially different from those in
the rest of the city; yet only a decade later there were fundamental differences. But of course other factors besides education contribute to status
and success in life. One of these is racial identity.

Table 5.3   Race and educational achievement of people aged 25 and
older in the Revitalizing and Remaining Areas of Washington, 1980

Years of schooling completed	White		Black	
	Number	Percentage	Number	Percentage
Less than 4 years of high school				
Revitalizing Areas	2,308	6.5	11,803	44.2
Remaining Areas	12,335	13.1	101,492	43.6
4 years of high school				
Revitalizing Areas	4,381	12.3	6,576	24.6
Remaining Areas	16,838	17.9	72,175	31.0
1-3 years of college				
Revitalizing Areas	4,995	14.0	3,777	14.1
Remaining Areas	14,062	15.0	31,959	13.7
4 years of college or more				
Revitalizing Areas	23,884	67.2	4,567	17.1
Remaining Areas	50,634	54.0	27,098	11.7
Total				
Revitalizing Areas	35,568	100.0	26,723	100.0
Remaining Areas	93,869	100.0	232,724	100.0

Source: Adapted from *Census of Population and Housing, 1970,* PHC (1), U.S. Bureau of the
Census (Washington, D.C.: U.S. Government Printing Office), table P2 and *Census of Population
and Housing, 1980,* STF 3A, table 48.

Race and Educational Achievement

Unfortunately, data on educational achievement by race were not available
from the 1970 decennial census in a form of use to the present analysis.
But 1980 census data provide at least a static measure of this condition and
permit comparison of the Revitalizing and Remaining Areas. Immediately
apparent are the vast differences in education levels between blacks and
whites. In the Revitalizing Areas only 7 percent of whites but 44 percent
of blacks attained less than four years of high school (see Table 5.3). At the
other extreme, those with four or more years of college, 67 percent of
whites and 17 percent of blacks reached that level. The percentage of
blacks in the lowest educational category was approximately seven times
that of whites, and the percentage of whites in the highest category was
about four times that of blacks. Thus, the educational differences between
blacks and whites in the Revitalizing Areas in 1980 were substantial.

Also important is educational attainment by race in the Remaining
Areas of the city. Whites in these areas had twice the proportion in the

lowest educational achievement classification as whites in the Revitalizing Areas had. Yet 67 percent of Revitalizing Area whites and 54 percent of Remaining Area whites were in the highest educational classification. Blacks, on the other hand, did not vary substantially between the two areas in the lowest educational achievement category. About the same percentage of blacks in each area had less than four years of high school. But a higher percentage of blacks in the Revitalizing Areas had four or more years of college education than those in the Remaining Areas. Thus, Revitalizing Area whites and blacks were significantly more accomplished educationally than their racial counterparts in the rest of the city. Educationally, blacks were more disadvantaged than whites in both areas but less so in the Revitalizing Areas than in the Remaining Areas.

Occupational Status

Another measure of socioeconomic status is occupation. The present analysis has aggregated census occupational groupings into four categories (see Table 5.4). Group 1, the highest achievement category, is composed of managerial, professional, technical, sales, and administrative occupations. Group 2 includes service occupations such as private household, protective service, and clerical occupations. Group 3 is composed largely of blue-collar occupations such as precision product, craft, repair, machine operation, fabrication, and labor occupations. Group 4, a minuscule share of most urban labor markets nationally, is made up of farming, forestry, and fishing occupations.

Because gentrifier households have been identified as generally college-educated and in white-collar occupations, we would expect that Washington's Revitalizing Areas would show significant gains in residents with Group 1 occupations.[7] In fact, the proportion of Group 1 residents rose from 62 percent of the 1970 population in the Revitalizing Areas to 77 percent of the corresponding 1980 population. In the Remaining Areas, however, the rise in Group 1 residents was from 57 to 65 percent. During the 1970s Group 1 residents in the Revitalizing Areas increased their numbers by almost 11 percent, while their counterparts in the Remaining Areas increased their numbers by less than 2 percent. In absolute numbers the city's Revitalizing Areas had a net gain of almost 4,100 of these high-status worker-residents, while the remainder of the city, with a considerably larger population and geographical area, had a gain of about 2,900

Table 5.4 Occupational status of employed people aged 16 and older in the Revitalizing and Remaining Areas of Washington, 1970 and 1980

	1970		1980	
Occupational status	Number	Percentage	Number	Percentage
Group 1[a]				
Revitalizing Areas	37,875	62.1	41,944	76.6
Remaining Areas	156,098	57.0	158,988	65.3
Group 2[b]				
Revitalizing Areas	13,496	22.1	7,402	13.5
Remaining Areas	56,955	20.8	44,701	18.4
Group 3[c]				
Revitalizing Areas	9,527	15.6	5,200	9.5
Remaining Areas	60,095	21.9	38,284	15.7
Group 4[d]				
Revitalizing Areas	125	0.2	232	0.4
Remaining Areas	805	0.3	1,356	0.6
Total				
Revitalizing Areas	61,023	100.0	54,778	100.0
Remaining Areas	273,953	100.0	243,329	100.0

Source: Adapted from *Census of Population and Housing, 1970*, PHC (1), U.S. Bureau of the Census (Washington, D.C.: U.S. Government Printing Office), table P3 and *Census of Population and Housing, 1980*, STF 3A, table 66.

a. Group 1 = managerial, professional, technical, sales, and administrative occupations.

b. Group 2 = service occupations, including private household, protective service, and clerical occupations.

c. Group 3 = precision product, craft, repair, machine operation, fabrication, and labor occupations.

d. Group 4 = farming, forestry, and fishing occupations.

such people. Comparison of similar data in a five-city study of revitalizing-neighborhood dynamics found approximately the same pattern.[8]

Although both the Revitalizing and Remaining Areas had decreases in Group 2 and 3 occupations during the decade, there were slight gains in Group 4 occupations. But because this category constitutes such an insignificant share of the labor market and population in the city of Washington, it merits no further discussion here. Nevertheless, the Group 2 and 3 categories, which together composed 38 percent of worker-resident occupations in 1970 in the Revitalizing Areas, made up 23 percent in 1980; in the remainder of the city, they amounted to 43 percent in 1970 and 34 percent in 1980. Hence, there was a slightly more dramatic drop in the less-prestigious occupations in the Revitalizing Areas than in the rest of the city.

These data suggest, then, that Washington's revitalizing neighborhoods, when compared with the rest of the city, have been disproportionately effective in countering the city's overall losses in higher-status people (that is, those with higher educations and those with upper-level, white-collar jobs), which have resulted primarily from out-migration. On the other hand, they have been disproportionately less effective in retaining lower- or moderate-status people. More important, perhaps, is the fact that losses among these people in the Revitalizing Areas do not show up as net gains in their numbers in the Remaining Areas; although the Remaining Areas tended not to experience losses as noteworthy as those in the Revitalizing Areas, their numbers have also declined significantly. While these data are not definitive, they add some weight to the assumption that the less-fortunate incumbents who vacate their homes in gentrifying neighborhoods do not migrate in large numbers to the nonrevitalizing areas of Washington. Alternatively, if they do so, they may be merely replacing many other households of similar circumstances that are lost to the city through death and out-migration. The net effect on the nonrevitalizing areas under this second assumption, therefore, would be losses in lower- and moderate-status people, though at less-substantial rates than those in revitalizing neighborhoods.

Previous Residential Location

A critical topic of concern in research on inner-city revitalization has been the relationship between reinvestment and the geographic mobility patterns of the population. In particular, concern has been expressed about the effect of gentrification on the retention of central-city residents and on the attraction of suburbanites to inner-city living. As discussed above, earlier research drew considerable attention to the finding that gentrifier-home buyers in several cities were not recent arrivals from the suburbs but rather had been living in the city prior to the decision to locate in a revitalizing neighborhood.[9] In short, the back-to-the-city hypothesis associated with gentrification was not supported.

But timely evidence on overall shifts among households in revitalizing neighborhoods has not been available until recently. Decennial census data permit comparison of the previous residential location (five years prior to each census) of people living in Washington in 1970 and in 1980. Table 5.5

Table 5.5 Previous residential location (five years earlier) of people aged five years and older in the Revitalizing and Remaining Areas of Washington, 1970 and 1980

	1970		1980	
Previous location	Number	Percentage	Number	Percentage
District of Columbia				
Revitalizing Areas	51,368	73.4	54,378	66.1
Remaining Areas	455,131	88.0	433,562	88.0
Suburbs of Washington				
Revitalizing Areas	3,006	4.3	5,402	6.6
Remaining Areas	9,673	1.9	20,103	4.1
Outside the Washington SMSA				
Revitalizing Areas	15,637	22.3	22,445	27.3
Remaining Areas	52,487	10.1	38,981	7.9
Total				
Revitalizing Areas	70,011	100.0	82,225	100.0
Remaining Areas	517,291	100.0	492,646	100.0

Source: Adapted from *Census of Population and Housing, 1970*, PHC (1), U.S. Bureau of the Census (Washington, D.C.: U.S. Government Printing Office), table P2 and *Census of Population and Housing, 1980*, STF 3A, table 35.

compares Washington residents who had lived previously in the city of Washington with Washington residents who had lived in Washington's suburbs and with those who had lived outside the Washington metropolitan area altogether. The last group could include not only those who had lived just beyond the suburbs but also those who had migrated from other parts of the nation or the world to live in the District of Columbia.

In 1970, 73 percent of those living in the Revitalizing Areas had lived in the city of Washington in 1965. By 1980, with revitalization in these areas well underway, the comparable measure—those who had lived in Washington in 1975—had dropped to 66 percent. Thus, the efficacy with which the Revitalizing Areas retained central-city residents declined during the 1970s. But this condition was offset somewhat by the increased proportions of Revitalizing Area residents from outside the city. Former Washington suburbanites, although a tiny minority in both censuses, raised their share from 4 to almost 7 percent. The proportion of Revitalizing Area residents from outside the metropolitan area rose from 22 to 27 percent of the total. No dramatic shifts occurred among any of these three subgroups, but the modest trend toward increasing the city's "capture rate" of suburbanites and "outsiders" is, perhaps, cause for cautious optimism.

When the Revitalizing Areas are compared with the Remaining Areas, the shifts associated with gentrification are more apparent. The Remaining Areas had a considerably higher share of continuing central-city residents. In both 1970 and 1980 this group amounted to 88 percent, showing great stability in the nongentrifying neighborhoods overall. But newcomers from the suburbs constituted a shift from 2 to 4 percent, and the proportion of outsiders changed from 10 to 8 percent. The Remaining Areas, therefore, showed a slight improvement in their capacity to attract suburbanites and a slight reduction in their ability to attract metropolitan newcomers to live in the city of Washington.

These data suggest that although the Revitalizing Areas were not as effective at retaining existing central-city residents, they were somewhat more effective than the rest of the city in attracting outsiders to move into Washington. In other words, gentrification and similar forms of neighborhood revitalization may contribute disproportionately to Washington's ability to attract residents to the city from outside the metropolitan area. On the other hand, both the Revitalizing and the Remaining Areas appear to have been effective in attracting former suburbanites to live in the city. Generally, these trends in Washington appear to comport with those in other similarly analyzed cities experiencing gentrification.[10]

Housing Conditions

Neighborhood revitalization is characterized not only by demographic changes but also by the relatively rapid improvement of housing quality. This process centers on housing rehabilitation and restoration, with moderate levels of new "infill" construction. Not so obvious, however, are the effects of gentrification on a neighborhood's housing supply. Previous discussions have pointed out that, typically, a neighborhood undergoing revitalization will have experienced a period of significant decline, perhaps having commenced after World War II. As middle- and working-class families left such areas in Washington to relocate in the suburbs, the single-family dwellings left behind were often subdivided into apartments or rooms, increasing neighborhood dwelling-unit densities. *A priori* impressions of housing conditions in revitalizing neighborhoods, on the other hand, suggest that gentrifiers often *reduce* the number of units per structure as a means of reclaiming space needed to accommodate the lower occupancy levels typical of middle-class households. This outcome, of course, may reduce area housing stocks, especially for households of low and moderate incomes.

Table 5.6 Year-round housing units by structure type in the
Revitalizing and Remaining Areas of Washington, 1970 and 1980

| | 1970 | 1980 | Change | |
	Number	Number	Number	Percentage
Structure type				
One unit[a]				
Revitalizing Areas	12,726	11,566	−1,160	−9.10
Remaining Areas	89,857	86,377	−3,480	−3.90
Two units				
Revitalizing Areas	2,709	3,555	846	31.20
Remaining Areas	7,620	6,362	−1,258	−16.50
Three or four units				
Revitalizing Areas	3,724	3,594	−130	−3.50
Remaining Areas	19,914	19,448	−466	−2.30
Five or more units				
Revitalizing Areas	35,188	34,193	−995	−2.80
Remaining Areas	106,652	111,762	5,110	4.80
Total				
Revitalizing Areas	54,347	52,908	−1,439	−2.6
Remaining Areas	224,043	223,949	−94	−0.04

Source: Adapted from *Census of Population and Housing, 1970*, PHC (1), U.S. Bureau of the Census (Washington, D.C.: U.S. Government Printing Office), table H2 and *Census of Population and Housing, 1980*, STF 3A, table 102.

a. Includes mobile homes and trailers.

One measure of this condition provided by the decennial census is the shift in the number of dwelling units by structure type from 1970 to 1980. Table 5.6 indicates changes in the supply of residential units in structures of various sizes. It indicates that in the Revitalizing Areas there was an overall decline of 1,439 dwelling units, or slightly less than 3 percent. This compares with a net loss of 94 units in the Remaining Areas of the city, a decline of less than one-tenth of 1 percent. The loss in the number of dwelling units in Washington's Revitalizing Areas was 15 times as large as that in the rest of the city. These data suggest the disproportionate effect that gentrification and other forms of revitalization have had on the overall supply of housing in the city.

Further insights can be gained by examining changes in the number of units by structural type (see Table 5.6). In the Revitalizing Areas there were losses in all structural types with the exception of two-unit structures. There was a gain of 846 two-unit dwellings, or 31 percent. This trend was in direct contrast with the losses in two-unit structures in the Remaining

Areas of the city. The reason for this is probably that many gentrifiers add a basement apartment to their homes to gain extra income. These so-called "English basement apartments" are ubiquitous on Capitol Hill, in Dupont Circle, and in other such neighborhoods and often appear to be built without building permits or other formal government approval. This hypothesis is further supported by a one-unit-structure loss of 9 percent in the Revitalizing Areas, a rate twice that in the rest of the city. This suggests that basement apartments have been added to many single-family struc-tures, which were reclassified as two-unit buildings. In some cases, of course, two-unit structures are created when investors merely subdivide a two-, three-, or four-story rooming house into two apartments, sometimes occupying one unit themselves. Nevertheless, whatever their configuration, these newly created units are almost invariably rented at middle-to upper-middle-income levels, thereby reducing the supply of housing for Wash-ington's low- and moderate-income households.

Also noteworthy are the contrasting figures for apartment buildings (structures with five or more units). While there was a loss approaching 1,000 such dwellings (3 percent) in the Revitalizing Areas, the Remaining Areas experienced a gain of over 5,000 units, or 5 percent. One possible explanation is that much of Washington's conversion of apartments to condominiums and cooperatives occurred in the Dupont Circle, Adams Morgan, and Capitol Hill neighborhoods, all included in the Revitalizing Areas.[11] Because some such conversions combine two smaller units into a single larger unit, a net reduction could occur in apartment-building units. A second explanation is that little private-market-rate rental housing has been built in the District in several years. Much of the new construction of rental units during the 1970s was in public or publicly assisted projects, few of which have been located in the Revitalizing Areas. Doubtless, more such subsidized buildings have been located in some of the Remaining Areas such as the far southeast and northeast.

The general implication of these data is that revitalization processes have disproportionately diminished the housing supply in the District of Columbia, when the Revitalizing Areas are compared with the rest of the city. Although revitalization brings inarguable improvement to housing and neighborhood conditions, it appears to do so at the expense of reduc-ing the supply of less-costly housing. Clearly, Washington lost far more housing units in the Revitalizing Areas during the 1970s than it gained throughout the rest of the city. Although the Revitalizing Areas had less than one-fourth as many households in 1980 as existed in the Remaining Areas, (see Table 5.1), they absorbed about 15 times the housing loss.

Another insight into housing conditions in Washington's gentrifying neighborhoods is revealed in census statistics that measure not housing supply but the adequacy of the housing stock in relationship to the needs of households for space. Two indexes used in the census are housing units with complete plumbing and overcrowded housing units. However, because outdoor toilets have been almost completely eliminated in most major cities, this measure is not as useful in Washington as that of overcrowdedness. A unit is defined as overcrowded in the census if it has more than one person per room living in it. This isolates the primary problem of housing in Washington, that of supply and space in relationship to household size. Furthermore, the data provide a comparison of conditions by race, giving a picture of the unequal housing circumstances of blacks and whites.

In 1980, 28 percent of overcrowded units in the Revitalizing Areas were occupied by whites and 72 percent were occupied by blacks. Thus, this type of housing inadequacy had a substantially greater effect on blacks than on whites. Considering that in 1980 the overall white-to-black population ratio in the city of Washington (27 percent white to 70 percent black) differed little from these figures, however, some observers may question whether this situation has a significant racial dimension. By comparison, though, the distribution of overcrowded units in the Remaining Areas provides a fairer barometer of the racial effect of this housing condition. While 28 percent of overcrowded units in the Revitalizing Areas were occupied by whites, only 6 percent in the Remaining Areas were so occupied. Although 72 percent of such units in the Revitalizing Areas were occupied by blacks, almost 95 percent were so occupied in the Remaining Areas.

Therefore, overcrowded housing was a condition that affected whites in the Revitalizing Areas considerably more so than it did whites in the Remaining Areas of the city. But it also affected blacks in the Revitalizing Areas substantially more so than it did whites in the same areas. Perhaps most surprising is that these conditions notwithstanding, blacks in the Remaining Areas of Washington were considerably more victimized by overcrowding than were blacks in the Revitalizing Areas. To put it simply, these data suggest that by the standard of overcrowded housing, whites in the Revitalizing Areas are proportionately worse off than whites in the rest of the city but better off than blacks in the Revitalizing Areas; blacks in the Revitalizing Areas, on the other hand, are better off than blacks elsewhere in the city.

Another assessment shows that of all white-occupied overcrowded housing in Washington, 40 percent is in the Revitalizing Areas and 60 percent is in the Remaining Areas. Yet of all black-occupied overcrowded housing in the city, only 9 percent is in the Revitalizing Areas, and 91 percent is in the Remaining Areas. One interpretation of these data is that the overcrowding effect of revitalization on whites living in revitalizing neighborhoods is disproportionately negative when compared with its effect on their black neighbors. But another interpretation is that because blacks are less able than whites to afford housing in a neighborhood undergoing reinvestment, they are more likely to be forced to move to nonrevitalizing areas, thus exacerbating housing crowding in those sections of the city. Overcrowding among whites in the Revitalizing Areas may be more a matter of choice (that is, the price one pays to live in a convenient, quaint neighborhood). For blacks almost anywhere in the city, however, overcrowding may be a simple matter of necessity.

Discussion

The foregoing analysis has revealed several noteworthy trends occurring in the Revitalizing Areas of Washington during the 1970s. The chief advantage of this analysis is that it yields one of the first fairly comprehensive geographic perspectives of gentrification in Washington, avoiding the narrower focus of earlier studies of one, two, or three individual neighborhoods. In addition, it draws on the best available source of data in terms of methodological sophistication, the decennial censuses. A third advantage is that for the first time, comparison of Washington's revitalizing areas with its nonrevitalizing areas has been possible. These comparative bases thus shed new light on the nature of one of the most important urban phenomena since the end of World War II—inner-city revitalization.

The analysis revealed that neighborhood reinvestment has been responsible for substantial socioeconomic shifts in Washington. But these dynamics are not revealed through simple analysis of overall net changes in the central city itself.[12] When Washington's Revitalizing Areas are compared with the rest of the city, it is clear that while reinvestment has not reversed the city's loss of middle-class households, it has contributed more to stemming that loss than has any other condition in the city. A significant middle-class population is of importance to the overall public welfare of the nation's capital, and the processes of reinvestment, especially private-market reinvestment, have been more effective in countering the net effects of the out-migration of its higher-educated, higher-status worker-residents than has any other dynamic. The finding that the Revitalizing Areas of the city added more higher-status worker-residents to the city's population than the rest of the city combined only underscores the importance of this phenomenon. Because higher educational achievement is more prevalent among whites than blacks in Washington, one inescapable conclusion about gentrification is that it has reduced the overall rate of decline in the District's white population. Although the District lost critical numbers of both blacks and whites during the last decade, the substantial appeal of gentrification to higher-educated, professional whites helped to maintain a ratio between the races in Washington in 1980 that was essentially the same as that in 1970.

The analysis further revealed that gentrification is more effective in attracting relative newcomers to the city than it is in retaining existing city residents. This is especially so of newcomers from outside the metropolitan area of Washington, although modest increases in former Washington suburbanites occurred also. These findings add further weight to the argument that Washington's gentrification experience has served to prevent the rather substantial loss of white households it would otherwise have suffered.

The relative socioeconomic benefits of gentrification notwithstanding, however, the reinvestment process in Washington was associated with a reduction in the supply of housing that was many times that in the geographically larger Remaining Areas of the city. Because much of today's inner ring of revitalizing neighborhoods surrounding the central business district once encompassed a significant share of the city's supply of low- and moderate-income housing, reductions in housing supply in those areas connote reductions in the city's overall stock of nonsubsidized housing for people of limited means. In short, gentrification has doubtless been responsible for much of the decrease in Washington's stock of housing affordable to needy households. The critically higher incidence of overcrowding among blacks in the Revitalizing Areas than among whites is one expression of this condition, although overcrowding among blacks was greater elsewhere in the city than in the Revitalizing Areas.

Postscript: Race and Revitalization in Washington

The political and public policy implications of neighborhood and CBD revitalization in Washington will be discussed later. It is important to point out here, however, that this chapter documents, as did Chapters 3 and 4, the existence of a fundamental process of competition for space in the national capital. This struggle has both socioeconomic and racial properties. Essentially, it pits major business interests that wish to redevelop in the core of the city or in some of its neighborhoods against those who are concerned for the most part with preserving the physical status quo of the city. This latter group is made up largely of people who champion the preservation of historical buildings and districts, and of preservationists of another sort—resident groups less interested in historicity but simply opposed to disruptive new development in their neighborhoods. The official role of the District government has been that of a mediator between development and preservation interests, although most observers would conclude that it is predisposed toward the objectives of the former.

This relationship represents a decided shift from that of the early 1970s, when private development threatened few neighborhoods other than the Georgetown waterfront and preservation was a less-salient issue than now. Most development in the CBD took place in the new downtown, where efforts to resist by incumbent business owners and residents were minimal. The final chapter was being written in this era of redevelopment—in which District and federal government control was paramount—slightly more than a decade ago. In that period fiscal and regulatory tools gave the public sector a firmer hand in decisions about planning issues. Riding the crest of social reform and civil rights politics, Urban Renewal and Model Cities programs, and public housing and community action projects, the interstate highway juggernaut, and other similar issues had often pitted government against residents and small-business owners trying to preserve the fabric of their neighborhoods. But at that time these groups were more frequently composed of racial minorities, usually speaking to the needs of (and often including) the economically disadvantaged. Their efforts were directed at agencies more heavily influenced by the white-dominated Congress and the executive branch of the federal government. Because home rule had not been fully instituted, District government policies, too, were more likely to be informed by white-dominated organizations such as the Board of Trade, real estate groups, and various professional and trade associations. As a result, urban planning conflicts routinely centered on social welfare issues such as increasing the supply of affordable housing and employment opportunities, heightening rent-control legislation, extending housing-rehabilitation assistance, preventing highway construction in low- and moderate-income neighborhoods, and improving neighborhood recreation facilities.

Today, with government intervention in urban policy issues vastly reduced, the District's political agenda (insofar as urban planning issues are concerned) is no longer dominated by struggle between black, working-class interests on the one hand and primarily white, middle- to upper-class interests on the other. To be sure, these issues arise from time to time, but today the momentum in urban planning politics is directed more routinely to struggles among whites. As such, planning conflict is less resolutely based on class and race than on the value distinctions of the white elite about the nature of the environmental fabric of Washington. Certainly, this view does not maintain that social welfare issues, and therefore struggle between working-class blacks and middle- to upper-class whites, has disappeared. Occasionally, controversies such as shelter for the homeless, subsidized housing, or rent control command public attention. But the battle lines in urban planning debates today are typically drawn between white-dominated groups serving interests viewed by many blacks as elitist.

However critical the effect of downtown and neighborhood revitalization on Washington's social, racial, and political makeup, other issues affect this matter as well. Chapter 6 explores one of these — the quality of public education and its role in achieving a stable, racially balanced population.

6

Revitalization and the Urban Schools

The rapid expansion in the rate of revitalization in Washington, primarily over the past decade, has brought a great deal of physical and economic renewal to the city's central business district and inner-ring neighborhoods. Yet with the shifting social-class and racial profiles that have accompanied this process have come differing expectations about the nature of some public services provided to residents of the Revitalizing Areas. In particular, the quality of education available in the city's school system has raised important questions about the long-term commitment of residents of gentrifying neighborhoods, especially whites, to continued central-city living. In many American cities such as Washington, the relatively poor quality of public schools has long been a reason cited by middle-class families for moving to the suburbs. At least since 1950, the perception has been that many suburban school systems provided a higher-quality education than did central-city school systems. Unless urban families could afford private schools, this reasoning went, their only alternative was to move to the suburbs by the time their children reached school age.

Of course, other factors such as urban crime, noise, congestion, and the cost of modern single-family housing have contributed to the decision of middle-class families to migrate out of central cities. But, for many, the public schools were paramount in their decision. And doubtless some families would have continued residence in central cities if public schools had been competitive with suburban schools in educational quality.

Nevertheless, when inner-city gentrification became a widespread pattern in Washington during the 1970s, there was reason to believe that perhaps gentrifier households would place less emphasis on public educational quality than had earlier generations of middle-class urbanites. Surveys of home buyers in two gentrification neighborhoods of Washington showed that many had few or no children, even though they were in the prime childbearing years. Sixty-one percent of the households in the Mount Pleasant sample and 74 percent of those in the Capitol Hill sample had no children.[1] Only 21 percent and 11 percent, respectively, had one child. Sixteen percent in Mount Pleasant and 8 percent on Capitol Hill had two children. Almost three-fourths of the former neighborhood's households and 55 percent of the latter's were made up of married or cohabiting couples. Slightly more than two-thirds of the household heads in each sample were aged 30 to 44. Therefore, these surveys showed that even though most of the gentrifiers were at the traditional life-cycle stage at which children are born and educational concerns mount, in fact relatively few had offspring.

Furthermore, less than 10 percent of either sample had children in the District's public schools. But this did not appear to be an expression of dissatisfaction with the city's school system, for an even smaller share had enrolled their children in private schools or as nonresident pupils in suburban public schools. When asked what neighborhood conditions they found most disagreeable, only 18 percent of Mount Pleasant and 10 percent of Capitol Hill respondents cited "inadequate D.C. public schools." Problems such as crime and parking were of greater concern. Thus, it appears that in 1976 and 1977 at least (the years of the surveys), public educational quality was an issue of low salience to many gentrifiers.

Even though more than 95 percent of each neighborhood's sample of respondents had completed college or graduate school themselves, concern about the quality of public education in District public schools was not a major issue among gentrifiers at the time the surveys were carried out. As one 26-year, female resident of Capitol Hill said in 1977, "Everything I've ever read about the District schools is that they're not very good. But it's all hearsay. I suppose if I did have children, I would not put them in the District schools. I would move to an area that had better schools." [2] This situation put these young, predominantly white households in a somewhat different position than their middle-class, nongentrifier counterparts elsewhere in the city. Ever since the years following the Brown v. Board of Education decision by the Supreme Court in 1954, white student enrollment in city schools had been declining. By 1970 whites made up 4.5 percent of the city's public school enrollment. From 1970 to 1981 white enrollment continued to drop, declining by almost 49 percent. Whites composed less than four percent of total 1981 public school enrollment. [3] (Their proportions remained about the same from 1970 to 1981 only because black enrollment had declined also). For many years, parents in the far northeast and southeast and in the upper northwest had been transferring their children to suburban schools or enrolling them in private schools. The spread of neighborhood revitalization in the 1970s thus represented something of a windfall for the national capital. Not only did it inject new

Table 6.1 Live births in the Revitalizing and Remaining
Areas of Washington, 1981, 1982, and 1983

Area	1981 Number	1982 Number	1983 Number	Change, 1981–1983 (as percentage)
Revitalizing Areas	1,455	1,477	1,551	6.6
Remaining Areas	7,877	7,901	7,973	1.2
Total	9,332	9,378	9,524	2.1
Revitalizing Areas as percentage of total	15.6	15.7	16.3	—

Source: "Resident Births (during 1981, 1982, 1983) by Age of Mother and Census Tract," from the unpublished files of the Government of the District of Columbia, Office of Births, Deaths, Marriage and Divorce Records, Research and Statistics Division.

middle-class wealth into the city's fiscal and economic structure, it brought a renewal of some of the city's physical fabric. Moreover, it appeared to many observers that gentrification would not only help to stem some of the city's losses to the suburbs but it would do so with fairly minimal demands on the public school system.

The small numbers of children in gentrifier households and the apparently low level of interest in public school quality among gentrifiers was undoubtedly part of a national trend toward fewer marriages, increasing divorces, and declining birth rates.[4] This trend, of course, translated itself into shrinking public school enrollments not only in most American central cities but in many older suburbs as well.[5] But the postwar baby-boom generation itself, which accounted for these dynamics, has aged since the mid-1970s. Women who entered the labor market in unprecendented numbers during the 1970s, deferring marriage and childbearing while advancing in their careers, are now reaching their mid- and late thirties, a point at which many women are electing to have children. These birth trends have arisen only in recent years, however, and are just beginning to assume noteworthy proportions.

Birth Trends in Washington

Total annual births in the city of Washington hovered between 9,200 and 9,900 between 1975 and 1985.[6] An analysis of births between 1981 and 1983 within the census tracts that encompass the revitalizing neighborhoods of the city (see Map 5.1 and the Appendix for methodology) shows a modest increase of 6.6 percent (see Table 6.1). Compared with the

Table 6.2 Number of live births to white and nonwhite women aged 30 to 39 living
in the Revitalizing and Remaining Areas of Washington, 1981, 1982, and 1983

	1981		1982		1983	
Area	White	Nonwhite	White	Nonwhite	White	Nonwhite
Revitalizing Areas	260	173	283	186	279	237
Remaining Areas	554	1,120	607	1,182	623	1,211
Total	814	1,293	890	1,368	902	1,448
Revitalizing Areas as percentage of total	.9	13.4	31.8	13.6	30.9	16.4

Source: "Resident Births (during 1981, 1982, 1983) by Age of Mother and Census Tract," from
the unpublished files of the Government of the District of Columbia, Office of Births, Deaths,
Marriage and Divorce Records, Research and Statistics Division.

remainder of the city (that is, the nonrevitalizing areas), where the rate of
increase was 1.2 percent, these data show that Revitalizing Area births are
rising at more than five times the rate of the rest of the city. But as earlier
evidence indicated, the large majority of gentrifier households are made
up of whites, typically in their thirties.[7] Thus, increases in births among
women in this group would more firmly indicate the direction of gentrifiers'
concern about public education.

Table 6.2 indicates that during 1981, 1982, and 1983 white women in
their thirties living in the Revitalizing Areas of Washington had almost
one-third of all children born to white women of this age group in the city.
Comparably, black women in their thirties in the Revitalizing Areas had
between 13 and 16 percent of all births to black women in their thirties
living in the city. In fact, although white women are outnumbered in the
city by black women by more than two to one, white women in the Revitalizing Areas had more children in the early 1980s than did black women
living in those areas. In the city overall, however, white women in their
thirties had fewer births than comparably aged black women.[8]

These data suggest, then, that birth rates among whites in Washington
have risen significantly in the 1980s, especially among white women in
their thirties living in the Revitalizing Areas of Washington. Thus, one
would expect that the issue of public education would be rising in salience
throughout the city, especially in Washington's gentrifying neighborhoods.
Rising birth rates raise questions about recent enrollments in the District's
public schools, particularly in those located in or near the Revitalizing
Areas.

Table 6.3   Enrollment in public elementary and junior high schools located in the Revitalizing and Remaining Areas of Washington, 1980 and 1983

	1980	1983	Change	
Category	Number	Number	Number	Percentage
Elementary				
Revitalizing Areas	7,221	6,999	−222	−3.1
Remaining Areas	45,536	41,181	−4,355	−9.6
Total	52,757	48,180	−4,577	−8.7
Junior high				
Revitalizing Areas	3,803	4,045	242	6.4
Remaining Areas	18,762	16,201	−2,561	−13.7
Total	22,565	20,246	−2,319	−10.3

Source: "Student Membership in Regular Elementary and Secondary Day Schools by Schools, by Grades, by Race, by Sex, and by Regions," Reports for 1980, 1981, 1982, and 1983, District of Columbia Public Schools, Division of Quality Assurance.

Public School Enrollment Patterns

Table 6.3 divides elementary and junior high school enrollments between the Revitalizing Areas and the Remaining Areas. It reveals that from 1980 to 1983 the District public elementary schools continued to lose students in both the Revitalizing and Remaining Areas. But the rate of decline (3.1 percent) in the Revitalizing Areas was only about one-third that in the Remaining Areas (9.6 percent). Hence, though the public schools throughout the city were losing pupils during the early years of the decade, the Revitalizing Area schools were less severely affected by this trend. Although the Revitalizing Areas had almost 15 percent of all students in city schools in 1983, only about 5 percent of the total citywide loss in students between 1980 and 1983 occurred there.

Do these findings indicate that confidence in neighborhood elementary schools is higher among gentrifiers than among families in the rest of the city? The answer is uncertain. But one insight comes from data on the shift in enrollment by race occurring citywide during the same time period (1980–1983). We would expect to see a slowing of the rate of decline (if not a stabilization or an increase) among whites if gentrifiers were entering more children in local public schools. Table 6.4 presents elementary school enrollment figures by grade level and by race for 1980 and 1983. It shows that in that period whites declined in enrollment at almost twice the rate (−16.8 percent) that of blacks (−9.2 percent). Even a one-third increase in the school system's tiny enrollment of other races, however, could not sub-

Table 6.4 Number of children enrolled citywide in Washington's
elementary schools by grade level and race, 1980 and 1983

Race	1980				1983				Change, 1980–1983	
	Pre-k	K	1–6	Total	Pre-k	K	1–6	Total	Number	Percentage
Black	2,456	5,447	41,081	48,984	2,686	5,605	36,208	44,499	−4,485	−9.2
White	188	296	1,998	2,482	209	295	1,561	2,065	−417	−16.8
Other	75	133	993	1,201	120	173	1,323	1,616	415	34.6
Total	2,719	5,876	44,072	52,667	3,015	6,073	39,092	48,180	−4,487	−8.5

Source: "Student Membership in Regular Elementary and Secondary Day Schools by Schools, by Grades, by Race, by Sex, and by Regions," Reports for 1980, 1981, 1982, and 1983, District of Columbia Public Schools, Division of Quality Assurance.

stantially affect the overall rate of decline. But obviously whites were continuing to show even less confidence in the elementary schools than blacks.

Yet one cannot resist pointing out a trend counter to this among the youngest age groupings (see Table 6.4). The decline in overall elementary enrollment occurred in Grades 1 through 6. In pre-kindergarten and kindergarten levels, though, blacks showed slight increases in numbers. White students either rose slightly or remained stable in numbers. Whether these conditions indicate increased confidence in elementary schools or merely a conviction that little harm can be done to young minds in pre-kindergarten and kindergarten grades remains to be seen.

However one may speculate about citywide statistics on racial patterns in enrollment, an informal scrutiny of white enrollment trends in individual elementary schools in the Revitalizing Areas confirms a pessimistic view about gentrifiers' attitudes toward the public school system. Most of the schools in these neighborhoods had fewer than ten white students each and were overwhelmingly composed of black or Hispanic students. An examination of six elementary schools with the highest white enrollments showed that there were 260 white students in 1980 and 228 in 1983, a 12 percent loss in three years.[9]

Clearly, enrollment in neighborhood public elementary schools among white, middle-class families is very low in Washington. Even though births have been rising among families in Washington's "pioneer" neighborhoods in recent years, there are few signs yet that their confidence in the public schools is very high. Nonetheless, it must be remembered that the city's public school system permits grade school students to transfer to schools in other neighborhoods of the city, space permitting. The schools in Washington that receive the most transfer students by far are those in the upper northwest. But even this alternative, taken advantage of by some parents in the Revitalizing Areas, has left only a few schools in the largely white upper northwest Washington area with significant enrollments of white students.

At the junior high level, there are five city schools located in revitalizing neighborhoods. Even though overall enrollment rose from 3,803 to 4,045 (6.4 percent) in these schools between 1980 and 1983 (see Table 6.3), in four of the five, white enrollment in both 1980 and 1983 amounted to less than 20 students. In the remaining school there was a decline from 65 to 47 white students (−28 percent) from 1980 to 1983.[10]

There are no senior high schools in the Revitalizing Areas. However, Woodrow Wilson High School, with the highest white student enrollment in the city, had 276 whites in 1980 and 254 in 1983, a decrease of 8 percent.[11] Whites made up 18 percent of Wilson's student enrollment in 1983. Located in upper northwest Washington, an area of the city over-whelmingly populated by whites, it is one of two senior high schools for which white parents have shown even a modicum of support. The other, the School without Walls, is a small experimental effort with about 211 students in 1983, of which 93 were white. Both schools draw much of their enrollment from outside their immediate neighborhoods.

Therefore, the record at this writing indicates that even though demand for primary education is clearly on the increase among families in Wash-hington's Revitalizing Areas, a marked departure from the trends of seven or eight years ago, the predominantly white gentrifier families in those neighborhoods to date have shown very little confidence in the city's school system. But where, then, are they sending their children to school? In Washington there are numerous private schools, from the nursery school level through primary and secondary grades. Many of these have been in existence for decades, if not generations. But a large number have appeared only in the past decade, many in response to dissatisfaction with the public schools. Some are located in the city and others, in the surrounding sub-urban jurisdictions such as affluent Montgomery County.

Private School Enrollment

Table 6.5 shows the total enrollment of children of District of Columbia residents in city public schools and in private schools (including parochial) both in the city and elsewhere during the early 1980s. Unfortunately, the statistics released by the city's school system do not indicate white student enrollment but rather aggregate whites with "other" minority students

Table 6.5   Number of children of Washington residents enrolled
in public and private schools by race, 1980–1981 and 1983–1984

Type of school	1980–1981				1983–1984			
	Black	Other[a]	RDU[b]	Total	Black	Other	RDU	Total
D.C. private schools	9,268	6,046	438	15,752	8,132	4,851	273	13,256
Non-D.C. private schools	1,146	2,865	434	4,445	1,310	1,189	256	2,755
Total	10,414	8,911	872	20,197	9,442	6,040	529	16,011
Change, 1980–1981 to 1983–1984 (as percentage)	—	—	—	—	−9.3	−32.2	−39.3	−20.7
D.C. public schools	93,746	5,479	0	99,225	83,287	5,569	0	88,856
Change, 1980–1981 to 1983–1984 (as percentage)	—	—	—	—	−11.2	1.6	0	−10.5

Source: "Data Resource Book," District of Columbia Public Schools, Washington, D.C.,
1980–1981, p. 10; 1981–1982, p. 11; 1982–1983, p. 11; 1983–1984, p. 13.

a. Other = all races other than black.

b. RDU = race data unavailable.

(mostly Hispanics and Asian Americans). However, because white students
vastly outnumber these other minorities in the city, we can safely interpret
the "Other" column as substantially composed of whites. Table 6.5 reveals
that contrary to popular perceptions, private schools are not dominated by
whites. There have been more black students in private schools in the
decade of the 1980s than whites. Nonetheless, the data also indicate that
both in 1980–1981 and 1983–1984 a much higher *proportion* of District
whites than blacks was enrolled in private schools. At the beginning of the
decade almost 62 percent of the city's white students were enrolled in
private schools; by 1983–1984 this proportion had dropped to slightly over
one-half. Thus, although these data indicate that there are vast differences
between blacks and whites in private school enrollment, there was a significantly higher share of whites still in the private schools as the mid-
decade approached.

The data also demonstrate that white enrollment in private schools was
declining in the early 1980s at a faster rate (−32 percent) than black enrollment (−9 percent). Indeed, while white enrollment in the public schools

actually rose by a slight 1.6 percent, it declined by almost one-third in the private schools. Table 6.5 indicates that private schools were losing students of all races at about twice the rate (21 percent) as that of public schools (11 percent). Therefore, while white enrollment in private schools is vastly out of proportion with that of blacks, there is evidence that if recent trends continue, this gap will narrow. At this writing, the pattern of the 1980s, however preliminary, is toward reduced white enrollment in private schools and a stabilization in their enrollment in public schools. Blacks, while declining in numbers in both the public and private schools, are maintaining about the same ratio of public to private school enrollment.

It seems, then, that the private schools continue to be an important option for both blacks and whites in Washington; however, their status appears to be slipping somewhat, especially among some white families. If rates of white enrollment decline in the private schools matched those in the public schools, we might conclude that the whole matter was due primarily to dwindling birth rates in the city during much of the 1960s and early 1970s. But this was not the case. We cannot conclude from this evidence that the public schools have been luring whites or blacks away from the private schools. Nevertheless, it may be that public education is in a better position today to regain some of its lost enrollment of middle-class students than it has been in since the 1950s. Further support for this argument is found in recent performance on educational tests in the District schools.

Educational Performance in the Public Schools

Students in Grades 3, 6, and 9 in Washington's public schools participate periodically in the nationally administered Comprehensive Tests of Basic Skills, Form T (CTBS). Scores on these tests are made available by the school system as the median of all scores achieved by students taking the test in individual schools at individual grade levels. Table 6.6 presents the median scores in reading, mathematics, and language and a composite score for all three of these. The Median Grade Equivalent (MGE) scores represent the grade at which students are performing, according to national norms. Thus, for example, an MGE score of 3.6 for the third grade of an individual elementary school would indicate that 50 percent of the students there were reading above and 50 percent below the level of students nationally who are in the third grade with six months of instruction at that grade level.

Table 6.6   Standardized test scores in Grades 3, 6,
and 9 in the Washington public schools, 1980 and 1983

Standardized test by year	Grade 3		Grade 6		Grade 9	
	MGE[a]	MPR[b]	MGE	MPR	MGE	MPR
1980						
Total reading	3.3	38	5.8	39	7.3	26
Total math	3.7	48	6.5	48	7.0	24
Total language	3.3	40	5.9	44	7.2	32
Total battery	3.5	43	6.1	42	7.6	27
1983						
Total reading	3.9	56	6.9	52	8.4	37
Total math	4.3	64	7.3	59	9.0	43
Total language	4.1	56	7.7	59	8.6	42
Total battery	4.0	57	7.2	56	8.8	40

Source: "A Summary of Reading and Mathematics Test Results as Measured by the Comprehensive Tests of Basic Skills, Grades 3, 6 and 9," District of Columbia Public Schools, May 1980, tables II, III, IV and "A Summary of Student Achievement on the Comprehensive Tests of Basic Skills, grades 3, 6, 9 and 11," District of Columbia Public Schools, December 1983, p. iii.

a. National MGE (Median Grade Equivalent) in Grade 3 = 3.8, Grade 6 = 6.8, Grade 9 = 9.8.
b. National MPR (Median Percentile Rank) in Grades 3, 6, and 9 = 50.

Table 6.6 also presents the Median Percentile Rank (MPR), another means of scoring students on the CTBS. The MPR indicates the percentage of students nationally who scored below the median for grade levels in the District school system. Thus, an MPR of 56 for the sixth grade would indicate that District sixth graders collectively achieved a median score that was higher than the median for 56 percent of sixth graders who took the test nationwide.

These data indicate that overall MGE and MPR scores in Grades 3, 6, and 9 in the District school system rose from 1980 to 1983. In fact, the consistency with which scores rose in reading, math, and language at each grade level is quite remarkable. But though gains occurred at all three grade levels, the amount of improvement was less dramatic with each higher grade level. Thus, the national MGE for Grade 9 (9.8) was not met in reading, math, or language. In fact, students in Grade 9 were achieving almost one year below the national norms and were well below the 50th percentile nationally. It seems, therefore, that efforts by the school system to improve student performance have been most successful in the lower grades.

Still, it is at the level of the individual neighborhood school that many parents make decisions about educational quality. Thus, even though citywide norms may not measure up to those of many suburban school systems or private schools, the reputations of local elementary schools is likely to be paramount in the minds of parents. If the neighborhood school is successful in achieving scores comparable with those of suburban or private schools, families may be more likely to enroll their children there.

In 1980 the District's school system listed all the schools in which third- and sixth-grade MGE scores in reading and math were at or above the national MGE. (Schools that had a third grade but no sixth grade were included on the list.) There were 17 schools on the list.[12] However, when the results of the 1983 tests were released, there were 47 schools that had achieved comparable levels.[13] Only one of these high-achieving schools in 1980 and six in 1983 were located in the Revitalizing Areas. In 1983 about one-third of these schools were located in the largely white northwest Washington quadrant. Most of these had MGE scores that were among the highest of all elementary schools in the city.

It is clear that significant progress has been made during the 1980s in the scholastic performance of many students in the city's public school system. If these trends continue, it is conceivable that, especially at the elementary school level, enrollment by white families—including those living in the Revitalizing Areas—may increase. With rising births in these areas and modest gains in enrollment in public pre-kindergarten and kindergarten classes, there is the slender possibility that the school system's growing proficiency in raising academic achievement will entice more white families to enroll their children at the elementary level.

But enrollment data for the early 1980s do not indicate a clear pattern of rising confidence in the school system among white families. Indeed, white enrollment in most of the primary and all of the junior high schools in the Revitalizing Areas was small, if not nonexistent, as recently as 1983. Although overall enrollment in these areas was dropping at a slower rate than in the remainder of the city, the higher rate of white decline in elementary school enrollment throughout the city suggests that recently rising test scores have not yet convinced white families to make a substantial commitment to public elementary education in the District of Columbia. It is only at the systemwide level (Pre-kindergarten to Grade 12) that enrollment statistics suggest a less negative trend among whites. At this level there is evidence that overall white enrollment in city public schools may be stabilizing, while white enrollment in private schools is definitely on the decline. In view of the less-dramatic progress of students in the higher grades on standardized tests, this trend is surprising. Nevertheless, overall white enrollment at the junior high and high school levels is so low in the public school system that exceptional performance at only one or two schools could misrepresent citywide trends. With births among white families on the rise and the opportunity for the District government to build confidence in the public schools, the city will approach a critical juncture during the remainder of the 1980s.

Over the past 15 years Washington's inner-ring neighborhoods have received hundreds of millions of dollars in private-investment. Many of these areas were formerly declining both physically and economically. Even after many observers had dismissed the hope that a substantial number of white, middle-class residents would remain in Washington, a new sense of confidence arose among younger whites. Consequently, the best opportunity the city has had in years to maintain an acceptable racial balance and to attract and hold middle-class, white families may be at hand. As the gentrifiers of the 1970s have aged, some have made a commitment to inner-city living that only a few conditions could change. Now bearing children in increasing numbers, the gentrifiers face the difficult decision about whether to enter them in the public schools, send them to private schools, or move to the suburbs. Only a substantial effort to raise educational quality by the District school system, with the support of the District government, will convince many white parents to "risk" the public school alternative. Recent evidence suggests that it is still possible for the city to retain a significant share of the population base represented by gentrifier families. While whites did not express a clear pattern of confidence in elementary schools in the city as recently as 1983, gains in public school educational performance may offer an opportunity to attract and hold white families who would otherwise move to the suburbs or enter their children in private schools. Indeed, there is evidence that efforts have been made at several neighborhood schools to attract not only middle-class, white children but middle-class, black children as well.

Educational Programs and Policies

Throughout the late 1960s and 1970s, the District's school system was characterized by consistent turmoil. Wrestling with the legacy of rapid social change brought about during the Civil Rights Movement and War on Poverty years, school officials in major cities throughout the United States sought to test a panoply of new pedagogical techniques and methods. This period was characterized by experimentation in public school systems such as Washington's. School administrators and teachers attempted to achieve desegregation goals while eliminating the "tracking" of students according to ability. They built "schools without walls," allowing freer interaction among students in the primary grades and a less structured system of discipline and decorum. A host of new courses and subjects such as the "new math" and "English as a second language" were introduced. School officials were implementing new personnel policies designed to bring more racial minorities into the teaching ranks and reduce the influence of many senior teachers and administrators thought to be lacking in sensitivity to the new ideas.

Throughout this period there were numerous changes in personnel in the District school bureaucracy. When the city turned from an appointed to an elected school board in 1968, school policy was further politicized. On top of this, parents were insisting on greater citizen participation in and in some cases community control of school matters. These conditions, in combination with a particularly acerbic and divisive atmosphere in school board politics during the mid-1970s, helped to undermine middle-class confidence in the public schools. Large-scale out-migration of blacks to the suburbs occurred during this period, doubtless in part due to dissatisfaction with District schools. In concert with the older pattern of white out-migration, these forces helped to erode respect for public education in the city.

It was Vincent Reed, a professional school administrator, who became superintendent in 1975 and instituted policies that gradually brought perceptible change to city schools. Under his leadership, the Competency Based Curriculum was implemented. It required that students master specified basic skills in reading, math, and other subjects and pass an annual examination before being promoted to the next grade. This back-to-basics, no-nonsense approach to learning represents a nationwide trend today and in part is a reaction to the failings of some of the educational ideas tested during the previous ten years.

But the innovations emerging during those earlier years were not uniformly ineffective. Perhaps the most successful effort to engender middle-class support for city schools was the Six Schools complex.[14] Composed of a cooperative arrangement between four elementary schools, a middle school, and an arts center, all located in the largely white upper northwest Washington area, the Six Schools complex was established in 1974 in response to declining white enrollment.

During the 1950s and early 1960s when desegregation and school busing programs were proliferating, white public school enrollment declined drastically. One result was that schools in predominantly white upper northwest Washington came under court scrutiny, and many were found to have higher per-pupil expenditures than schools in other parts of Washington. The *Hobson v. Hansen* judicial decision resulted in a policy that per-pupil expenditures be equalized at each elementary school.[15] On top of this, school officials reduced busing in the city because the school system had become so overwhelmingly populated by black students that effective desegregation was impossible. It was felt that further losses of white students to suburban and private schools was also undesirable.

In the elementary school attendance districts served by the schools later to become the Six Schools complex, a decline in the number of black students bused from other sections of the city coupled with diminished white enrollment brought the threat of school closings. With lower birth rates becoming a national trend in the early 1970s, the school system could not justify operating several half-empty school buildings. In 1971 enrollment in these neighborhood schools had totaled 1,034. One year later the figure was 869, and by 1973 it had dropped to 713.

From 1973 to 1974 parents in the six attendance districts worked with the school system to form the Six Schools. They pooled teaching staff and budgets to provide more specialized educational opportunities and turned one of the schools into a resource center for the other five. Students living in the Six Schools attendance boundaries were allowed to attend classes in any one of the buildings. One of the schools was transformed into a middle school with grades five through eight, in order to extend the reach of the Six Schools philosophy. A heavy emphasis was placed on educational experiences such as field trips and dance and sculpture instruction not normally found in inner-city public school curricula. Each school developed a specialization (for example, English and Spanish language instruction). A 16-member advisory council was established. It was composed of elected Parent-Teacher Association (PTA) representatives and school officials and has no authority except to recommend policies and procedures to the school board.

Enrollment in the Six Schools rose by about 100 students from 1973 to 1976. By the time of the complex's tenth anniversary in 1984, enrollment had risen to 925 students. Of these, 532 were from the Six Schools attendance district and 393 were from other districts in the city. There are waiting lists for outsiders, who are admitted on a space-available basis. By 1983 scores on the Comprehensive Tests of Basic Skills among the Six Schools' third graders ranged from almost one year to more than three years in advance of national norms; among sixth graders scores were more than three years beyond national norms.[16] Clearly, the Six Schools complex is one of the most successful educational efforts in the city school system. It has proven popular with northwest Washington white families as well as with some whites living in the Revitalizing Areas and black, middle-class parents in other sections of the city.

If the Six Schools initiative has been successful in affluent northwest Washington, another effort to pool school resources in the revitalizing southwestern part of the city yielded just the opposite result. The Tri-Schools Plan brought together middle-class elementary pupils, both black and white, with elementary pupils from two schools serving a public housing project composed almost entirely of black families. The middle-class families had been drawn to the neighborhood after urban renewal had wiped out a low-income community, replacing it with new housing, shops, and offices (see Chapter 4). The three neighborhood elementary schools attempted to comply with desegregation policies underway in the late 1960s yet keep children close to home by avoiding long-distance busing. Children rotated from one school to another among the Tri-Schools every year or two. As a result, many middle-class children were gradually transferred to private schools. Parents complained that annual school changes meant that it was impossible for teachers, parents, and students to know one another well. There were complaints that teachers and administrators could not easily be held accountable for poor pupil performance because of the frequent shifts. Often, schools would blame a student's previous school for lagging grades. Even some poorer residents were unhappy, pointing out that their children had to cross heavily travelled streets to walk to school.[17]

Clearly, the Six Schools complex was a larger undertaking and had stronger support from parents than the Tri-Schools experiment had. Neither did it require frequent relocation of pupils. Most important, many parents have been satisfied that the Six Schools program is providing an acceptable education for their children. Nonetheless, the Six Schools complex is unique in Washington, and since admission for pupils from outside its attendance boundaries is highly competive, it offers little to the children of parents living in the Revitalizing Areas of the capital. Although a small number have sent their children to one of the few open-enrollment elementary schools outside of the Six Schools area of northwest Washington, most must choose between neighborhood public schools and private schools, or they must move to the suburbs and send their children to public schools there.

Nowhere is this problem better illustrated than in the Capitol Hill neighborhood. Located to the east of the Capitol, the Supreme Court and the Library of Congress, Capitol Hill is the largest of the contemporary neighborhoods undergoing gentrification. Some families living there have sent their children to private schools in other parts of the city—primarily northwest Washington—or in the suburbs. For some, the expense of tuition is a significant burden. Coupled with this is the effort to transport young children to and from school each day. Some parents send their children in taxicabs or must endure long trips at rush hours before and after the workday.

But gentrifiers on Capitol Hill have been successful in establishing new private schools. For example, the Capitol Hill Day School was formed in the late 1960s by early "pioneers" who renovated houses and settled in the neighborhood.[18] Two churches collaborated in sponsoring the school and providing space for its operation. As more children were born on the Hill, the school grew. Pressed for space by the late 1970s, day school parents succeeded in leasing an empty public school building in the neighborhood at $2,000 per month for 20 years. The school board allowed the day school to defer payment for the first five years of its operation, instead paying $3,300 per month for the remaining 15 years of the lease. For its part, the school system found a way to generate income and maintain an architecturally valuable property. For the day school, an opportunity came from the agreement to gain substantial new space and a new legitimacy among parents on the Hill. But it is revealing that the school system permitted this arrangement, a symbolic acknowledgement that the public schools on Capitol Hill could not be made appealing to these parents.

Parents of Capitol Hill Day School children have volunteered thousands of hours of labor to raise money for equipment and operations. Several have turned their house-renovation talents to scraping, caulking, repairing, and painting their newly acquired building. Funding for renovation work came from a $65,000 federal historic preservation grant and a $270,000 private bank loan. In addition, however, 80 families with children in the school made loans of from $200 to $5,000 to supplement these funds.

By 1980 the Capitol Hill Day School was composed of about one-third minority children. Parents have a substantial effect on school policies, procedures, and pedagogical philosophy and, as in the Six Schools, offer innovative opportunities to broaden childrens' cultural and artistic experiences. For parents who elect not to undertake this time-consuming route, however, and who do not send their children to established private academies, there is one elementary school on the Hill that has succeeded to date in attracting and holding enough whites to maintain an integrated educational experience.[19]

The Peabody School's enrollment of white students ranged from 120 to

146 from 1980 to 1983, approximately one-third of its total enrollment. Much like parental participation in the Six Schools and Capitol Hill Day School, parental involvement at Peabody is enthusiastic. Many parents participate in fund-raising activities to supplement Peabody's budget from the school system. One effort in 1981 raised more than $12,000 to buy textbooks and playground equipment, pay salaries for part-time teachers, and buy laboratory supplies. As one parent leader noted:

> We sell pumpkins, we sell cookies, we sell peaches and we sell Christmas trees. We even did a centennial cookbook. . . . Many white parents are afraid of public schools because of the negative press. The fundraising is for public relations as well as the money. We are saying that we as middle-class parents are not afraid to send our kids to public school.[20]

Offering extra classes in dance, instrumental music, art appreciation, woodworking, creative writing, and drama, the school has a waiting list for admission of pupils living outside its attendance boundaries. Its third-grade students performed more than three grades above the national norm in their combined reading, math, and language score in 1983. Still, even these attributes have only temporarily held a sizable share of white students in any of the Hill's public schools. Once children complete the Peabody School, they must contend with the junior high schools. Capitol Hill realtors note that families are likely to put their houses up for sale at this point, moving to northwest Washington or to the suburbs. Some Hill residents have noted that friends have left the neighborhood because of inadequate public schools. But no evidence exists to show the magnitude of this condition. Nor is it clear what effect such out-migration from Capitol Hill will have on overall demand for housing on the Hill or on the continued spread of property renovation and restoration.

If gentrifier families choose to send a child to Hine Junior High School, located in the revitalized area of the Hill, they face several problems. First, with a much larger attendance district than the elementary schools, the school has to minister to the needs of large numbers of low- and moderate-income blacks. In 1984 about one-half of its 554 students qualified for the federally subsidized lunch program.[21] While scores on standardized tests have risen at Hine, only 75 to 80 percent of its students, a low percentage by citywide standards, took the Comprehensive Tests of Basic Skills in 1983. Of these, combined scores were from approximately one-half to one year below national norms. Of course, many Hine students scored considerably below these medians. The effort needed to span the gap between low achievement and the higher expectations of white families on Capitol Hill is sobering.

Not only do academic standards worry gentrifier families, crime and the safety of their children concern them as well. Although Hine has realized substantial progress in maintaining order and discipline among students, many parents still remember the late 1960s and the 1970s when students claimed to have been beaten by teachers, a student was shot and killed by another student, and a teacher was convicted on ten counts of various sexual crimes against students.[22]

Sensational crimes, however, are only part of the concern of the parents of students in public schools. More commonly, white parents, and some black parents as well, cite incidents of harassment by children from different cultural and economic backgrounds than those of their own. Older children sometimes terrorize younger ones, threatening to hurt them unless they give up their lunch money. In other situations racial tensions may be more subtle. Members of a Dupont Circle family found that teachers at the neighborhood elementary school resented their activist role in school matters. One of the parents had taught French as a volunteer, had raised money for the school, and had headed the PTA. Elected to the school board in 1979, she withdrew her son from the elementary school a year later and entered him in a prestigious private day school. The parents had grown weary of alleged petty harassment against their five-year-old son from children of black and Hispanic families. After other white children were withdrawn from the school, their son was left without any white friends to provide a buffer against childhood cruelties based on cultural and class differences.[23]

However difficult problems of crime and personal safety are for white primary and junior high school children, they may be compounded in high school. Woodrow Wilson High School in northwest Washington has the highest public secondary school white enrollment in the city. In 1983 about 18 percent of its 1,440-member student body was white. Although its principal has struggled successfully to reduce incidents of crime and intimidation by poorer blacks directed primarily at middle-class, white students, as recently as 1980 these conditions were alleged to be almost a daily occurrence at Wilson.[24] In spite of the improvements, many white parents retain the perception of Wilson as unsafe. Wilson's image problems have been compounded by criticism of educational standards, lack of the kind of prestige associated with private school attendance, and fears of interracial dating. However, parents and school officials felt that Wilson was the victim of out-of-date perceptions among whites. Thus, they held a series of meetings with local real estate agents and told about the school's rising test scores, declining incidence of crime, and new advanced courses. The agents were asked to make white home buyers in Washington aware that Wilson was no longer the high school it had been even a few years earlier.[25]

The extreme difficulty District officials face in attempting to offer a high school education that will effectively serve both moderate-income, minority students and middle- and upper-middle-income whites is apparent in Washington's new Banneker High School. Attempting to reduce the loss of white students to private and suburban schools, Superintendent Vincent Reed, a reformist educator, sought approval from the school board for the creation of a model academic high school in 1980. With competitive entrance standards, it would attempt to attract the brightest students from all neighborhoods, races, and income classes. Residents of the predominantly white Capitol Hill neighborhood wanted to locate the school in the building then housing the Hine Junior High School in their neighborhood. Fearing that whites would take over the school and charging that it would become an elitist institution, some black school board members objected. Realizing that inadequate city high schools would continue to lose the city many of its white students, including those in gentrifying areas, Reed had pushed for the Hine School.[26]

Ultimately, Banneker was located near Howard University in a black neighborhood with a mixed middle-, moderate-, and low-income profile. Opening in 1981, it formulated a more rigorous grading scale than other city high schools and required more credits for graduation. Four years of English and three years each of math, science, social studies, and a foreign language are required. One year of Latin and a semester of computer science also are required. Howard University faculty members are involved in the school's academic programs. During the four years each student has to spend 270 hours of time in community service activities such as tutoring younger schoolchildren. Fewer than two out of three students who started in Banneker's first class graduated in 1984. Every one was offered admission to at least one college, and several chose from two or more offerings, including Massachusetts Institute of Technology, Vassar, Amherst, Bowdoin, Johns Hopkins, Stanford, and Yale.

Nevertheless, there were no whites in the first graduating class. Six whites were in lower grades at Banneker, however. One was the daughter of a city council member and former school board member. But the original hope that a model academic high school would attract significant numbers of talented whites and blacks to study together in an integrated setting has not yet been realized. One important reason is the school's location on a busy street in a somewhat run-down area of the city. Doubtless, had it been located on Capitol Hill or in another predominantly white neighborhood, it would have attracted a larger white student body. But it may also have drawn whites from Woodrow Wilson, a school whose integrated composition is already precarious. In its present location, even with the scholarly atmosphere of Howard University nearby, Banneker must struggle with the fears many white parents—and black parents as well—have for the safety of their children.

In December 1983 and January 1984 Banneker students reported a total of five incidents involving robberies, assaults, threats, and verbal abuse on the streets outside the school. Students travelling to Banneker by the city's transit system were increasingly the victims of crimes. A former Banneker student government president was beaten up and his watch was taken. Purses and jewelry were snatched, and one student was held up by a teenager with a knife. The school's principal was threatened by a gang of 15 to 20 youths and told to go back into the school building one evening.[27] These incidents confirmed many white parents' fears about entering their children in Banneker. But they also pointed out that white youths are not the only victims of school-time violence. Even middle-class, black youths are vulnerable, and class and cultural differences are probably at least as much a part of the underlying factors in interracial crime as is race.

In further efforts to increase student safety, the school system and the District of Columbia Police Department have developed a program to reduce crimes against students in the vicinity of public school buildings.[28] Banneker parents were instrumental in initiating the effort. But it is doubtful that white parents in Washington will succumb to the appeal of Banneker's admirable academic curriculum as long as the school continues in its existing location. The school board seems to have lost the one opportunity it had to attract and hold substantially more white students than it now has in the senior high schools of the city. And certainly Banneker will offer little promise to parents in the Revitalizing Areas.

Future Directions for Educational Policy

However difficult the problems of the senior high schools, experimental programs such as the Six Schools have demonstrated that the special curricular expectations of numerous white parents—expectations routinely associated with private schools—can be met in the public elementary school system. In fact, many black parents have endorsed the Six Schools effort, competing actively to send their children across the city to attend.

The Six Schools and other special educational efforts in which gentrifier families have been involved have demonstrated that at least at the elementary level, the District public schools and the District government may have the opportunity to reduce the city's loss of middle-class families significantly. The out-migration of whites and blacks to suburban communities, for many an emblematic rejection of District public schools, could be decelerated. To date, however, neither the school board, nor the city council, nor the mayor of Washington appears to have recognized this opportunity. To capitalize on it would require that the city school system establish more elite educational opportunities. And, unlike the ill-fated Banneker High School experiment, these schools would have to be located in safer areas.

Yet, as the preceding pages show, Washington's public schools already have an *informal* ability-grouping policy. Most school officials would not publicly admit to this condition. Rather, they have indicated that school transfer permission is granted for "severe hardship"; but hardship includes "gross inconvenience to parents" and "unavailability of a specific curricular offering" at the pupil's regularly assigned school.[29] Thus, where space in the desired school is available, enrolling a child is relatively easy.

To be sure, to argue that middle-class consensus appears to favor expansion of ability-grouping opportunities will raise the specter of the "track systems" popular in the wake of the earliest school desegregation efforts. Widely disliked by most black parents, the separation of students by ability in individual schools frequently meant that few blacks were admitted to the most selective tracks. The District school system had minimized the use of ability grouping during the late 1960s and 1970s in most areas of the city. But attempts to rid schools of this practice too often brought complaints from middle-class parents that the brighter pupils were unchallenged and the less-able pupils felt that efforts to compete were futile. It may be no accident that the substantial rise in black out-migration to the suburbs occurred during this period. Primarily middle-class families, many may have experienced the same frustrations with "trackless" education in Washington as white families had.

Whatever the case, there is substantial *a posteriori* evidence that public education in Washington is likely to have little effect in increasing white or black middle-class student enrollment without some form of ability grouping. But there is also recognition that this policy, perhaps repugnant to some, is not as likely to cause the extreme separation of students by race as occurred during the 1950s and 1960s. Undoubtedly, segregationist sentiments among some whites then partly motivated support of tracking policies, but the resulting racial separation was also due to the fact that black children were less likely to have parents with high school or college educations. Not having had as much exposure to informal, home-based educational experiences as affluent, white children had, black students were usually at a disadvantage when thrown into classrooms with them. As the number of black parents with high school or college educations in Washington has risen in the past 15 years, however, their children are less likely to be burdened by the extreme racial disparities in ability common 15 or 20 years ago.

It is precisely this group—black families—that has become part of the middle-class hegira, in part to seek better educational opportunities in the suburbs. Should the District schools pursue a systemwide policy of providing expanded opportunities for children of greater abilities, it might be possible to attract a mixture of whites and blacks to schools with curricula and entrance requirements similar to those at the Six Schools complex. It is not clear, in other words, that ability grouping in the 1980s necessarily implies racially segregated schools or classrooms.

Rather, ability grouping leads naturally to the "magnet school" concept in public education, which candidly recognizes that the primary purpose of public education is to raise each pupil to his or her highest level of educational performance, regardless of race. As Chapter 8 will show, magnet school programs have recently been instituted in Prince George's County, where the second highest concentration of blacks in the Washington area resides. Most of these blacks have migrated out of Washington over the past 15 years, many influenced in part by frustrations with the District's school system. The next few years should provide important evidence of the degree to which magnet schools combine the twin objectives of integration and excellence in education.

Conclusion

There is evidence that birth rates in Washington's revitalizing neighborhoods have risen, at least since 1980. Faced with declining fertility, many working women in their thirties have chosen not to defer childbearing further. Thus, among whites in this age group, and especially among those living in the Revitalizing Areas, rising birth rates have raised new questions about public education. Most of these people were themselves the products of private or suburban public school educations. By national standards they are highly educated and could be expected to have high aspirations about the quality of the education of their offspring.

The gentrification phenomenon represents an opportunity for the District government and the school board to reduce, or at least stabilize, middle-class out-migration to the suburbs. But it also suggests that it may be possible to stabilize the racial composition of the city's population and perhaps even raise the white population base to achieve a more balanced ratio of whites to minorities. However, it seems unlikely that many white families with children, especially those in the revitalizing neighborhoods, will elect to remain in the city if they decide not to enroll them in the District of Columbia public schools or in nearby private schools. So far, there is only the slightest evidence that parents are experimenting with pre-kindergarten and kindergarten classes. As of yet, public elementary school enrollment among whites, especially gentrifier children, remains low. But white private school enrollment is not rising either and, in fact, was declining more rapidly during the early part of the present decade than was public school enrollment.

Recent gains in student performance on standardized national tests in the city's public schools, especially in the elementary grades, show that the quality of instruction has improved since the mid-1970s. Furthermore, experiments such as the Six Schools and the Peabody School have demonstrated that public elementary school education can be enhanced enough to attract significant shares of white, middle-class students to racially mixed environments. Efforts to establish private neighborhood elementary schools such as the Capitol Hill Day School have shown the level of commitment of some gentrifier parents to continued urban living. They have shown that the availability of an acceptable primary school, even one with resources vastly inferior to those of the District's school system, will keep many of them in the city.

Still, the District is faced with a problem of established perceptions about the quality of public education. Undoubtedly, few parents are aware of the gains in test scores among city schoolchildren. Some rely on word of mouth and hearsay, creating a kind of neighborhood mythology about some schools. If the city government is to arrest a second wave of white out-migration to the suburbs, to say nothing of growing black out-migration, it will have to publicize rising educational performance in the elementary schools. This will require an extensive and personalized effort to reach individuals and small groups of parents. Both white and black middle-class households must be persuaded that their perceptions about neighborhood schools are out-of-date. But the issue is most critical with respect to white parents simply because there are so few white children left in the public schools.[30]

Of course, not all gentrifier parents will be satisfied, even with accurate knowledge about educational performance. For some, only the prestige of a private school will do. For them, there is the appearance of indemnification—that their children may have a better chance at an Ivy League college in the future. For other parents, fears about their children's safety and happiness in the public schools will override any news about rising scholastic performance. Still other parents in revitalizing neighborhoods will reject city living altogether, moving to suburban communities in Montgomery and Fairfax counties to escape crime, seek more open space, and live in larger houses. For them, regardless of public school quality, city living will no longer be desirable. Nevertheless, even with the drawbacks of city living, it is likely that a concerted effort by the District government and the District public schools could significantly reduce continued out-migration of middle-class families to the suburbs and could increase white enrollment in the District's public schools. Unfortunately, there is no comprehensive program to relate such critical public services as education to the overall social or economic health of the nation's capital. The District of Columbia's *Comprehensive Plan for the National Capital* is silent on these issues, confined instead to reviewing school space needs over the next several years.[31] Should the District experience continued net out-migration of whites during the remaining years of this century, it will become evident that the public sector has lost this decade's opportunity to stabilize its racial and socioeconomic composition.

Part Two, which follows, examines population and public school trends in Washington's suburbs, with special attention to Prince George's County. Thus far, our concern has centered primarily on the revitalization of the city's core and the implications this has had for the future racial and socioeconomic balance of Washington. Revitalization dynamics have been determined largely by white households, and our attention has focussed on issues related to white population maintenance in the city. But what of the thousands of black households leaving Washington for the surrounding suburbs? What of the many other minority-group members who have migrated to the Washington area in recent years? What effect have they had on suburban population and school conditions?

Part Two

Minorities and the Suburbs

7

Patterns of Race and Class

Just as inner-city decline and revitalization have constituted a major planning issue in American cities for several decades, so also has minority representation in suburban communities. As in most major metropolitan areas, suburbs in the Washington SMSA were characterized by white in-migration and population growth, especially from the mid-1930s to the mid-1960s. The presence of racial minorities was modest and limited mostly to black farmers and sharecroppers, whose farms were gradually engulfed by the tide of suburban subdivisions in the post–World War II years. The relative inaccessibility of these areas to minorities became a national policy issue during the 1960s. Federal legislation providing for equal employment opportunity helped many minorities to gain incomes permitting them to afford suburban housing. The Fair Housing Act of 1968 prohibited discrimination in the sale or rental of housing. Suburban large-lot zoning policies, preventing the construction of economical higher-density housing units (for example, apartments and town houses) were modified. More important, increased public awareness, citizen action, and mass media attention helped to create a climate in which discrimination became less tolerable.[1]

With new laws and new attitudes in place, minority populations in suburban jurisdictions began to grow. In most of the inner-tier counties surrounding the District of Columbia (see Map 1.1), net black in-migration rose substantially from 1965 to 1980. By the late 1970s, though, large net out-migrations of whites were occurring in some jurisdictions. For example, although Prince George's County had a net in-migration of 58,500 whites from 1965 to 1970, it experienced a net out-migration of 94,500 whites from 1975 to 1980.[2]

This chapter traces the path of minority suburbanization in the Washington area during the 1970s. Data from the 1970 and 1980 decennial censuses provide by far the best measures of shifts in the representation of blacks. But the relatively recent influx of other minorities is not accurately reflected in these censuses. Therefore, our knowledge of their representation is necessarily more limited.

Before proceeding, a word about methodology is justified. The geographic dimensions of racial change in the Washington suburbs, as in most metropolitan areas, involve several jurisdictions. Therefore, the analytical problems are more complicated than those exemplified by the preceding examination of similar dynamics in a single jurisdiction—the city of Washington. Not only are there wide variations between suburban jurisdictions in the level of minority growth experienced, considerable variation exists between neighborhoods or census tracts within several of these communities. Lacking the resources necessary to carry out a comprehensive analysis of small areas (yet not wanting to confine the study to only one or two jurisdictions), I have chosen to limit my comparisons to jurisdiction-level statistics. This has the disadvantage of obscuring vast racial and other variations in the smaller areas. Patterns of racial segregation, for example, cannot be fully understood. Nevertheless, while a more penetrating analysis would perhaps illuminate race and class conditions more fully, even at the level of the following study, sharp variations between communities and between racial and ethnic groups are clearly evident. This level of scrutiny will satisfy the purposes of this book and will set the stage for consideration of the implications of race and class shifts for suburban public educational systems.

Blacks in the Washington Metropolitan Area

Before exploring Washington's suburban jurisdictions, it is useful to remember that the national capital area departs from most other large metropolitan areas in several important respects. It is a fairly well known fact that the District of Columbia has the highest proportion of blacks of any major central city in the nation. It is not as well known, however, that among large metropolitan areas (that is, those with 300,000 or more blacks), Washington's SMSA ranked sixth in *number* of blacks in 1980. Only the metropolitan areas of New York, Chicago, Los Angeles, Philadelphia, and Detroit—each with substantially larger overall populations than Washington's—had more black residents than Washington's nearly 839,000 (see Table 7.1). In the relative size of metropolitan black populations in the nation, Washington's 28 percent was second only to New Orleans's 33 percent. It was slightly larger than the black populations of the Baltimore (26 percent) and Atlanta (25 percent) metropolitan areas.

Table 7.1   Population by race in the Washington metropolitan area, 1980

Jurisdiction	White	Black	Other	Total
Washington SMSA	2,016,147	838,983	133,041	2,988,171
District of Columbia	171,768	448,906	17,659	638,333
Virginia				
Arlington	126,121	14,028	12,450	152,599
Alexandria	74,726	23,006	5,485	103,217
Fairfax[a]	556,270	35,802	33,734	625,806
Loudoun	51,529	5,018	880	57,427
Prince William[b]	148,821	13,607	4,237	166,665
Maryland				
Montgomery	495,485	50,756	32,812	579,053
Prince George's	391,427	247,860	25,874	665,071

Source: Verna E. Martin, "Socio-economic Characteristics of the Black Population of Metropolitan Washington, 1980," COG Census Report 4, Metropolitan Washington Council of Governments, Washington, D.C., 1983, table 1-1.

a. Includes Fairfax city and Falls Church.

b. Includes Manassas and Manassas Park.

Thus, on at least one of these two measures of black population, the national capital metropolitan area outranks every large SMSA in the United States.[3]

Even more important is the fact that black family median income in the Washington metropolitan area is substantially higher than that in any other large SMSA. In 1979 one-half of all black family incomes in the Washington metropolitan area exceeded $19,075. The next highest black family median income was in the Los Angeles SMSA ($16,469). Black family median incomes in the remaining SMSAs with large black populations ranged from $16,069 to $11,798. The Washington metropolitan area's black population on the average, then, was considerably more affluent than were other black populations located in the nation's large urban concentrations.[4]

These data, then, provide a context within which to probe jurisdictions within the Washington SMSA. While the capital metropolitan region has one of the largest and most financially successful black populations in the nation, the distribution of blacks within the region varies significantly from jurisdiction to jurisdiction. The District of Columbia continues to have by far the largest black population. In 1980 there were almost 449,000 blacks living there, compared with less than 172,000 whites (see Table 7.1). In addition, nearly 18,000 people of other racial identities (for example, American Indians, Asians, and Hispanics) were included in the popula-

Table 7.2 Black population in the Washington metropolitan area, 1970 and 1980

Jurisdiction	1970 Number	1980 Number	Change Number	Percentage
Washington SMSA	703,745	838,983	135,238	19.2
District of Columbia	537,712	448,906	−88,806	−16.5
Virginia				
Arlington	10,076	14,028	3,952	39.2
Alexandria	15,644	23,006	7,362	47.1
Fairfax[a]	16,381	35,802	19,421	118.6
Loudoun	4,648	5,018	370	8.0
Prince William[b]	5,925	13,607	7,682	129.7
Maryland				
Montgomery	21,551	50,756	29,205	135.5
Prince George's	91,808	247,860	156,052	170.0

Source: Verna E. Martin, "Socio-economic Characteristics of the Black Population of Metropolitan Washington, 1980," COG Census Report 4, Metropolitan Washington Council of Governments, Washington, D.C., 1983, table 1-3.
a. Includes Fairfax city and Falls Church.
b. Includes Manassas and Manassas Park.

tion. The next largest concentration of blacks was in suburban Prince George's County, where approximately 248,000 blacks were living. The remaining 142,000-plus blacks in the capital metropolitan area were living in the other six suburban communities surrounding the District of Columbia. Between them, the District's 53.5 percent and Prince George's 29.5 percent accounted for more than four-fifths of the SMSA's black population. The next most sizable share of the area's black population was in Montgomery County (6 percent). While the Washington metropolitan area has one of the largest and most affluent black populations nationally, blacks are concentrated primarily in only two jurisdictions. Nevertheless, it is quite significant that substantial growth in black suburban population occurred between 1970 and 1980. Most of the shift is attributable to outmigration from the District of Columbia (see Table 7.2). The District's black population declined by almost 89,000 between 1970 and 1980 (−16.5 percent). Meanwhile, in every suburban community, there were proportional gains in black population. The largest occurred in Prince George's County, where blacks increased in number by 170 percent or more than 156,000 people. In adjacent Montgomery County the black population increase amounted to over 29,000 or 135.5 percent. Across the Potomac River in Virginia, Prince William County experienced the next highest

Table 7.3   Female-headed families with children under
age 18 by race in the Washington metropolitan area, 1980

Jurisdiction	Percentage of black families with children headed by females	Percentage of white families with children headed by females
Washington SMSA	38.0	11.7
District of Columbia	50.0	15.3
Virginia		
Arlington	39.0	17.0
Alexandria	46.0	19.0
Fairfax[a]	26.0	11.2
Loudoun	25.0	9.0
Prince William[b]	9.0	10.0
Maryland		
Montgomery	30.0	11.0
Prince George's	31.0	12.2

Source: Verna E. Martin, "Socio-economic Characteristics of the Black Population of Metropolitan Washington, 1980," COG Census Report 4, Metropolitan Washington Council of Governments, Washington, D.C., 1983, tables 2-6, 2-7.
    a. Includes Fairfax city and Falls Church.
    b. Includes Manassas and Manassas Park.

proportional gain. Almost 7,700 additional blacks (129.7 percent) established residence there. Although Fairfax County's increase of 118.6 percent was smaller than that of neighboring Prince William County, the number of blacks in Fairfax County increased by over 19,000, a substantially larger increment than Prince William's gain of under 8,000. Overall, the black population in Washington's metropolitan area rose by more than 135,000 (19.2 percent) during the 1970s.

Female-Headed Households

Normally, one-parent families have a more difficult time maintaining a basic standard of living. The historical dependency pattern of women and discrimination in employment markets have ensured that female-headed families have had to wrestle with the most trying economic burdens. Thus, significant gains in this household type may have important implications for welfare policy in the region.

One measure of this condition is the percentage of female-headed households with children under age 18 among blacks and whites in 1980. Thirty-eight percent of black families with children were headed by females in the

Table 7.4 Median family income among whites, blacks, Hispanics and Asians in the Washington metropolitan area, 1979 (in dollars)

Jurisdiction	White	Black	Hispanic	Asian/ Pacific Islander
Washington SMSA	$31,820	$19,075	$22,370	$21,820
District of Columbia	35,825	16,410	14,795	19,250
Virginia				
Arlington	31,300	17,540	19,175	18,110
Alexandria	30,250	14,720	20,905	18,575
Fairfax[a]	34,500	20,220	27,900	25,430
Loudoun	27,520	19,085	28,260	28,640
Prince William[b]	27,200	21,410	25,170	22,835
Maryland				
Montgomery	35,135	23,620	26,140	29,020
Prince George's	27,360	23,140	20,670	23,785

Source: Verna E. Martin, "Socio-economic Characteristics of the Black Population of Metropolitan Washington, 1980," COG Census Report 4, Metropolitan Washington Council of Governments, Washington, D.C., 1983, table 3-1.
a. Does not include Fairfax city or Falls Church.
b. Does not include Manassas or Manassas Park.

Washington SMSA; about 12 percent of white families with children were headed by women (see Table 7.3). In virtually all of the jurisdictions in the area, the proportion of female-headed, black families was higher than the counterpart figure for whites. But the District of Columbia had the highest figure. One-half of all black families with children and about 15 percent of white families with children were headed by women in 1980.

All jurisdictions experienced sizable growth in black, female-headed households with children during the 1970s; however, the greatest growth rates were not in the District but in the suburbs. Paralleling black suburbanization rates of growth in this group ranged from almost 120 percent in Loudoun County to over 500 percent in Prince George's County. In the District the rate was slightly above 19 percent. Nonetheless, the highest concentrations of black, female-headed households with children in the SMSA in 1980 were located in just two jurisdictions—the District and Prince George's County. In those two communities there were almost 40,000 such households or approximately 85 percent of the female-headed, black households with children in the region. By contrast, about 8,100 or 26 percent of white, female-headed households with children in the region were living in those two jurisdictions. The largest single concentration of

Table 7.5   Distribution of black families by family income
range in the Washington metropolitan area, 1979 (percentage)

Jurisdiction[a]	$0–$14,999	$15,000–$24,999	$25,000–$34,999	$35,000+
Washington SMSA	38.5	26.0	18.2	17.2
District of Columbia	46.0	25.0	15.0	14.0
Virginia				
Arlington	41.0	29.1	16.7	13.0
Alexandria	51.0	26.6	13.6	8.6
Fairfax[b]	36.0	25.0	20.0	19.0
Loudoun	40.0	28.2	20.7	11.3
Prince William[c]	32.4	28.1	23.0	16.4
Maryland				
Montgomery	28.2	24.6	18.3	28.7
Prince George's	27.3	27.7	23.4	21.4

Source: Verna E. Martin, "Socio-economic Characteristics of the Black Population of Metropolitan Washington, 1980," COG Census Report 4, Metropolitan Washington Council of Governments, Washington, D.C., 1983, table 3-4.

  a. The total percentage for each jurisdiction does not come to 100 because of rounding errors.

  b. Does not include Fairfax city or Falls Church.

  c. Includes Manassas and Manassas Park.

white, female-headed households was located in Fairfax County, where the number totaled about 9,500.

Income

Discussions about households with children and those headed by females lead naturally to concern about income patterns among blacks and whites. Although not all female-headed families have low incomes, the incidence of these households with low-incomes is relatively high nationwide. In spite of the Washington SMSA's comparatively high overall income structure— even among blacks—there are substantial economic disparities between blacks and whites. For whites, the median family income in 1979 was about $31,800, and for blacks it was about $19,100 or about 60 percent of the white median income (see Table 7.4). Within the city of Washington the white median was about $35,800; the black median was about $16,400 or 46 percent of the white median. Thus, the racial income gap in the nation's capital was even greater than that for the region. White income was more than double that of blacks in the central city. Washington's

Table 7.6   Changes in black median family income in the
Washington metropolitan area, 1969–1979 (percentage)

Jurisdiction	1969–1979	1969–1979 (constant dollars)
Washington SMSA	117.4%	10.9%
District of Columbia	93.3	−1.3
Virginia		
Arlington	102.7	3.4
Alexandria	103.6	3.8
Fairfax[a]	152.6	28.8
Loudoun	214.4	60.4
Prince William[b]	196.7	51.4
Maryland		
Montgomery	124.4	14.5
Prince George's	117.8	11.1

Source: Verna E. Martin, "Socio-economic Characteristics of the Black Population of Metropolitan Washington, 1980," COG Census Report 4, Metropolitan Washington Council of Governments, Washington, D.C., 1983, table 3-2.

a. Does not include Fairfax city or Falls Church.

b. Includes Manassas and Manassas Park.

whites were the highest income group among blacks and whites in the SMSA, but the city's blacks had the second lowest income; only Alexandria's blacks had a lower median family income.

But measures of central tendency such as median income can mask the range of variation in economic circumstances. For example, 46 percent of the District's black families had incomes below $15,000 in 1979, although 38.5 percent of black families in the metropolitan area were in the same circumstances (see Table 7.5). At the upper-income scale, 14 percent of black families in the District earned $35,000 or more, while slightly more than 17 percent of those in the metropolitan area did so. Therefore, the District's black income structure is skewed toward low and moderate incomes, while the metropolitan area shows a moderately larger middle and upper income structure. Similarly, changes in black median family incomes between 1969 and 1979 reveal that the District had the lowest growth rate (see Table 7.6). Blacks there had a 93 percent gain in income. In Arlington and Alexandria the growth rate was about 10 percentage points higher. In the more affluent suburbs of Maryland and Virginia, income growth rates ranged from 118 percent in Prince George's County to 214 percent in Loudoun County. Adjustments for inflation indicated that black families in Washington, Arlington, and Alexandria had almost no change in real income between 1969 and 1979. Yet black families in the remaining jurisdictions had constant-dollar increases of from 11 to 60 percent.

Poverty Levels

While the weight of income advantage among blacks in the metropolitan area was with those living in the suburbs, there was one notable fact that augured well for the central city. The District's black family poverty-level population decreased by almost 7 percent during the 1970s. This meant that by 1979 there were approximately 6,700 fewer black families with incomes below the federally defined poverty level. Yet because the number of black families in the city declined by more than twice this amount in the same period, the decline in poverty level did not keep up with the population change. The poorest of Washington's residents, therefore, did not have the opportunity to migrate that blacks with higher incomes had.

In suburban jurisdictions, however, there were gains in black poverty-level population in all but one community—Loudoun County. These gains ranged from about 7 percent in Fairfax County to almost 126 percent in Prince George's County. Arlington and Alexandria increased their numbers of poor blacks by slightly more than one-fourth, while Montgomery and Prince William counties increased theirs by approximately two-thirds. While gains in black population in the Washington area suburbs outpaced increases in black poverty levels, the rise in poverty associated with new black populations has led to the recognition that being poor and black is no longer synonymous with living in the central-city.

Educational Attainment

Another useful measure of black population shifts in the Washington area is educational achievement. An increase in the number of black college graduates is a measure of the rising importance of post–high school education in the Washington area's highly competitive employment market. During the 1970s the number of District of Columbia blacks aged 25 or older with at least a college education rose by almost 52 percent. Considering that the population of blacks in all age groupings (except those 65 and older) diminished in this period, that is a rather remarkable demographic shift. By 1980 there were almost 10,800 more black college graduates in the city than there had been a decade earlier. In the suburbs, where black populations had been on the rise, there were gains ranging from 243 percent in Arlington County to 631 percent in Fairfax County. Notably,

Table 7.7   Percentage of people aged 25 and older within racial or ethnic groups with college degrees in the Washington metropolitan area, 1980

Jurisdiction	White	Black	Hispanic	Other	Total population
Washington SMSA	39.5	14.8	27.5	43.7	33.2
District of Columbia	57.5	12.2	25.0	43.0	27.4
Virginia					
Arlington	45.5	17.5	20.8	34.9	42.5
Alexandria	47.3	13.2	33.6	37.2	40.9
Fairfax[a]	42.9	22.3	32.0	42.9	41.7
Loudoun	24.8	8.6	17.5	30.9	23.4
Prince William[b]	23.6	13.8	25.3	24.0	22.9
Maryland					
Montgomery	43.3	31.8	32.0	55.1	42.8
Prince George's	23.1	15.6	20.6	37.8	21.0

Source: Verna E. Martin, "Socio-economic Characteristics of the Black Population of Metropolitan Washington, 1980," COG Census Report 4, Metropolitan Washington Council of Governments, Washington, D.C., 1983, table 4-2.

a. Does not include Fairfax city or Falls Church.

b. Does not include Manassas or Manassas Park.

Prince George's County experienced a rise of 296 percent, amounting to almost 14,600 new black college graduates. By 1980, then, 75 percent of all black college graduates in the Washington metropolitan area were living in the District or in Prince George's County. Slightly less than two-thirds of the increase in these graduates occurred in those two jurisdictions.

Still, even after these substantial educational gains, the proportion of black college graduates lagged far behind that of whites in all of the jurisdictions. In 1980 about 12 percent of blacks and 58 percent of whites aged 25 and older in the city of Washington had college degrees (see Table 7.7). In spite of the fact that blacks outnumber whites by more than two to one, approximately five times the proportion of whites as blacks had higher levels of education. The pattern of higher educational achievement levels among whites was repeated throughout metropolitan Washington's suburban jurisdictions. The narrowest gap existed in Prince George's County, where about 23 percent of whites and 16 percent of blacks had college educations. Still, notwithstanding the sizable gain in black graduates in Prince George's County during the 1970s, the percentage of black college graduates there in 1980 was small.

Summary

Recent evidence indicates that the disparity in opportunity between central-city and suburban blacks in the national capital metropolitan area declined between 1970 and 1980. Substantial increases in black suburban residency occurred, and measures of income and education show that suburban blacks were narrowing the black-white socioeconomic gap—although it was still sizable in 1980. Still, the increased access for blacks to suburban living has raised a worrisome prospect. As predominantly middle-class, black households—especially families—leave the District for the suburbs, the gap between whites and blacks in the District will continue to grow. Perhaps it is too early to speculate. But it is conceivable that yesterday's racial disparity between the suburbs and the central city may become tomorrow's racial disparity within the central city. While greater access for blacks to suburban living is to be applauded, the loss to the District of Columbia in middle-class families, both black and white, raises the possibility of a city populated primarily by a youthful, affluent minority of whites and an aging, poorer majority of blacks.

Also distressing is the fact that while black suburbanization has grown admirably in the Washington metropolitan area, progress has been skewed largely in the direction of one jurisdiction—Prince George's County. With more than four-fifths of the metropolitan area's black population now concentrated in the District and Prince George's, it can hardly be said that blacks have achieved equality with whites in access to suburban housing.

Nevertheless, measures of suburban socioeconomic change show that poverty levels and the incidence of female-headed households with children have been rising in the suburbs while declining in the city. Should these trends continue through the 1980s, some suburban jurisdictions could be faced with social problems ever more similar to those confronted by the District of Columbia throughout much of the mid-twentieth century.

Other Minorities in the Washington Metropolitan Area

Clearly, the black population in the national capital metropolitan area has experienced profound changes during the past decade or two. Yet blacks are not the only minority group to have realized significant changes in their numbers or demographic circumstances. The remaining groups are referred to by the U.S. Bureau of the Census as "other minorities." Among them are Hispanics, American Indians, and Asians/Pacific Islanders. Because American Indians constituted only a tiny proportion of the area population in 1980 (less than one percent), this section will discuss only those groups referred to by the Census Bureau as Hispanics and Asians/Pacific Islanders. (The latter group is herein referred to as Asians.)

According to the 1980 census almost 95,000 Hispanics were living in the Washington metropolitan area, composing about 3 percent of the SMSA population. Of that amount, approximately 18,000 (19 percent) were concentrated in the city of Washington, and the remainder were in the suburban jurisdictions.[5] The largest share of Hispanics was located in Montgomery County (23 percent) and the next largest in Fairfax County (20 percent). Prince George's County had 14 percent of the Hispanic population.[6]

But members of the Hispanic community, as well as other observers in the Washington metropolitan area, have criticized Census Bureau procedures in the decennial census, arguing that Hispanics were vastly undercounted. Language problems, the rapid rise in undocumented workers, and the influx of refugees trying to escape political conflicts in Central America had created a special problem in the enumeration of many Hispanic people. An attempt to estimate the Hispanic population in the Washington metropolitan area based on adjustments of the 1980 census indicated that perhaps 160,000 Hispanics were living in the city and its suburbs by 1981. Of this number, over 49,000 (31 percent) were thought to be living in the District of Columbia. If these estimates are accurate, they indicate that Hispanics composed approximately 5 percent of the metropolitan-area population and 8 percent of the District population.[7]

The Asian population was slightly more than 82,000 in the capital metropolitan area in 1980; this amounted to less than 3 percent of the area's population. Of this sum, about 6,600 or 8 percent of metropolitan-area Asians were residing in Washington. Asians made up 1 percent of the central-city population. The remainder were concentrated in Montgomery (22,800), Fairfax (22,700), and Prince George's (16,500) counties. These three suburban jurisdictions accounted for three-fourths of the metropolitan Asian population.[8]

It is apparent that neither Hispanics nor Asians made up a substantial share of the population of any of the jurisdictions in the Washington metropolitan area at the beginning of this decade. Nonetheless, it is significant that while Hispanics have a larger presence than Asians in the District of Columbia, both groups have substantially larger shares living in the suburbs—and especially in Fairfax, Montgomery, and Prince George's counties—than in the District. Perhaps more important is the *rate of increase* in recent years in the numbers of Hispanic and Asian people who have settled in Washington and certain of its suburban communities. It is thought that much of the increase in these minorities has been due to the influx into the United States of refugees from Central and South America since the late 1970s and of refugees from Southeast Asias (especially Vietnam) since the mid-1970s. For example, it is estimated that 543 Vietnamese, Cambodian, and Laotian refugees moved into Arlington County from July 1982 to June 1983. Yet both Asians and Hispanics are difficult to enumerate, and 1980 census data are already out of date for that reason.

Income

Even though statistical evidence of the current population of Hispanics and Asians is insufficient, the growth in their presence in the Washington metropolitan area is readily apparent to those who live there. But evidence of socioeconomic contrasts between these groups is also lacking. Data from the 1980 census, although helpful, are clearly obsolescent in light of recent migration patterns. Generally, this evidence shows that median incomes for Hispanic and Asian families in 1979 were higher in most jurisdictions than were incomes for black families (see Table 7.4). Only among Hispanic families in the District of Columbia and Prince George's County were incomes lower than among blacks. In the Washington metropolitan area overall, black family incomes were 60 percent those of white families, while Hispanic family incomes were 70 percent and Asian family incomes 69 percent those of white families.

Educational Attainment

Educational achievement, another measure of well-being, showed similar variations. In all but one Washington suburban jurisdiction (Montgomery County) in 1980, the percentage of college graduates aged 25 and older was significantly higher among Hispanics and "other" races (mostly Asians) than among blacks (see Table 7.7). While proportions of college graduates were generally higher among whites than among Hispanics, proportions among other races in several communities were higher than those among whites. In the region as a whole, almost 44 percent of people of "other" races, compared with less than 40 percent of whites, had college degrees. Almost 28 percent of Hispanics and almost 15 percent of blacks had these credentials.

The impression that emerges from very limited evidence is that most minority groups in the Washington metropolitan area other than blacks were only moderately less well off socioeconomically than whites. Even if timely, appropriate data sources were available to measure conditions among other minority groups, it appears that the numbers would not be significant compared with the more serious social problems confined largely to a small number of concentrations of Asians and Hispanics. Most of these appear to be populated by Cambodians, Vietnamese, and Laotian refugees or by Central Americans from Honduras, Guatemala, Nicaragua, and especially El Salvador. The large majority are probably relatively recent arrivals to the area. While some have been resourceful in their adaptation to American life and have established economically sound livelihoods, substantial numbers will probably struggle for several more years. Among immigrants who have lived in the metropolitan area for several years, as well as the American-born offspring of immigrants, it appears that many have reached a reasonably comfortable middle-class status. In short, problems of inequity, poverty, discrimination, and other social ills appear to be confined primarily to relatively small concentrations of newcomers living in parts of the District of Columbia, Arlington, Alexandria, and a few parts of inner Montgomery and Prince George's counties. And even in these communities, there is ample evidence among newcomers of enterprise and initiative to improve their socioeconomic condition.

Minority Suburbanization in the
Washington Metropolitan Area

Since the late 1960s few conditions in the Washington metropolitan area have had as profound a set of implications for life in the capital as has the rise in suburban residence of minorities. Both blacks and other minorities have sharply increased their presence in the inner tier of counties outside the District of Columbia. However, it is among black households that the most striking shifts have occurred. For many years the capital has had one of the highest proportions of black households in the largest central cities of the United States. It is not surprising, therefore, that the suburban population of blacks is vastly greater than that of Hispanics or Asians. (However, while suburban blacks *outnumber* other suburban minorities, the *percentage* of all SMSA blacks in the suburbs in 1980 was smaller than the percentages of Hispanics or Asians; although 47 percent of

SMSA blacks were suburbanites, the proportion was 78 percent for Hispanics and 92 percent for Asians.) Furthermore, overwhelmingly, blacks in the Washington metropolitan area are native Americans and consequently do not have the language or acculturation problems that newcomers from Third World countries are likely to have.

Nevertheless, while metropolitan Washington blacks are considerably better off than metropolitan area blacks nationally, as a group they lag considerably behind whites, Asians, and Hispanics in the Washington metropolitan area. Clearly, economic gains among many blacks—mostly the young and college-educated—have been a primary factor in their increased access to suburban homes. But much of the Washington metropolitan area's black suburbanization has come at the expense of its central city. As large numbers of middle-class blacks have vacated the city, they have left in their wake a population composed of greater shares of elderly and poor blacks. In the suburbs too, though, there have been disturbing rises in black poverty-level and female-headed households. The largest concentrations have been in Prince George's County, where black population gains have also been the highest in the region.

Black migration into Prince George's County has been a subject of public attention at least since the late 1960s. For example, a guide to housing in the Washington metropolitan area published by the *Evening Star* newspaper in 1969 described the early stages of black suburbanization in Prince George's County; it noted that the county was "the least equipped of Washington's suburbs in terms of tax resources and public-policy attitudes" to do anything about the poor public services blacks were receiving.[9] Not only was the county ill-prepared, the real estate industry was rife with agents who practiced blockbusting and racial steering, and some insurance companies had redlining policies.[10] Arbitrage, a process in which property is bought for less than it is worth (and sold for more than it is worth), was another common real estate practice. Hence, many blacks were forced to pay more for their houses than the value indicated by current market prices.[11]

A scholarly study of four Prince George's communities in the path of black migration during the early 1970s found that relatively little open hostility was expressed by white incumbent residents; yet there were some explicit racial incidents that made it clear that generally, blacks would not be welcomed with open arms.[12] All four communities were populated by predominantly middle-aged whites with working- or lower-middle-class backgrounds. The complicated nature of their attitudes toward blacks moving in at this time was explored in a celebrated participant-observer study of one of these communities carried out by Joseph T. Howell.[13] By 1980 several thousand more black families had settled in Prince George's County. Again, overt hostility from whites was far less common than were subtle signs of dissatisfaction. Thus, some blacks said they were snubbed by their white neighbors or experienced petty acts of vandalism. By far, the most routine signal blacks received, however, was "white flight" or the rapid, almost panic-stricken effort by some whites to sell their homes and move away.[14]

Much of the appeal of Prince George's County to black households has been its proximity to northeast and southeast Washington, areas with heavy concentrations of blacks. A study of racial out-migration from Washington to the suburbs from 1975 to 1980 found that most suburban-bound blacks who left Washington relocated in the Maryland suburbs.[15] Almost 95 percent of this group moved to Montgomery, Prince George's, and Charles counties; the remainder moved to the Virginia suburbs. White suburban-bound Washingtonians were more evenly divided, with 53 percent moving to the Maryland suburbs and the remainder to Virginia. Nevertheless, Prince George's County has received the lion's share of black attention. Of all black suburban-bound Washingtonians, about 86 percent moved to that county, but only 12 percent of their white counterparts did so.

The vast differences in suburban settlement patterns of black and white exiles from Washington raise the specter of racial discrimination in housing. Have blacks concentrated in Maryland, and especially Prince George's County, because of higher incidences of racial discrimination in the Virginia real estate industry?

Insofar as rental housing is concerned, new light has been shed on the subject. In 1986 a federally funded study compared the treatment black and white apartment seekers received in Washington and its suburbs.[16] Black and white "auditors" (that is, people who pretended to be looking for an apartment) were sent to individual apartment buildings. In each case, the black auditor was followed a short time later by a white auditor; auditors were matched according to income and background, wore similar clothing, and asked to see comparable apartment types. It was found that whites received preferential treatment over blacks in 54 percent of the test cases in the metropolitan area, and whites and blacks were evenly treated in 41 percent of the cases. The northern Virginia apartment landlords, however, favored whites at about the metropolitan average (56 percent of the time), while Montgomery County's landlords did so more frequently (64 percent of the time) and Prince George's County's did so less often (44 percent of the time). District of Columbia landlords favored whites in 50 percent of the cases.

The study showed conclusively that racial discrimination is very much a factor in rental housing choice, and there is little doubt that an audit of black and white home buyers would turn up similarly disparate racial treatment. But further complicating the housing search for blacks are the wide variations in housing prices in the Washington suburbs. In 1984, for example, the median sales price for all housing in Prince George's County was $82,000, the lowest median in the metropolitan area. In Montgomery County it was $118,000 and in Fairfax County, $124,000.[17] This, of course, helps to explain why Prince George's has become such a powerful magnet to black, middle-class families. Furthermore, while discrimination against renters was great in all the jurisdictions tested, we might have expected rates to be highest in Virginia. This would have helped explain the over-whelming black avoidance of that state. Yet it was suburban Maryland that had both the highest and the lowest rates of discrimination, while Virginia's rate was comparable to the metropolitanwide rate. Perhaps the 1975–1980 out-migration patterns cited above are not representative of 1986 patterns, and blacks, finding no perceptibly greater renter discrimi-nation in Virginia than elsewhere, are now more actively seeking housing in Virginia.

Whatever the explanations for black settlement patterns, less is known about other minorities in the Washington suburbs. As shown above, they constitute a much smaller proportion of the population than American blacks. Too, much of the recent gain in Hispanics and Asians in the Wash-ington metropolitan area has been due not to out-migration from the Dis-trict but rather to *immigration* from Central America and Southeast Asia. Although combined these groups made up only about 6 percent of the metropolitan-area population in 1980, the recent rise in their numbers almost certainly has increased this figure by a few percentage points. While the largest single concentration of Hispanics resided in the central city in 1980, there was a greater total living in the surrounding suburban counties. Among Asians, the smallest concentration was in Washington, and larger groups lived in the suburbs. Visual evidence, however imprecise, suggests that post-1980 in-migration to the area has brought more Hispanics than Asians to the District. Perhaps the largest communities of Asians have settled in Arlington and Alexandria. Generally, the longer-term Hispanic and Asian residents have shown great enterprise and appear to find economic security. More recent arrivals will probably follow the path of their predecessors.

The relatively rapid rise in minority suburbanization in the national capital metropolitan area has numerous social dimensions. But just as among middle-class whites in the city of Washington, the public schools have become a major sounding board in the struggle among suburban minorities to improve their social circumstances. For most, no single path offers more promise for upward mobility than a sound education. As Chapter 8 will show, the suburban school systems vary substantially in the extent to which they are able to fulfill such expectations.

8

Minorities and Suburban Schools

Just as white, middle-class gentrification in Washington's core has raised questions about public services such as education, minority suburbanization has done so in the inner tier of jurisdictions surrounding the city. Yet the effectiveness of suburban public schools in educating minority students is an issue that is more advanced in public debate and public policy than is quality education for white, middle-class city residents. In part, this situation may be due to the simple fact that for many years American suburbs have been valued more highly than central cities for the quality of their educational systems. For many households, part of the justification for moving to a particular suburban community has been the better educational opportunity offered by local public schools there. On the other hand, few people base their choice of residence in Washington on the quality of the public school system.

One measure of public attitudes about public education is a survey of residents of the capital metropolitan area conducted at a time when both minority suburbanization and gentrification were in the early stages of acceleration. In 1973 it was found that 53 percent of respondents believed that their local public schools were doing a "very good" or "good" job of educating residents. Eighteen percent rated their schools "fair," 11 percent "poor," and 18 percent had no answer. Dissatisfaction was highest in the District of Columbia and lowest in the wealthier suburbs of Montgomery and Fairfax counties. When the survey was repeated two years later, only 43 percent of the metropolitanwide sample gave their schools a "very good" or "good" rating. Twenty-two percent rated them "fair," 12 percent "poor," and 22 percent had no opinion.[1] Again, dissatisfaction was highest in the District and lowest in Montgomery and Fairfax counties. Therefore, not only was the overall level of public confidence in public schools declining, it was lower among District residents than among suburban residents; among suburban residents the city of Alexandria and Prince George's and Arlington counties were considerably less well regarded educationally than were Montgomery and Fairfax counties. For example, one-half of 1973 respondents in Prince George's County rated their public schools "very good" or "good"; two years later only 39 percent rated them so.

In a 1983 survey by the *Washington Post*, one-third of the respondents in Prince George's County rated the public schools "poor" or "very poor." [2] In that study 29 percent said that the schools were worse than they had been in 1978 and 32 percent said that they were about the same. Only 13 percent felt that the schools were better. As the following discussion will show, even with the increased access to suburban schools that many minority families have realized, dissatisfaction with public school quality is a continuing problem.

The purpose of this chapter is to document rising minority enrollment patterns in those inner-tier jurisdictions where significant growth in minority residence has occurred. It will also trace the experience of suburban school desegregation, probe academic measures of minority pupil performance in suburban schools, and discuss relations among whites and minorities in schools.

Enrollment Shifts

Although no recent surveys have assessed attitudes about public education on a metropolitanwide basis, the issue was becoming increasingly controversial during the late 1970s as court-ordered desegregation plans were being implemented and suburban minority enrollment was increasing. In Prince George's County, for example, white enrollment declined from 119,000 students in 1972 to about 70,300 in 1978; during the same period black enrollment rose from 40,400 to 58,800. By 1979 the combined presence of black and other minority students made up 51 percent of Prince George's public school enrollment. In 1980 blacks alone accounted for almost 60,800 students, while whites made up 56,000. Three years later, blacks constituted almost 56 percent of the Prince George's County school system enrollment. [3]

While these rapidly changing racial dynamics were underway, the county was wrestling with a court-ordered busing program to achieve racial balance in individual schools. When busing was mandated in January 1973, black student majorities existed in 46 schools. Even though a temporary improvement occurred after busing began, the continued migration of black families into the county helped to create imbalances in other schools. Thus, by the end of 1979 almost one-half of the schools exceeded the

Table 8.1   Number of children enrolled in public schools
in the Washington metropolitan area, 1970 and 1980

Jurisdiction	White		Black		Total[a]	
	1970	1980	1970	1980	1970	1980
Washington SMSA[b]	456,912	321,966	196,113	192,218	663,146	545,782
District of Columbia	6,496	3,611	137,502	93,756	145,330	99,366
Virginia						
Arlington	20,947	9,859	2,715	2,414	24,768	15,139
Alexandria	12,271	4,452	4,888	5,406	17,555	11,011
Fairfax	127,455	109,176	4,214	8,530	133,368	126,860
Loudoun	8,275	11,808	1,486	1,316	9,809	13,447
Prince William	29,008	31,448	1,574	3,086	30,927	35,577
Maryland						
Montgomery	114,844	77,386	6,454	11,912	125,343	98,843
Prince George's	127,798	56,031	31,994	60,793	160,897	121,893
Charles	7,891	12,756	5,249	4,524	13,167	17,514

Source: Lawrence Feinberg, "Black Students in Suburbs Top City Enrollment," *Washington Post*, December 14, 1980, p. A32.

a. Includes Asians, Hispanics, and American Indians.

b. SMSA totals include Falls Church, Manassas and Manassas Park (Virginia), which are not shown separately. Consequently, SMSA totals are greater than the sum of the jurisdictions in each column.

court-set guidelines that required between 10 and 50 percent black enrollment in each school.[4]

It soon became apparent that Prince George's County's school desegregation problems were hardly unique. A study of desegregation in 23 school districts (including Prince George's County) in the United States found that busing accelerated the decline of white enrollment in the public schools. Even though many jurisdictions and school systems had been losing whites prior to the commencement of desegregation programs, the study's author concluded, the rate of decline rose after such efforts were underway.[5] Although this study was highly controversial, producing several critical rejoinders from busing advocates and some scholars, it found considerable support among other scholars. Nevertheless, it is clear that the racial-balance problem in Prince George's County was exacerbated by both rapid black in-migration and rising white out-migration.

A substantial share of the gain in Prince George's County's black enrollment resulted from student transfers from the District of Columbia school system.[6] In 1970 blacks composed about 95 percent of District public school enrollment (see Table 8.1). By 1980 the proportion of blacks was about the same, but there were almost 44,000 fewer black children in District schools and more blacks attended suburban schools (about 98,500) than attended District schools (about 93,800). Furthermore, almost two-thirds of suburban black public school students in 1980 were attending Prince George's County public schools.[7]

In two other suburban jurisdictions, black students approximately doubled their numbers in the 1970s. Montgomery County's black enrollment rose from 6,500 to 11,900 and Fairfax County's, from 4,200 to 8,500 by 1980. But in both counties white enrollment declined substantially. Montgomery County whites dropped from 114,800 to 77,400 and Fairfax County whites, from 127,500 to 109,200. During this same period, even though Arlington and Alexandria did not experience substantial changes in black enrollment, they had more profound percentage losses in white enrollment than did Fairfax and Montgomery counties. Arlington declined from 21,000 to 9,900 whites and Alexandria, from 12,300 to 4,500 whites, both losing more than one-half of their white student bodies.

Of course, diminishing white student populations in the suburbs are not related entirely to "white flight" from the school systems or from the counties themselves. The notable drop in birth rates among younger white females during the mid-1970s limited the number of white children entering public schools. This factor was related to reduced rates of marriage and higher rates of divorce and separation. But there can be no doubt that white resistance to the increasing presence of blacks in their neighborhoods and local schools had a profound influence on declining white enrollment in Prince George's County. Small wonder, then, that white student bodies, while declining in the District of Columbia and all of the first-tier suburban counties, were increasing in the second-tier counties of Charles, Loudoun, and Prince William during the 1970s. And these patterns were underway as school desegregation efforts were being carried out in most of the first-tier counties.

Nevertheless, black student enrollment statistics tell only part of the suburban school story. Even though minorities other than blacks made up less than 6 percent of metropolitanwide enrollment in 1980, their numbers were increasing rapidly in several jurisdictions. In Arlington County, for example, Asians and Hispanics composed about 6 percent of total student enrollment in 1972. But by late 1983 they made up 25 percent of total enrollment.[8] Most were from El Salvador, Nicaragua, Vietnam, and Cambodia. In neighboring Alexandria, enrollment of these "other minorities" rose from 5 percent in 1973 to 14 percent ten years later. By 1983 slightly more than 1,300 "other minorities" (mostly Hispanics and Asians) were studying in Alexandria public schools.[9] Similarly, in several of the Fairfax County school districts closest to Arlington and Alexandria, foreign-student enrollment has increased sharply in recent years. But data on countywide attendance does not reflect this. Nevertheless, Asian and Hispanic students constituted about 7 percent of total county school enrollment in 1980 but had risen to 11 percent by 1984.[10]

The shifting composition of suburban populations in the inner-tier counties during the past decade and a half has brought declining white enrollment and increasing black and other minority enrollment in public schools. Although many (perhaps most) black suburban students formerly attended District of Columbia schools, most Hispanic and Asian students appear to have migrated to the inner-tier counties directly from their home countries or from temporary locations in the United States. Whatever the case, the inner-tier suburban school districts have wrestled with unprecedented numbers of racial and ethnic minorities even as the presence of whites was slipping considerably.

School Desegregation

As minority populations and student enrollments have grown in many metropolitan school systems, the issue of school desegregation has provided a continuous counterpoint to the periodic issuance of enrollment statistics by community school boards. Just as central-city and rural bureaucracies had to wrestle with the prospect of busing and redistricting during the late 1950s and 1960s, the suburbs now have to deal with the equitable distribution of racial groups in local schools, a problem brought on by minority suburbanization. Perhaps because the historic 1954 *Brown v. Board of Education* decision by the U.S. Supreme Court occurred in Washington, the issue of school desegregation has been particularly poignant in the national capital metropolitan area. This factor in concert with the presence of a large and articulate black population has helped to raise political consciousness about racial issues to a level that can be matched in few other metropolitan areas in the United States.

Among the first area suburban school districts to struggle with desegregation were Alexandria city and Prince George's and Arlington counties. Desegregation commenced in Arlington in 1959. Court-ordered busing began in Alexandria in 1971 and in Prince George's in 1973. Extensive shuffling of black and white students among predominantly black and white neighborhood schools helped to bring a temporary improvement in racial balance. But declining birth rates among whites, as well as continued black in-migration from Washington, the transfer of white students to private schools, and the out-migration of white families to other communities, led to resegregation at many schools. In Prince George's County, for example, by the end of 1979, 7 of 19 senior high schools, 21 of 41 junior high schools, and 73 of 145 elementary schools had enrollments that were more than 50 percent black. In addition, three elementary schools were more than 90 percent white.[11]

Several Prince George's County schools were closed as a result of declining overall enrollment during the early 1980s. Between 1980 and 1983 enrollment fell from approximately 122,900 to 108,200 students. By 1983 black enrollment had increased to almost 56 percent.[12] A reorganization of the school system established middle schools, encompassing seventh, eighth, and ninth grades and reducing high school to three grade levels. This technique helped to reduce racial imbalance throughout the school system during the early 1980s, but still a federal district court found that whites or blacks were overrepresented in 25 of 114 elementary schools and 4 of 28 middle schools. The court ruled that even with a more liberal standard—that schools with between 10 and 80 percent black enrollment would not be considered imbalanced—the Prince George's school system was not entirely in compliance with desegregation requirements. In fact, racial imbalance had increased slightly between 1982 and 1983.[13]

In response to the problem and to declining overall enrollment, in 1984 county school administrators proposed closing 22 elementary and middle schools and redrawing some attendance boundaries. Busing would continue to be used to achieve racial balance as required by the court order.[14] The U.S. District Court of Baltimore rejected this proposal and considered instead recommendations from a study panel chaired by Dr. Robert L. Green, president of the University of the District of Columbia at the time and a nationally recognized expert on desegregation policy. The Green proposal recommended closing up to 40 schools and busing larger numbers of black students, primarily from inside the Capital Beltway, to schools in the predominantly white neighborhoods outside the beltway; similarly, white pupils outside the beltway would be bused to schools inside the beltway.[15]

But this plan seemed to do nothing to alleviate opposition to increased busing. As a result, the county school board proposed another alternative, the so-called magnet-school plan. Devised by a new school superintendent, John A. Murphy, it would set up 30 magnet schools, some offering programs for a select group of about 700 "talented and gifted" pupils. These educational enrichment curricula would presumably be attractive enough to convince white and black parents to send their children to the special schools. Other magnet schools would offer the incentive of before- and after-school day care for the children of working parents. Racial guidelines would be used in selecting students for each magnet school so as to balance enrollment.[16]

Meanwhile, the black community in the county was divided in its attitudes about approaches to desegregation. For example, a group of eight black elected officials in state and county government rejected this plan unless a back-up program of busing was instituted in the event that the magnet schools failed to achieve a balanced racial profile.[17] In addition, the county's chapter of the National Association for the Advancement of Colored People (NAACP) expressed similar concerns and recommended nine amendments to the magnet-school plan.[18] But even before the magnet plan was announced, the Black Coalition Against Unnecessary Busing, a group of black parents in the county, announced its opposition to further attempts to bus children for desegregation purposes. Instead, it called for more neighborhood schools, even if racially imbalanced, and greater concentration of school resources on schools with the lowest test scores. The group was joined by the South Prince George's Coalition on Black Affairs, which was also unhappy with the Green plan.[19] Thus, the magnet-school plan was designed to neutralize opposition not only among large numbers of white parents but also among some black families, and it has engendered more promise that a compromise can be reached than any other measure thus far proposed. The district court gave preliminary approval to the plan but required that back-up busing be available and that the implementation schedule be accelerated.[20] Sensing the growing consensus in the county for its proposal, the school board reached an agreement with the county NAACP on further revisions to the magnet-school plan. In addition, the board approved an administrative reorganization that would result in the promotion of six blacks to high management posts. These events were viewed as promising because the board and the NAACP had been at loggerheads for over a decade.[21]

By the end of its first year of operation, the county's magnet-school program had succeeded in raising the level of interracial enrollment in several schools. Seventeen of 33 schools under a court order to desegregate had reached court-required standards. Moreover, nearly 1,000 of the 4,000 applications for the program's 1986–1987 school year were from pupils in private schools, a solid indication that the program appealed even to some of those who formerly had avoided the public schools. An unfortunate side effect, however, was the high number of black children on the program's waiting list; of 2,255 pupils on the list, 96 percent were black. Thus, white children were much more likely than black children to be admitted.[22]

At the present time, then, the county appears to be closer to resolving the school imbalance problem than it has at any time since the original 1972 court order to desegregate was issued. But the burden of expectations placed on the magnet-school plan is sobering. Furthermore, an accord was being reached on the plan just as the results of a survey of county public school educators were released. The report found that nearly one-half of those surveyed were so unhappy that they wanted to leave the teaching profession. More than two-thirds reported incidents of verbal abuse from students, and 21 percent said they had experienced physical abuse. More than one-third cited discipline problems that affected their teaching substantially.[23] It is clear, then, that the school board in Prince George's County has a very difficult time ahead. Not only must it resolve the school imbalance controversy, it must do so with an educational staff that is decidedly less than enthusiastic about current conditions. Just as important, the magnet-school plan and teacher dissatisfaction with salaries will require substantial increases in the school board's budget. Whether county taxpayers and state legislators will agree to this is yet to be seen.

In the city of Alexandria the school system has faced a far less severe racial imbalance condition than has Prince George's County. Since 1971 Alexandria has conducted a busing program to achieve racial balance in elementary schools. Under threat of a court order, the school board established the program so that schools with predominantly black enrollment were paired with schools with predominantly white enrollment, and students were transported between schools to achieve desegregation. Much like Prince George's County, Alexandria succeeded in reducing the extremes of imbalance, which had persisted before desegregation began. But a combination of white flight from the community and from its public schools, as well as an influx of predominantly Hispanic and Asian students, left the Alexandria school system in 1985 with an even more complicated racial balance problem. Even though court-ordered school desegregation plans throughout most of the United States have not been required to take nonblack minorities into consideration, Alexandria officials have been uncertain how to proceed. Just as black-white desegregation policy centered on the elementary schools, where imbalance was usually greatest, so also has discussion of the newer minorities.

As in most communities, busing in Alexandria was not popular with most whites and many minorities. A computer simulation of elementary school racial patterns under a hypothetical reduction of busing found that imbalance would be exacerbated and overcrowding would occur at some schools. Even though there had been sizable shifts in racial patterns in several neighborhoods since busing began, the simulation projected that increased attendance at neighborhood schools would inflate segregation conditions. The federal guideline used by Alexandria to define segregated conditions required that racial profiles in any school not vary from the overall systemwide racial proportions by more than 20 percent.[24]

After several months of study and public debate, the Alexandria school board approved a new plan, which combined school-attendance boundary changes, reduced busing, and established a magnet school. Adopted in May 1984, the plan was opposed by two of the three black members of the nine-member school board. The plan incorporated some of the concessions of the earlier computer simulation study, permitting children in some neighborhoods with racial mixtures to attend neighborhood elementary schools. Busing would be continued in other neighborhoods where greater imbalance would result if children were to attend neighborhood schools. The magnet school would be established in a predominantly black neighborhood of Alexandria. It would feature a math and science curriculum, with computer literacy being a central vehicle for teaching. Student progress would be measured individually, and students would advance by mastering skills one at a time. The purpose would be to offer an alternative education sufficiently attractive to draw more affluent students from public and private schools in other parts of the community while achieving an acceptable racial composition.[25]

Almost 500 students were admitted from the neighborhood district in which the school is located. Applicants from outside the district had to apply for admission. In the first round of applications for the autumn of 1984, there were not enough "outside" white applicants to fill the quota for whites and too many "outside" minority applicants for the minority quota. Thus, all the white applicants were accepted, while minority applicants had to compete for their positions.[26] By the 1986–1987 school year, only 31 of 430 pupils in the school were white. The problem of low white enrollment was due in part to the school's curriculum, which many have criticized as not sufficiently improved over those of conventional elementary schools.[27]

Other school districts in the Washington suburbs have struggled with the issue of racial imbalance in the public schools. In Fairfax and Montgomery counties, where minority enrollment is proportionately smaller compared with Prince George's County and Alexandria, the issue has been raised primarily in areas located closest to the District of Columbia. Because Fairfax and Montgomery are considerably larger than Alexandria and have smaller minority populations than Prince George's, countywide desegregation programs have been viewed as infeasible and unnecessary. However, targeted busing programs and proposals have raised controversy in an area of Montgomery County located close to the boundaries of the District of Columbia and Prince George's County.[28]

Busing in Arlington County has been employed in the primary grades for several years. There, however, almost all the children being bused are black and from the southern portion of the county. They are sent to schools in the northern sections where whites predominate. In the fall of 1986 school officials agreed to review their current desegregation plan, a modification of one first established under a 1971 court order. Pressure from disgruntled black parents, who disliked having their children bear the brunt of busing, led to this decision.[29]

However controversial the problems of desegregation, they are secondary to the issue of the quality of education received by minority and white students. The next section examines the capital-area suburban school districts' experiences with one measure of educational excellence—student performance on standardized examinations.

Pupil Performance

However tension-producing the issues of racial imbalance and desegregation may be in the Washington metropolitan area, the central educational concern of both white and minority parents is pupil performance. Desegregation programs have as their core assumption that the social and intellectual development of children in a pluralistic democratic society is incomplete in communities with significant racial diversity but essentially segregated schools.

Undergirding this assumption are beliefs that less-privileged, minority children may improve their academic performance if given the opportunity to share the classroom with middle-class, white pupils. A corollary is that school board per-pupil expenditures will be more equitably apportioned from school to school if whites and minorities are mixed. Therefore, parents and school personnel alike look to pupil performance on standardized tests to measure the worth of assumptions about the benefits of racial balance.

Recent data from the 1983 Scholastic Aptitude Test (SAT) revealed that high school seniors in Washington's metropolitan area achieved widely varying average scores from school district to school district. In the city of Washington the combined math and verbal score was 702, in the bottom one-fifth of scores nationwide. Prince George's County's score was 848, somewhat under the average national score of 893. Alexandria city and Arlington, Fairfax, and Montgomery counties all had scores between 908 and 968. However, seniors in Washington succeeded in raising their average score 15 points between 1978 and 1983, while those in the other area school systems had declining average scores.[30] In a city with a student population that is approximately 95 percent black, many observers have noted the significance of this achievement.

But comparisons of white and minority student progress *within* school districts tend to find less positive results. For example, even though Fairfax County seniors had the second highest average SAT score in the metropolitan area in 1983, the county's 23,000 minority public school students "consistently scored lower than whites on achievement tests."[31] A *Washington Post* article reported, "The school system's 10,000 black students have had significantly lower average scores than whites in almost all tests. The 3600 Hispanic students did somewhat better and the 9000 Asian students did almost as well as white students in some tests."[32] A 1983 Fairfax County study revealed that on the average blacks received lower course grades and minimum competency scores than did whites. In addition, they repeated grades more frequently, went on to college less frequently, had higher dropout rates, and had lower representation in programs for the gifted and talented. Generally, Hispanic students fell between blacks and whites, using these measures. Asian students were usually slightly less successful than whites in most of these areas, although they had better average performance in course grades than did whites.[33]

By late 1986 Fairfax County had measured modest progress in minority achievement under a special program that increased staff and funding at 80 schools with significant minority enrollment. There were small gains in black scores on some standardized tests and a decline in the number of blacks in special education courses. However, black children's grades had not changed notably by the end of the first year of the program. Follow-up assessments will be made as the program progresses.[34]

In Arlington, black student test scores repeated the pattern of other communities. In late 1986 they lagged behind white pupil test scores in all grades tested and by as much as 46 percentage points in the 11th grade. This pattern had remained unchanged over the previous two years.[35] In response, the school board earmarked $130,000 for individual schools to develop their own programs to raise black achievement. Although most other minorities also achieved lower scores than did white children, the board decided to limit its effort to blacks. This was because blacks do not qualify for local and federal funding under language education programs, as do non-English-speaking minorities. Furthermore, black parents exerted pressure on the board to concentrate the program on the needs of black children.[36]

In Montgomery County, where Walt Whitman High School was recently rated one of the top 15 public high schools in the United States, county residents take great pride in the reputation of their school system. Five of the seven high schools in the Washington metropolitan area with the highest average 1983 SAT scores were in Montgomery County. Nonetheless, a study by the county school system found that minority students were achieving at a substantially lower level than were whites in most measures of scholastic progress. With minority enrollment composing 27 percent of the student population in the county public schools, it was found that blacks and Hispanics scored markedly lower on standardized tests. They were overrepresented in low-level courses and underrepresented in advanced courses. In addition, they were less likely to go on to college than were whites or Asians and were suspended more often from school. Finally, the study found that they were not as likely to receive remedial assistance as were nonminorities.[37]

Another study, prepared by a committee of citizens and black organizations in Montgomery County, discovered that black and Hispanic students scored in approximately the 50th percentile on the California Achievement Tests; white and Asian students were generally in the 70th and 80th percentiles, respectively. The report noted that about two-thirds of blacks and one-half of Hispanics failed to pass a state examination in math proficiency; 70 percent of whites and 77 percent of Asians passed the exam.[38]

Prince George's County high schools, where black enrollment is higher than in any other Washington suburban high school system, has struggled with student performance levels, which have been below national norms. Between 1980 and 1984 both verbal and math mean test scores on the SAT ranged from 18 to 27 points lower than national means. Furthermore, variation among county high schools was wide. Most impressive was Eleanor Roosevelt High School, which had the highest combined SAT score (1,050) of all public high schools in the Washington metropolitan area; about 37 percent of the school's enrollment was black. With a selective program in science and technology, Roosevelt High School was established in 1976 as a kind of magnet school, drawing from among the most able students in the county.[39] The impressive achievements of Roosevelt High notwithstanding, Prince George's County has continued to wrestle with lower minority-student performance levels. In 1980, for example, when about one-half of county public school students were black, slightly less than 13 percent of the enrollment in courses for gifted and talented students was composed of blacks.[40]

Certainly, student academic performance is the primary concern of most parents and school officials everywhere. But evidence of poor minority achievement on standardized tests is only the most prominent source of conflict about minority-student opportunity in the suburbs of Washington. Also important is concern about unequal treatment of minority students by school system personnel. Throughout the decade or so of efforts to reduce racial imbalance in suburban public schools, minority parents, especially blacks, have complained that black children are sometimes treated differently from white children. In 1979 it was noted that blacks were suspended twice as often as whites for disciplinary problems in Alexandria schools. Although a citizens' committee found no substantial evidence of discriminatory practice, it expressed the suspicion that two standards of behavior—one for whites and one for blacks—were in effect.[41] A similar study in Montgomery County found that in the six school years between 1979–1980 and 1984–1985, black senior high school suspensions ranged from 11 to almost 16 percent of black enrollment, while white suspensions ranged from approximately 6 to 8 percent of white enrollment. Asian and Hispanic suspension rates generally fell between these ranges.[42] Higher rates of suspension among black and in some cases Hispanic students have been found in other school systems in the Washington metropolitan area, but data are not usually made public.[43]

It is not only suspension or expulsion data that raise minority parents' concerns, however. One Fairfax County high school in the planned suburb of Reston, Virginia, has been the target of complaints from some black parents that even in their affluent community, racial discrimination is present. With a 13 percent black student population in 1986, the school's advanced and honors programs had a black enrollment of less than 6 percent. This and several other complaints from some black parents were the basis of a charge of racial discrimination. School administrators and an independent panel of community residents found that most complaints were unsubstantiated but concluded that some school staff members were insensitive to black student needs or had difficulty teaching blacks.[44]

These kinds of figures, not surprisingly, raise suspicions among many who support racial-balance efforts. There is the fear that outright racial antagonism by some white teachers and administrators may account for differences in the way minority pupils are treated in disciplinary matters. There is also the recognition that differing cultural patterns, especially among blacks and Hispanics, may be perceived by whites as belligerence or unwillingness to cooperate. Alternatively, some fear that student misbehavior may be a sign of rebellion against unequal treatment in the classroom. Whatever the validity of these suspicions, the existence of doubt about the equality of treatment of minority students points to the overall concern about race relations in the public schools.

Race Relations

Probably the most elusive indicator of the success of efforts to achieve a balanced racial profile in public schools is the character of relations between white, black, Hispanic, and Asian students. Also important are conditions between students, teachers, and administrators. Race relations, of course, do not express themselves in statistics, at least not in any meaningful way. But occasional observations suggest that school desegregation has helped to reduce the extremes of bigotry, especially between black and white students.

According to one view of pupils in Alexandria public schools, younger children are most accepting of one another and exhibit the least evidence of racial intolerance. By the fourth or fifth grade, however, they begin to show signs of awareness about children of other races. When they reach junior high school, at a time when most teenagers are facing puberty, they have begun to separate themselves according to cliques, interest groups, and social class preferences, and blacks and whites are seen less frequently together. Because junior high tends to weed out many students with disciplinary cases, by senior high school age, most students find that conflict between the races has been reduced. Although interracial contact is not widespread and teenagers tend to fraternize mostly with members of their own race, sports, music, and drama organizations and similar activities provide opportunities for blacks and whites to rub elbows.[45]

Nevertheless, there is evidence that even the social benefits that many observers assumed would result from interracial student bodies are not always as pervasive as many had hoped they would be. For example, a veteran teacher in Alexandria's most prestigious high school, Patrick Welsh, recently enumerated many of the difficulties that teenagers experience.[46] Laced throughout his article are examples of misunderstanding and in some cases outright racism among students at the high school. But it is clear that conflict occurs not only between whites and minorities but also among whites and among blacks. Both white and black students divide along socioeconomic lines, the author points out. White "preppy" students may show antagonism for whites from less-affluent, working-class backgrounds. Blacks who perform well academically may be picked on by blacks who see such accomplishments as rejection of less-able black students. Students usually cluster in the school cafeteria not only according to race but also along interest-group and class lines. Thus, black "jocks" may sit at one table, black band members at another, and black academic achievers at a third. White "punkers" may hang out in one group in the hallways, white jocks in another, and white computer enthusiasts in a third. Separate clusters may be made up of Hispanics, Asians, or other minority groups.

A white female complained of pinching and lewd behavior by black males, but a black female pointed out that she, too, has been the victim of such behavior by blacks. On the other hand, another white female said that black males treated her well but that some white males called her names and treated her shabbily. Foreign students, especially those still struggling to master the English language, are often the victims of both white and black racism, Welsh points out. Not only are they set off by their language and customs but for those who are especially talented scholastically, derision by American students is sometimes based on jealousy.

The special difficulties encountered by a bright, black eighth grader in Montgomery County also document the complexities of race relations.[47] The thirteen-year-old girl described occasional racism among white students, some of it based on adolescent insensitivity and inexperience and some of it, on cruel and senseless remarks. Assigned to advanced courses, she found that there were few, if any, blacks in her classes. In fact, most of the 45 blacks in the 450-student school were in courses for average or below-average performers. She related the trials of balancing the taunts and subtle peer pressure she received from other black students with the intended and unintended racially discriminatory behavior of whites. Her experience conveys the especially critical role that peer acceptance plays during adolescence and the complications that race brings to this problem.

The normal insecurities of puberty may be compounded by the challenges of a racially mixed school environment. The young black girl described the lack of confidence she felt about her intellectual abilities in classes that were overwhelmingly composed of whites. She felt that many of her white peers believed that she had not earned her admission into the advanced classes and that she was not as academically accomplished as they. Each mistake she made in her studies, she feared, would spell the end of her plans to become a corporate lawyer. Her friendship with a black girl, one of only 20 in her grade, was motivated out of a need for companionship with someone who could understand her difficulties and share feelings of racial insecurity. But there was evidence that her friend, not as academically talented as the honor student, may have made her feel that to do well in courses dominated by whites was to reject her own blackness.

White and minority students appear to develop many interracial friendships, especially through group activities such as school bands and athletic teams. But observers note that outside of these pursuits, students tend to "hang with their own kind." And although open violence is uncommon, it has happened. During the first years of school desegregation in the early 1970s, for example, periodic fighting between black and white students occurred at some schools.[48] In more recent years, when Hispanic and Vietnamese students began to grow in numbers at a Fairfax County high school, a "rumble" broke out between whites and the new minorities.[49] Confrontations such as these do not typify race relation in Washington's metropolitan-area schools. Yet tension among students at a given school is only one measure of race relations. Interaction between students and teachers and administrators may also call forth charges of racial intolerance.

A recent meeting at a high school in Montgomery County revealed how perceptions of racism, whether real or imagined, can compound conditions in a tension-ridden atmosphere. Amid angry shouts, parents and students complained about uneven discipline, with black students more severely and frequently punished than whites. The crowd at the meeting, predominantly black, singled out one black and one white teacher, who were accused of prejudicial actions. Black students tallied a two-page list of examples, which, they claimed, showed differential treatment of blacks and whites. Among the criticisms were the following:

1. Lunchroom monitors refused to take disciplinary action when white students threw food on black students.
2. Black students and white students were disciplined differently.
3. A teacher encouraged students to skip an assembly honoring the Reverend Martin Luther King, Jr.
4. "Black Experience" class was taught by white teachers.

5. No tribute was paid to singer Marvin Gaye by playing his songs over the school's audio system at lunch hour after he died, although when John Lennon died, his records were played all day.[50]

Other complaints centered on the school newspaper, which some students felt had not covered the Reverend Jesse Jackson's political views as well as those of other Democratic presidential primary candidates. Criticism emerged about cartoons that were said to show blacks "in an exaggerated manner."

The school's principal acknowledged that some complaints were founded on fact and were fair. Others, he felt, were misperceptions, some of which may have been based on faulty information. Whatever the case, it is apparent how delicate a balance must be maintained in the Washington metropolitan area in schools where minorities and whites are in attendance. To minority students, for whom the day-to-day issues of race are ever-present, each slight, whether intended or inadvertent, is a possible expression of the very real racism that exists in the larger society. Where the climate in a given school becomes tinged with suspicion, teachers and administrators must take extraordinary measures to reduce tensions. Matters of balanced treatment of blacks and whites that might go unchallenged when students feel that racism is minimal take on larger proportions when distrust has taken root. Thus, even issues that to outsiders may seem trivial become very important to students who are on the cutting edge of society's efforts to achieve true racial equality.

Racial Progress in the Suburban Schools

Varying degrees of conflict have arisen in Washington's suburban school districts over issues related to race in education. But clearly, the most complicated and salient concerns have revolved around the problems of black students. In Prince George's County, with the largest black student body of all suburban Washington communities, the problems of achieving racial balance—by any reasonable definition—and the challenge of improving educational achievement are most difficult. In Arlington and Alexandria, school systems are faced not only with maintaining racial balance between blacks and whites but also with unresolved issues about maintaining balance between these groups and Asian and Hispanic students. In the wealthier counties of Fairfax and Montgomery, minority-student populations are smaller, but the minority students are more likely to come from professional families; while racial balance is a less-controversial issue, minority parents and students tend to be more involved in school matters and seem to articulate better their concerns to school officials. Even in Fairfax and Montgomery counties, nevertheless, minority students, especially black and (to a lesser extent) Hispanic children, have performed less well collectively than whites. This helps to explain, perhaps, why suspicions exist among some blacks that school system discrimination accounts for disparities in performance. Doubtless, the higher educational and socioeconomic status of many black parents in Montgomery and Fairfax counties indicates correspondingly higher expectations about their children than those of parents in other Washington suburban jurisdictions.

Generally, attitudes in the Washington metropolitan area about achieving racially balanced school systems and erasing racial differences in educational performance are less sanguine—and more realistic—than they were a decade ago. But the heavy emphasis of the 1970s on school desegregation and racial balance as a means of reducing educational disparities has shifted considerably. As the minority presence has grown in the inner capital suburbs, the problems of reaching, to say nothing of maintaining, desirable levels of racial balance in the schools have become apparent. The problem has only been complicated further by declining white populations and white enrollment in schools. Mandatory busing continues to be a device for reducing racial disparities in individual school enrollments in some communities. However, educators have tended to rely increasingly on magnet schools and voluntary incentives to promote parental cooperation and reduce the propensity of some white families to move away or send their children to private schools.

Simultaneously, greater stress is being placed on remedial and compensatory curricula for minority students, whatever the racial composition of the school attended. Requiring strict attendance, regularly testing pupil performance, and raising teachers' expectation levels for minority-student performance have been identified as necessary adjuncts. Yet it has been only very recently that some suburban school systems around Washington have released to the public standardized achievement test scores by race; the consistent pattern of significantly lower scores among blacks—and to a lesser extent, Hispanics—has served to magnify the issue in public policy realms. These data have shown that even in school districts with several years of experience with busing and desegregation, troubling disparities in pupil achievement persist.

It is apparent that many public school officials have been reluctant to release such data by race. Some have suspected that minority children would be stigmatized by racial comparisons. Some have felt that such revelations could be used by those opposed to minority progress to undermine desegregation and compensatory programs. Other educators have simply feared that release of test scores would bring charges of racism.

Doubtless, most teachers, administrators, and elected officials are aware that reporting test scores by race does not show the very substantial differences in socioeconomic circumstances between most minorities and most whites. Indeed, Chapter 7 provides evidence of the variation, especially between whites and blacks in Washington's suburbs, in household or family levels of income, education, and poverty. Until test scores by race can be standardized according to social and economic background, we cannot be sure how much of the variation in performance by race is due to the scourge of deprivation. This, in turn, raises the question of how much progress in educational attainment can be contributed by the schools and how much must come through social welfare assistance in housing, income, health, and the like.

However disparate are views about race and educational performance in the Washington suburbs, the new candor about the existence of sizable gaps in test scores appears to be ushering in a period of experimentation and testing of curricula, instructional methods, and personnel policies. Meanwhile, even though the difficulties of school desegregation continue to plague school officials, especially in Alexandria city and in Prince George's and Arlington counties, efforts persist to reduce racial imbalance in individual schools. Optimism about the effects of busing and of voluntary efforts to reduce interracial differences in performance has nevertheless been clouded somewhat by varying findings and conclusions of empirical research projects nationwide. (This topic is discussed briefly in Chapter 9.) [51] It is clear that until there is a greater consensus among scholars, however, public and political support for other than voluntary desegregation policies in the Washington metropolitan area is likely to undergo continued erosion.

Whatever the *educational effects* of racial balance, the question of its *social effects* requires a second dimension of evaluation. In a society founded on the aspirations of equality, what influence does the mixing of whites with black, Hispanic, Asian, and other minorities have on increasing interracial harmony? No definitive studies of students in the national capital metropolitan area have been undertaken at this writing. But informal testimony from individual teachers and other observers suggests that while racial balancing efforts may not erase racial stereotyping by students, teachers, administrators, and parents, the grossest misperceptions are less likely to persist. Even though social interaction between blacks and whites, for example, may be confined to limited times during the school day, regular exposure to one another in a setting and routine overseen by adults appears to undermine some of the most prevalent aspects of racial tension.

To be sure, racial conflict has occurred at many schools in isolated circumstances and at infrequent times. For every incident that has attracted public attention, perhaps a thousand more go undetected. But even these would seem to pale by comparison with the routine day-to-day cordiality and mutual respect that characterize race relations throughout most suburban schools with white and minority attendance. The long-term effects of these less-dramatic interactions on future educational, employment, and housing opportunities for minorities may be the real test of the worth of efforts to increase racial balance.

Nevertheless, at least for the near future, resistance among whites continues to raise doubts about the feasibility of achieving more than isolated progress in reducing racial imbalance in individual suburban schools. When surveyed, whites in the Washington metropolitan area have been less likely than blacks to believe that desegregation programs have improved the quality of public education; in a 1986 survey 33 percent of whites and 54 percent of blacks saw improvements.[52] These differences in attitudes help to account for the out-migration of whites from many of Washington's inner suburban neighborhoods, a phenomenon that has undermined the social effect of minority suburbanization. This factor, the shifting of children to private schools, and until recently, declining birth rates among whites account for the transition of some neighborhood public schools from largely white to largely minority enrollments. When queried, white parents seldom object openly to racially mixed enrollment patterns. But they are more likely than blacks to be concerned when their children are in the minority in school. Survey data show that 56 percent of blacks but only 42 percent of whites would be comfortable in sending their children to a school where they were in a racial minority.[53] Yet when queried under other than anonymous circumstances, many whites cite inadequate academic standards, resources, and test scores at individual schools in support of withdrawing their children. Ironically, affluent minority families, especially in Montgomery and Fairfax counties, sometimes point to the same problems for their children. It appears that where white and minority students in individual schools are drawn from similar socioeconomic levels, the difficulties of maintaining acceptable educational standards are reduced. The more common pattern, however, is much like that in the District of Columbia public schools, where middle-class students are expected to attend schools with students from widely varying economic circumstances. Given this prospect, most white parents in the city and many in the suburbs opt to move away from the neighborhood (if not the larger community altogether) or enroll their children in private schools.

Part Three

Race, Politics, and Public Policy

9

The Evolving Social Geography of the
Washington Metropolitan Area

More than a decade and a half has passed since Washington experienced its episode of civil disorder during the national urban riots of the 1960s. As in other cities, the riot symbolized the lowest ebb in the churning waters of social unrest that accompanied the Civil Rights Movement. It would be several years before many whites could restore their trust in the future of business and residency in the District of Columbia. On the other hand, while the riots were deplored by many blacks, they underscored the depth of frustration and anger many felt about the implications of that future for their own interests. At the time of the riots, the black population in the metropolitan area was heavily concentrated in the central city, while whites vastly dominated the surrounding suburbs. A popular metaphor among militant activists referred to the "white noose around the black neck of the inner city," recalling the lynchings of southern blacks by the Ku Klux Klan in earlier decades.

As the preceding chapters have shown, the national capital metropolitan region has undergone some stunning changes since the 1968 violence. Partly as a result of shifting social values, a complex web of federal, state, and local government legislation and litigation, and rising black affluence, the geographical and social status of race relations has undergone a major transformation. Blacks are no longer as heavily concentrated in Washington. About one-half of all blacks in the metropolitan area now live in the suburbs, although most of these reside in Prince George's County. Moreover, most suburban blacks live in the older communities inside the Capital Beltway. Other minorities, especially Asians and Hispanics, are scattered in several locations, primarily in Arlington, Alexandria, and Prince George's County. But they, too, tend to be concentrated in the older, inner tier of suburban communities.

Accompanying this trend has been a much more gradually evolving rediscovery of the historical commercial and residential center of the capital city, largely by white businesses and households. There can be no doubt that revitalization has had a powerful effect on economic conditions, particularly on the city's fiscal health because of substantial increases in tax and other revenues. But there are important social costs that partially undermine the positive economic effect of Washington's reinvestment cycle. Clearly, revitalization in the core has not only reduced the low- and moderate-income and minority populations there, it has shrunk the supply of privately owned, low-cost housing and contributed to the high degree of overcrowdedness in black-occupied dwelling units in other areas of the city. Had the District government been able to add substantially to the supply of subsidized new and renovated housing during the 1970s, the loss of housing for needy people in the core might not have become as critical a social issue. But enormous cutbacks in the federal budget for many housing programs, especially public housing, have contributed to the District government's inability to realize this goal.

Overcrowding in housing not yet touched by the reinvestment process may be one means by which poor people have coped with the dwindling supply of appropriate shelter. But it is a subject of speculation among some observers that another coping technique might be that of fleeing to the older, inner suburban sections in jurisdictions such as Prince George's and Arlington counties. While black out-migration from the District of Columbia tends to involve mainly middle-income households, it is conceivable that some of the city's poorer families have sought shelter in the older dwellings and garden apartment complexes within approximately one mile of the District line. If so, the District may be unwittingly exporting part of its poverty problem to the suburbs.

The Social Terrain

The summation of the effects of inner-city revitalization and minority suburbanization is a metropolitan area whose social and economic patterns have shifted considerably since 1960. Four sectors of the national capital metropolitan area bear brief discussion.

1. The *core of Washington* is no longer characterized by disinvestment, slums, and a high density of minority groups. It is becoming an enclave of middle- and upper-income residents and workers, largely whites, with expensive housing, stores, and restaurants. A growing body of galleries, museums, theaters, and concert halls serves the cultural interests of these

people. Historic preservation has become an implicit, if not explicit, communal mucilage for many white, middle- and upper-class residents who support it. An ethos of historicism underlies much of the revitalization movement, but it is an ethos to which relatively few minorities seem to subscribe.

2. The *remaining areas of the city* outside the core have shown greater stability in recent decades. Upper northwest Washington continues to be overwhelmingly white and middle to upper class. Much of the northeast of Washington is composed of lower-middle- and middle-class minority families with numerous neighborhoods of well-maintained, single-family dwellings. Parts of the far southeast, especially in the Anacostia area, hold some of the city's most seriously deprived minority families; other sections, however, are composed of stable middle-income neighborhoods with predominantly white or black residency patterns. Substantial sections of both the northeast and southeast underwent black in-migration and white out-migration during the 1950s and 1960s. But for the most part, their racial identities have remained fixed since the 1970 census.

3. In several communities located in the *inner tier of suburbs* (roughly, the area encompassed by the Capital Beltway), there has been a sharp decline in white households and a rapid rise in minority households. In others, for example, Chevy Chase and Bethesda, the changes have been less dramatic. The net effect has been that the inner tier has shifted from its earlier identity as a haven largely for working- and middle-class whites. These groups persist but in dwindling numbers in many sections of the inner tier. Joining them have been sizable numbers of blacks and smaller numbers of Asians, Hispanics, and other minorities of similar socioeconomic circumstances.

4. Most of Washington's *younger suburban areas* lie beyond the capital beltway. These areas have built up primarily since the late 1950s. Although they contain smaller percentages of minorities than the inner tier, their minority populations tend to be more affluent. But their identities have changed relatively little since minorities began to migrate out of Washington in large numbers in the late 1960s and 1970s.

Hence, the geography of racial and socioeconomic change in the Washington metropolitan area has primarily affected the core and the inner suburbs. Both areas have experienced relatively rapid population changes —the core from predominantly black to increasingly white and the inner tier from predominantly white to increasingly black, Hispanic, and Asian. Although the District of Columbia has had a declining population base since the 1940s, the U.S. Census Bureau recently estimated that its population remained steady at 623,000 in 1983 and 1984.[1] If these estimates are accurate, they may indicate that births and in-migration associated with the city's core at last have balanced out the city's losses due to deaths and out-migration—especially black out-migration to Prince George's County. The remaining years of the present decade should be scrutinized very closely to determine whether the city has finally reached a steady state in its population status.

Nevertheless, in both the District's core and the inner-tier counties, the quality of public education raises provocative issues about the expectations of the newer in-migrants. Even though the bulk of gentrifier households in Washington's core are childless, recent evidence shows that birth rates have risen dramatically. While some public elementary schools in the core have shown slight gains in white enrollment in the lowest grades, to date there has been no noteworthy effect on the school system.

It is possible, however, that the school system will experience a marked rise in white enrollment in the core or in the upper northwest. If so, the District's school system bureaucracy will face an important challenge. With only a few exceptions, it has not been successful in attracting and holding the children of white families in the core and several other sections of the city. (Nor is its hold on black, middle-class families in other areas of the city as strong as it once was.) But the real test will come when the bumper crop of newborn whites reach elementary school age in the latter half of the present decade. If parents decide to give their neighborhood schools a chance, the school system will have to confront the issue of tailoring curricula to meet the needs of growing numbers of students from privileged backgrounds while continuing to serve those of less fortunate circumstances. This is likely to exacerbate concerns about tracking, elitism, and dual school systems. If the public schools recognize that enriched, ability-based curricula are absolutely essential to holding young, middle-class whites and blacks, they may be able to decelerate the out-migration of these people to the suburbs. If the school system does not commit enough school resources to this end, it will effectively confirm that the future of the city of Washington is directed to a two-stratum urban society.

One stratum will be composed of middle- and upper-income people, both minority and white, with relatively few children, most of whom will attend private schools; primarily consumerists and careerists, they will take little interest in public school issues.[2] The other stratum will be made up largely of the poor—mostly minority families and elderly singles and couples. The complicated problems of poverty will relegate most parents to the struggle merely to get their children through the school system, with little thought to improving curricula or resources. Conspicuously missing will be a significant population of middle-class, black and white families.

In effect, Washington has been given the opportunity to stabilize, if not increase, its white population base, largely as a result of the revitalization that has occurred in its core. But there are complicated political factors that becloud this opportunity. These will be discussed in Chapters 10 and 11.

Desegregation: Dissension and Consensus

In the surrounding inner-tier suburbs of Washington, the issues of public education are also crosscut with racial and socioeconomic dimensions. Moreover, the schools take on more stature because suburban residency is so much more firmly based on the desire for quality academic preparation. As thousands of minorities have moved into these jurisdictions seeking better schooling for their children, they have at once imposed new burdens on local school boards and raised new expectations. In recent years busing for desegregation purposes appears to have lost some of its earlier support among white liberals and blacks in the Washington area and nationally. Legal and political factors, however, continue the inertia of busing, while empirical research on desegregation yields mixed findings about its effectiveness in raising educational performance.

One school of thought, ably represented by Robert L. Crain, Joe T. Darden, Rita E. Mahard, Willis D. Hawley, Meyer Weinberg, and others, acknowledging varying test scores, grades, and IQ scores, argues that there are enough positive outcomes to justify continued efforts to desegregate public educational systems.[3] Another school, equally well represented by Nancy H. St. John, Martin Patchen, Harold B. Gerard, Norman Miller, and others, insists that substantial proportions of black students have had little, if any, gain in such achievement measures in desegregated settings.[4]

There seems to be a consensus within both schools of thought, however, that desegregated schools are more effective when certain conditions are present. Among these conditions are that desegregation begin in preschool or kindergarten rather than in the higher grades, that the principals and staff be absolutely committed to desegregation, and that there not be vast differences in the numbers of minorities and whites at individual schools.[5] Additionally, some researchers have found that in one metropolitan area the greatest gain in test scores occurred among pupils from neighborhoods that were about half black and half white or mostly (but not entirely) black. While it may be that racial composition is in turn related to socioeconomic background in the study, the results suggest that housing and neighborhood racial and socioeconomic patterns have a bearing on performance as well.[6]

Nevertheless, the difficulty of producing many of the optimal conditions for raising minority-student performance under desegregation has undermined some of the earlier enthusiasm for busing in the Washington metropolitan area. The issue is further clouded by varying performance among minority groups. There appear to be distinct disparities between the educational fortunes of many suburban black students and those of other minority groups. While evidence is limited, it seems that the performance of black children overall has been more problematic than that of Hispanics or Asians. Understandably, this pattern is perplexing for black parents, recognizing that their children are native Americans with few of the problems of acculturation and language typical of immigrant children. Suspicions about racially discriminatory behavior among white teachers and administrators arise within some—perhaps most—black families. Complicating these feelings are the real and imagined racial slights and insults that sometimes occur among children, especially in the middle and upper grades. Both white and minority children may be the victims. Some minority parents and students have also linked racial differences in school penalty rates with racial discrimination.

For thousands of black families in the Washington metropolitan area, especially those in Prince George's County, the suburban schools represented an opportunity to escape what was perceived to be an inferior educational system in the District of Columbia or other central-city school systems. While most would agree that suburban public education is an improvement, some black parents are undoubtedly disillusioned. Their children have not progressed as dramatically as they had hoped. Some have blamed teachers and administrators, while others point to the bad influence of poorer students who attend some of the inner-tier schools.

Meanwhile, in many black households both parents are forced to work to maintain their middle-class standard of living. As a result, some children have poor supervision. This situation may be complicated in some families by the fact that parents who have only recently attained the ranks of the middle income are not able to instill values about educational diligence in their children. They expect the school system to impart a respect for learning and habits of industry and initiative and are frustrated when it cannot do so. Of course, these perceptions are hardly unique to black parents; many whites and other minorities similarly place too much dependence on the school system. But for black families, the consequences of an inadequate education are likely to be more severe than those for many whites.

Meanwhile, the inner-tier jurisdictions have been plagued by substantial white out-migration. As white residency and white public school enroll-ment patterns have declined, the difficult job of balancing individual schools has been further complicated. Although some of the loss of white pupils is related to decreasing birth rates among whites, there can be little doubt that much more is due to other factors. To be sure, some whites believe that some blacks are intellectually inferior; most fair-minded people, how-ever, recognize that the enormously crippling legacy of slavery and dis-crimination has placed blacks in a unique position in American society. Still others attribute black student performance to the effects of poverty or the alleged breakdown of family structure. Many whites associate some blacks with crime and antisocial behavior and fear for the safety of their own children. Few parents are happy with the inconvenience of busing. Whatever the motivation, thousands of inner-tier suburban whites have fled the approach of racial minorities.

Thus, the inner-tier suburban school districts find themselves wrestling with the same issues of white out-migration that the District of Columbia has confronted since the 1950s. But the District now has the added prob-lem of dealing with black, as well as white, middle-class out-migration. While the public school systems in the District and inner-tier counties, of themselves, will not resolve these problems, they are a critical ingredient—perhaps the most critical—in addressing the policy issues of out-migration. In both the suburbs and the central city, the linchpin of this problem lies in the political structure and the elusive nature of race relations, which Chap-ters 10 and 11 will discuss.

It should be emphasized, though, that the political ramifications of racial change in both the city and the suburbs go well beyond public education. As elsewhere, the politics of race is manifested in local government em-ployment practices, police treatment of citizens, zoning and real estate practices, and similar matters. To examine all of these with other than superficial treatment, of course, would require that this study be expanded to include a second volume. Hence, we will have to contain our explora-tion of the political dimensions of racial change within the single issue of public education. Most would agree, nevertheless, that public policy has gone furthest in the schools in attempting to alter historical relationships between whites and minorities. For this reason, therefore, the Washington and suburban school systems seem to offer the most promising possibilities for political analysis.

10

Race, Politics, and
Public Education in Washington

The city of Washington has had a black-majority population at least since the 1960 decennial census. Nevertheless, it was not until 1967 that Walter Washington, the first black mayor of Washington, was appointed by President Lyndon B. Johnson. The mayor had very limited powers then and had to seek approval from the District Committee of the House of Representatives for almost any action. The city council was also appointed, and its powers, too, were constrained. In 1968 the school board was allowed to hold elections, the only local government body to have this privilege. After passage of the Home Rule Act by Congress and a referendum by District voters, the city was given the right to elect its own mayor and legislators. In the city's first elections Walter Washington was voted mayor and took office in 1975. City council members also ran for office for the first time.

The current mayor, Marion Barry, was first elected in 1978 and reelected in 1982 and 1986. A former civil rights activist, Barry served on the District's school board and the city council during the 1970s. Although seen by many older whites and blacks as brash and unrestrained, he won the support of a plurality of mainly younger, more liberal voters. By the end of 1983 he was one of 16 black mayors in cities with populations of 100,000 or more.[1] After Chicago, Los Angeles, Philadelphia, and Detroit, Washington is the largest American city with a black mayor. Elected by a slim majority in 1978, Barry overwhelmed his 1982 opponent, Patricia Harris, former U.S. secretary of Housing and Urban Development under President Carter, in a landslide vote.

Just as the mayoralty has been dominated by blacks, so also has the city council, a 13-member body. One member is elected from each of the city's eight wards and 5 are elected at large. All but 2 members on the first elected council were black. Currently, there are 4 whites (including David A. Clarke, the council chairman) and 9 blacks. The school board is a 12-member body, of which 8 are elected by wards and 3 at large; 1 student representative is also a member. For its entire existence as an elected body, the board has been composed almost entirely of black members.

Similarly, most of the city's public employees are minorities, the large majority of these, black. This makeup is reflected in a 1981 poll of District residents, which found that 18 percent of blacks and 5 percent of whites in the sample had at least one member of their household employed by the District government. Furthermore, it was found that of blacks with annual household incomes of $30,000 or more, 30 percent had someone working for the District; among their white income counterparts only 6 percent were so employed. Clearly, black residents, and especially black middle-class residents, are considerably more dependent for employment on the District government. Not surprisingly, whites in the survey tended to view the District government's work force as too large and overpaid; blacks, on the other hand, saw it as smaller than necessary and underpaid.[2]

It can be said that the racial profile of the political and governmental structure of the city of Washington roughly reflects the racial profile of the city's population. The fact that a majority of D.C. government jobs are held by blacks is remindful of the Irish-dominated political machines of the late nineteenth and early twentieth centuries. Wresting power from Yankee-controlled governments in cities such as Boston and Providence, the Irish wasted no time in adding their own to city payrolls. Other ethnic groups in other cities have performed similarly.

Race and Political Hegemony

If blacks dominate Washington's local government, there appears to be less consensus as to whether they have comparable influence on local political life. According to some observers, at the heart of political dynamics is an underlying ethos among many blacks that whites are attempting to reclaim political hegemony in the city. Mayor Barry has acknowledged that some blacks and Hispanics "feel there is some kind of conspiracy on the part of some people, somewhere, to put them out of the city and to move in and take over the city."[3] Black *Washington Post* columnists Juan Williams and William Raspberry, both perceptive observers of Washington life, have found similar views.[4] For example, Williams wrote, "For many years in Washington, some political observers have held the notion that there is a 'master plan,' orchestrated by rich whites, to systematically rid the city of blacks and the poor by manipulating city elections and raising the prices of housing dramatically."[5] Whites such as Stuart Long, owner of several bars and other real estate located in gentrifying areas of Washington, see no conspiracy but agree that the white share of city population will rise in the future. Long, an active campaign fund-raiser for and friend of Mayor Barry, thinks that eventually, a white could become a viable candidate for mayor of Washington.[6]

Understandably, some blacks are uncomfortable with predictions such as these, especially from white real estate business people. In 1981 one reporter interviewed three dozen real estate agents in the city, all of whom admitted to pressuring elderly, black homeowners in gentrifying areas into selling their homes; they also admitted to steering white, two-income couples to these neighborhoods in the hope of stimulating more reinvestment and further demand for properties.[7]

Interestingly, the white-conspiracy theory is not new in Washington. As early as the late 1930s and early 1940s in Georgetown, Washington's first gentrification area, there were rumors that white real estate agents were conspiring to force blacks to move away so that they could move higher-income whites into their neighborhoods.[8]

Regardless of suspicions, the theory that whites are trying to force blacks out of the city by causing real estate prices to rise falters on some grounds. Although many black suburbanites who have left the city lament the high cost of housing in Washington, they also point to the inferior quality of city schools. Many seem to have moved to the suburbs in search of better public education and more affordable housing. Hence, most appear to have the *choice* of remaining in the city. Like many suburban-bound whites, they have exercised a *preference* for the attractions of communities outside the city.

Few, if any, whites subscribe to the white-conspiracy theory, and certainly many, probably most, blacks do not either. But regardless of whether revitalization in the city's core is thought to be deliberately orchestrated or merely the inevitable byproduct of economic and demographic forces, there is widespread agreement, it seems, that the city's white population will grow in influence. Typically, the business community in the city, which is still dominated by whites, is seen as the primary force behind the city's shifting racial dimensions. With relatively few manufacturers in the city, business interests are made up mostly of banking, real estate, and retail institutions and professional organizations such as law firms. A 1981 poll of city residents found that almost 54 percent of blacks and 46 percent of whites thought that the business community had more power than the elected mayor and city council members.[9]

Part of the reason for this perception is not that the business structure is necessarily more powerful than those in comparable cities; rather, it has to do with the peculiarities of the Home Rule Act. The District government has no voting member of Congress. Any laws passed by the city council can be overturned by the House District Committee (although they rarely are). The mayor must gain approval from Congress for the annual budget. The District's judges are appointed by the President. Having no state legislature, the District cannot build urban alliances to counterbalance the influence of private-sector interests. Thus, the vacuum created by constrained political authority in the city is easily filled by well-organized groups such as the Metropolitan Washington Board of Trade, the Apartment and Office Building Association, innumerable trade associations, and the local chapters of national organizations such as the American Bar Association and the National Association of Realtors. To a lesser extent, organizations for public employees such as the police, fire fighters, teachers, and sanitation workers also influence the city's political structure.

Economic Development and Housing

The effect of the power of business in Washington is felt most in the central business district and somewhat less in commercial corridors located in several neighborhoods. Ironically, Mayor Barry, who often championed the welfare of poor blacks before he became an elected official, is now viewed (fairly or unfairly) by many in Washington as prodevelopment and probusiness. Once critical of white commercial interests that had helped to perpetuate racial segregation and other discriminatory practices before he arrived in Washington, Barry has become a favorite with many business people. Twin forces, which help to explain the shift, have been at work.

First, the national political climate has emerged from Carter-era support for moderate social welfare programs to the Reagan administration's reduction or elimination of such programs, with an emphasis on volunteerism, economic growth, and self-sufficiency instead. It would be easy to conclude that Barry's transformation was due merely to adaptation to shifting partisan winds. Yet the mayor has made little secret of his support for real estate development or of the contributions his political campaigns have received from Washington's highly organized real estate and business communities. He is quick to claim credit for the boom in Washington's business and real estate, which has occurred since he took office in 1979.

However, some business people have privately opined that market forces, federal tax credits, the new Metro system and other conditions deserve the lion's share of credit for the building resurgence in the city.[10]

According to one assessment, whatever the causes of the real estate explosion, the Barry administration is definitely supportive of it. Barry has actively encouraged new business investment, especially in the old downtown. Furthermore, he conditions his support on the requirement that developers hire and train minority youths, subcontract with minority-owned businesses, and invite ownership participation from minority business people. Developers have complained that they compete among themselves to sign up Barry's friends or those of other high city officials in order to win project approval. In some cases, a minority partner may contribute little or no financial backing yet reap substantial profits. At least one black city council member has complained that the beneficiaries of Barry's minority policies have been too few in number.[11]

Although the mayor has won plaudits for his prodevelopment policies, historic preservationists have lashed out at his insensitivity to Washington's architectural legacy. On top of this, community activists in Georgetown and the upper northwest have bitterly criticized his unfaltering support for new office/retail complexes in their neighborhoods. So acerbic did the issue become that Barry had to require a comprehensive zoning review along a rapidly redeveloping section of Wisconsin Avenue NW where a neighborhood group had organized a write-in campaign to defeat the mayor in the 1986 election. Moreover, the city council condemned the mayor a few months before the election for dragging his heels in implementing the Comprehensive Plan. The plan had been adopted by the District in 1984 and had not been detailed sufficiently by mid-1986 to permit its use in controlling growth. Many believe Barry, fearing developer reaction, was waiting until after the election to complete the plan.

While Mayor Barry's development record earns mixed reactions from affluent whites, his efforts at stimulating economic development in predominantly black neighborhoods have met with broader citizen approval. Barry's administration has helped to engineer construction of four shopping complexes, as well as renovation of a warehouse and construction of an industrial park, in declining areas of northeast Washington. He has built District government office buildings in two other older neighborhoods as anchors to encourage private-sector investment nearby. A new insurance office building, a private medical center, and an interstate bus terminal have also been completed under the mayor's leadership. Stung by criticism when his administration failed to compete successfully for federal subsidies such as the Urban Development Action Grant program, Barry has improved his performance in recent years, as demonstrated by some of his newest development successes.

Perhaps even more popular among blacks than Barry's economic development triumphs have been his housing projects. Since 1979 approximately 3,000 units of housing for low- and moderate-income families, the elderly and the handicapped have been built or renovated. As in other American cities, most new housing was funded under various federal programs. As these monies have receded under the Reagan administration, the District has slowly pledged more local budget resources to housing. At first the District government was reluctant to draw on its own revenues in addressing the city's serious housing shortage. Suffering a revenue decline in the early 1980s, the city faced mounting dissatisfaction among the black poor. As the 1986 election drew nearer and tax revenues grew, the Barry administration wisely increased local funding for housing.

One popular approach has involved lending District funds to assist lower-income households in purchasing a home in the city. Another program helps tenant groups acquire their buildings, using both federal and local government financing. A third effort allocated $20 million of city funds over two years to replace the federal Section 8 rental-assistance program for low- and moderate-income residents. In addition, the city has initiated a system designed to reduce land costs for low-income housing developers: The District will buy land on which eligible projects are built, leasing it back to developers with a promise to permit them to repurchase it later. The city argues that lower tax burdens and carrying costs will help landlords to offer more moderate rents.

However much the mayor's detractors criticized his historic and neighborhood preservation record, the rise in employment, tax revenues, economic activity, and housing opportunities that have occurred during his first two terms can only be looked upon with envy by other mayors. Confidence about the city's physical and economic future has not been this lofty since the early part of the twentieth century. With much of the central business district revitalized and most of the surrounding inner neighborhoods redeveloped or rehabilitated, Washington is in better shape than it has been in several decades. Mayor Barry's problems in economic development and housing in the poorer sections of the far southeast, the southwest, and the inner northwest will persist, however, until he solves two problems.

First, he has not been forceful enough in choosing his real estate development issues. Essentially, he is supportive of almost any new office or commercial construction proposal, regardless of its design, siting, effect on traffic, or the like; he is viewed as having little interest in these matters and, at best, only passing concern for the historical or architectural losses necessary to make way for redevelopment. As a later section in this chapter will argue, his failure to recognize this helped to deliver the predominantly white Ward 3 to his Republican opponent in the 1986 mayoral election. Barry's unrestrained support for high-rise-building construction angered many residents. In effect, he was merely applying the same have-your-cake-and-eat-it-too philosophy to northwest Washington that he applies virtually everywhere else in the city. This philosophy is undergirded by the mayor's belief that economic development comes with no strings attached; thus new office and commercial projects are approved with little regard for the increased noise, air pollution, and traffic and parking congestion which inevitably follow. Because Barry was timid about proceeding forcefully to complete and implement the District's Comprehensive Plan, he had no vehicle other than the city's go-along-to-get-along zoning system by which to manage the development process. District law requires that the zoning ordinance and map not be inconsistent with the Comprehensive Plan. Therefore, Barry has the means at hand to create a more thoughtful and sophisticated system with which to reconcile economic-growth and quality-of-life issues. Because Barry has linked growth in tax revenues, as well as minority advancement, to real estate development, he has been only too happy to encourage the process almost anywhere in the city. Nonetheless, he needs to realize that these worthy goals cannot persist at the expense of neighborhood quality. In short, his administration must learn to make choices among development proposals and demonstrate that the mayor stands for a balance between growth and quality of life in the city.

A second problem the mayor must resolve is his failure to direct the benefits of Washington's explosive economic development to the city's social and economic problems. Currently, few Washington voters have a clear idea how new office buildings, boutiques, "upmarket" shops, and tourist hotels can serve the social purposes with which Barry once so proudly identified. In fact, as Chapter 5 points out, it is precisely due to the soaring rise in neighborhood reinvestment that much of inner Washington's low- and moderate-income housing was lost to the city's poor during the 1970s. New development projects have increased city revenues substantially, and Barry should establish devices that will *visibly direct* some of the resulting windfalls to housing production, rent subsidies, neighborhood improvement loans, the rehabilitation of older buildings, and similar programs. For example, an adaptive-use trust fund from such revenues could help finance restoration or renovation of buildings in the old downtown or in older neighborhoods for reuse as artists' apartments and studios, community centers, housing for the elderly, or other socially beneficial purposes. A linkage program, such as those in San Francisco and Boston, could tie permission for height increases for downtown office buildings to a requirement that developers build or help finance the construction of low- and moderate-income housing in appropriate neighborhoods of the city. With the assistance of the city council, Mayor Barry will have to convince many citizens that endless new construction brings more than financial gain to business people, real estate investors, and a few who benefit under his minority-participation programs. It is partly this poor accounting for the District's gigantic rise in revenues through real estate that has led to the erosion of the mayor's integrity in the public view (discussed below).

The "Chocolate City Dream"

Anyone with hindsight might find Mayor Barry in a rather troubling situation. When he took office in 1979, he was viewed by many as the embodiment of the ideals of the War on Poverty, the Civil Rights Movement, and the new black-youth militancy so popular in the 1960s and 1970s. With a majority of black voters, the city of Washington was perceived by many to be one of the most promising urban centers in which these ideals might be approximated, if not realized. The phrase "Chocolate City" appeared on bumper stickers and became shorthand reference among blacks for a community that had not only black control but the ability to drastically reduce, if not eliminate, poverty and indemnify equality. There was a sense that if the dream could not be realized in Washington, it probably could not be realized anywhere.[12]

Today Mayor Barry officiates over a city with a declining middle-class-family population and an increased presence of singles and couples without children. An urban underclass, composed largely of minority households, hangs precariously in pockets located in various parts of the city. As elsewhere, the middle and upper classes have substantially higher voting rates than those of lesser means. It is against this backdrop that the forces that undermine the Chocolate City Dream have unfolded.

First, the substantial out-migration of moderate- and middle-income blacks to suburban communities is helping to fulfill one major goal of the

Civil Rights Movement at the expense of another. Opening up the suburbs through fair housing laws and less-discriminatory bank lending policies has reduced the likelihood that the current size of Washington's black electorate can be maintained. The continued fulfillment of freedom of choice in housing and neighborhood location for all citizens has thus hindered fulfillment of another worthy goal, the opportunity to exercise political and governmental power in pursuit of the truly equal urban society. Thoughtful people agree that minority suburbanization is a fair and necessary social condition, and the Washington experience has shown that given a choice, thousands of minority households rank suburban living conditions above political hegemony and the Chocolate City Dream. In this regard, their aspirations have proven to be no different from those of their white, middle-class counterparts who left Washington in large numbers during the 1950s and 1960s.

As one writer pointed out:

> Many middle-income blacks don't want their children sharing the life styles of poor children; they move to protect their own children from "black speak" (black English), and the practice of "less is better than more," both considered contagious.
>
> They should slow their pace a bit, however, because middle-income blacks can't have it both ways. They can't claim that whites should stay put in mixed neighborhoods and schools, "sacrificing" children in the name of integration, while retaining for themselves some right to run.[13]

A second force, however, while less momentous, has also contributed to the uncertainty of the Chocolate City Dream. Its most visible manifestation has been the surge of gentrification in Washington's core neighborhoods since the late 1960s. More recently, the massive investment in the central business district, especially the old downtown, has lent further dimensions to this force. The net effect has been the near-stabilization of the white population in Washington and the persistent growth of white-controlled economic might. While black voters continue to control the outcome of elections for mayor and for most city council and school board posts, there has been widespread support for many black candidates among liberal whites as well. The evidence has only recently emerged, however, that a split along racial lines is beginning to develop in voting patterns. The 1984 presidential primaries, the local elections for city council in the same year, and the 1986 mayoral election provide the evidence.

Race and Voting Patterns, 1984

The unparalleled 1984 campaign by the Reverend Jesse Jackson provided a test of the racial voting patterns of District whites and blacks given the opportunity to choose a black candidate for the Democratic party presidential nomination. The result was that Jackson won 67 percent of the city's Democratic vote, with Walter Mondale and Gary Hart winning 26 and 7 percent, respectively. Yet in largely white precincts, including several in the revitalizing core, Mondale far outpaced Jackson. In Ward 3, the only white-dominated ward in the city, Mondale received 58 percent of the vote, Hart 28 percent, and Jackson 14 percent.[14] Although voter motivations are varied and complex in any election, the sharp division of voting patterns along racial lines has not been overlooked by local political observers.

But the political climate in Washington was further tested during local elections for city council in 1984. District election laws require that two council positions be held by non–Democratic party candidates. In the at-large contest for one of these positions, a white candidate, Republican Carol Schwartz, defeated the Reverend Jerry A. Moore, Jr., a black Republican and 15-year veteran of the council, in the primary. Schwartz, a former school board member, received her heaviest vote in the four wards with the most registered Republicans and the highest concentrations of white voters. These wards included several of the revitalizing neighborhoods. Moore, on the other hand, had his strongest support in four wards in which registered voters are predominantly black. These are located mostly in northeast and southeast Washington.[15]

Both Walter E. Fauntroy, the District's nonvoting member of Congress, and Mayor Barry charged that "racism" in the primary helped to explain the voting pattern. The Reverend Mr. Moore dissociated himself from these remarks. Six Democratic members of the city council, including its white chairman, David A. Clarke, supported a write-in effort for Moore during the election campaign. But Schwartz was elected, again drawing her heaviest support from the largely white-populated Ward 3, where she is a resident, and from the revitalizing sections of the city's core, where rising numbers of whites have settled.[16]

With Schwartz's election the city council has a total of 4 whites out of 13 members, the largest white representation since the Home Rule Act took effect almost 13 years ago. (In 1978 Betty Ann Kane, also white and an ex–school board member, was elected on an at-large basis. She is a resident of one of the city's gentrifying neighborhoods.) Although blacks are still in the electoral majority, the rise in white voting strength on the council doubtless symbolizes for some blacks not only an erosion of black voting power but also a political expression of the revitalization of the city's core by whites. More important, both national and local electoral processes in 1984 demonstrated that whites and blacks in the nation's capital are still willing to vote predominantly along racial lines.

Of course, this is not to argue that whites voted only for whites or blacks only for blacks. For example, Phyllis Young, a black federal worker, ran for an at-large seat on the school board in November 1985, beating an incumbent black woman viewed by some voters as acerbic and divisive. She carried not only three predominantly black wards but largely white Ward 3 as well.

Still, the Jackson and Schwartz voting patterns show a certain predilection among blacks and whites to lean toward candidates of their own race. These elections were not the first evidence of this; rather, they came at a time in national political life when the American electorate had demonstrated a definite turn to the right. Accompanying this conservative swing has been a shrinking federal outlay for welfare programs and government employment, to say nothing of less vigorous enforcement of affirmative action and equal opportunity programs and policies. Thus, there is little surprise in events in the District of Columbia that hint that black political power may be slipping. Nor is it so remarkable that some black residents suspect that a white conspiracy is afoot to reclaim the District's city hall.

The Uncertainties of Power

Largely since the 1984 elections, Mayor Barry's administration has been beset by other problems that cause discomfort in some circles. Executive directors of two city commissions and the head of the Housing Finance Agency have left their posts as a result of alleged improprieties. Moreover, the president of the University of the District of Columbia, a public institution, resigned after questions were raised about his expenditure of university funds. The former head of the Department of Administrative Services was fired by the mayor for alleged corruption and mishandling of city contracts and leases. District funds were also invested in a private security firm whose financial soundness had been ineptly investigated by District officials. (The firm later went bankrupt.)

Furthermore, a former District government employee was sentenced to 18 months in jail for dealing in cocaine. Although the mayor denied buying drugs from her, his legal counsel revealed that Barry had had a "personal

relationship" with the woman and had visited her apartment during a 12-
to 18-month period ending in the fall of 1982.[17] (The mayor is married and
has one son.) In proceedings on drug use by District employees, the white
U.S. attorney for the District, appointed by President Reagan, raised
questions about Barry's relationship with the woman. It was reported that
Barry subsequently accused the D.A. of trying to " 'lynch' [him], figur-
atively speaking, just as whites lynched black leaders with ropes in bygone
times." On another occasion, he maintained that the news media were
charging guilt by association and innuendo, adding, "People are now being
tried by the media as opposed to being tried by their peers."[18]

As the *Washington Post*, the city's premier daily newspaper, has increased investigative reporting of the Barry administration's activities,
tensions between the District building and the mass media have risen.
Although the *Post* endorsed Barry in the 1978 and 1982 mayoral campaigns, Barry has been quite vocal in his sensitivity to penetrating articles
in the newspaper. Not only have *Post* stories raised questions about the
conduct of several Barry administration officials, who subsequently left
city government, but District minority-contracting procedures have been
scrutinized by the newspaper as well. Requests for information by the *Post*
have brought comments from the mayor that the *Post* has termed "loaded"
with "racial innuendo." The *Post* also noted that Mayor Barry said that a
Post employee told him the newspaper was out to "get" his administration.[19]

Further plaguing the mayor was the case of Ivanhoe Donaldson, formerly one of his highest-ranking appointees in the District government.
Mr. Donaldson pleaded guilty to tax fraud, obstruction of justice, and
misappropriation of more than $190,000 in District government funds. A
close political advisor and friend to the mayor, as well as former chairman
of the District's Democratic party, Donaldson had already left the District
government for private-sector employment when the charges arose. He is
now serving his sentence in a federal prison.

Understandably, some observers see these events as not only politically
motivated but also racially inspired. Any questioning about the honesty
and competence of an elected or appointed official is bound to be perceived by some observers as a deliberate attempt to dislodge that person.[20]
But it may be viewed by others as an expression of doubt about the ability
of blacks to run city government with honesty and effectiveness. Public
displeasure was no surprise, then, when former Attorney General John
Mitchell, now a financial consultant, compared the city's fiscal operations
to the running of the "Amos 'n' Andy Taxi Company." Uttered in late 1984,
this remark caused widespread indignation and charges of racism. The

uncertainty felt by many blacks in the District of Columbia is apparent, so recently have they gained true political power in the city. Both Mayor Walter Washington and Mayor Barry have commented on the uphill battle black city officials have had in attempting to convince whites that minorities are equally capable of running the city honorably and knowledgeably. Conditions and events such as these, then, have done nothing to allay festering notions among some blacks of a white conspiracy. Indeed, two writers for the *Washington Post* suggested that it is "possible" for the mayor "to arouse fears among his legions of supporters of a white renaissance or takeover whenever he feels his administration is being threatened." [21]

Interracial mistrust notwithstanding, the city still demonstrated substantial support in 1985 for Mayor Barry's overall record of accomplishment. A survey of District residents found that almost two-thirds of those polled rated his performance as mayor as either excellent or good. But again, race was a differentiating factor. Among whites, 42 percent disapproved of his performance, while among blacks, 27 percent disapproved. And of all residents, about one-third felt that the mayor's efforts to maintain high ethical standards in his administration were unsatisfactory. A slightly larger percentage felt that the mayor cared "more about a few special interests," while about one-half thought that he cared "equally about the needs of all." [22]

Race and Voting Patterns, 1986

The theme of integrity in government, coupled with growing dissatisfaction among whites over the mayor's seeming lack of concern with rising commercial development in neighborhoods of the affluent northwest, conspired to further embarrass the Barry administration in the 1986 mayoral campaign. By August of that year, ten high- and mid-level city government officials had been convicted of crimes connected with their municipal duties since Barry had taken office in 1979. When shortly before the 1986 election he was asked at a press conference about unethical behavior in his administration, the mayor distinguished between dishonesty and ineptitude in city employees. "[In my] culture . . . we just forgive people easily," he noted. "We're not as hard on people." [23] He faulted himself for not taking more decisive action against those who did not perform competently. The mayor thus seemed to imply that the distinctions between activities that constitute dishonesty and those that suggest mere incompetence were sometimes hazy. Given this elusiveness, he implied, blacks are more willing to assume the latter than the former about a public official whose activities are questionable.

In another interview the mayor opined that his support was stronger in the racially integrated wards of the city, such as the gentrifying areas, and weaker in wards that have largely segregated residential patterns, such as Ward 3. He also noted that residents who work for the District government were more likely to be aware of its many positive activities and therefore more appreciative of his administration. Because few white Ward 3 residents work for the District, he implied, they receive their impressions from the mass media, which concentrates on the negative. Finally, he felt that Ward 3 harbored many newcomers to the city who were unaware of the many improvements in District management and services Barry had made since 1979; therefore, he suggested, their views were shortsighted.[24]

The issues of corruption and incompetence dogged the mayor throughout the last two years of his second term. But in the few months prior to the 1986 campaign, they received even greater attention. For example, a few months before the general election, it was learned that the mayor's wife had received $1,150 worth of designer clothing in 1982 as a gift from a lobbyist who had met or communicated dozens of times with the mayor.[25] The *Washington Post*'s account of this story and others raising questions about the mayor's integrity have continued to heighten tensions between the mayor's office and the primary newspaper in Washington. Further frustrating Marion Barry was the announcement in August 1986 that a federal grand jury was investigating his expenditure of city funds for personal uses. The investigation, undertaken by the U.S. attorney and the Federal Bureau of Investigation, examined whether the money had been advanced by the District government for official uses but later diverted to cover the mayor's personal expenses. The mayor's legal counsel, Herbert O. Reid, charged that there was an "obvious link" between the U.S. attorney and the *Washington Post* indicating that they had shared information about the case.[26] With the increased attention given to the mayor by the *Post* during his reelection campaign, he grew more restive about "racial polarization" in the city and blamed it in part on the news media. He charged that the media concentrated on negative stories about his administration and ignored the positive.[27]

Beyond the issue of integrity in government, the mayor suffered from perceptions about the sources of contributions to his primary and reelection campaigns. Developers, builders, and other real estate interests had donated more than $128,000, investment and financial business people had given in excess of $126,000, and attorneys had added another $135,000.

Minority-owned businesses gave more than $132,000.[28] Some of the contributors had had business dealings with major developers in the city or with the District government itself.[29] While it is not unusual for politicians to receive financial support from such sources, Barry's close ties with the real estate and business communities in the city, in the growing climate of public distrust over the integrity issue, were considered by some voters to be proof enough that the mayor's business dealings were improper.

The 1986 primary and general election again brought to public attention the name of Carol Schwartz. Through no fault of her own, her 1984 campaign for city council had underscored the latent issue of racially divided voting patterns. Again in 1986, without any mention on her part of race, it was ironic that that issue would persist as a subtheme in her attempt to defeat Mayor Barry. Schwartz pounded heavily on the themes of misfeasance, malfeasance, and nonfeasance in the Barry administration. An eight-year veteran of the Board of Education, she had served only two years on the city council when she ran against the mayor. She was viewed as a loner on the council and had not succeeded in sponsoring a single major piece of legislation. Her campaign speeches, however, captured the dissatisfaction of many Washington voters over increasing reports of dishonesty and incompetence in the District government.

In the primary elections in September 1986, Barry was defeated in largely white Ward 3 by black Democrat Mattie Taylor, even though Barry rolled to easy victories in the remaining wards of the city. Schwartz captured the city's Republican nomination and predominated in Ward 3's primary. Embarrassed by his defeat there, Barry acknowledged during the general campaign that reforms were needed in his administration and that he had exercised faulty judgment on some issues. Schwartz campaigned in the general election not only for the city's Republican vote but for the votes of disaffected Democrats as well.

On election day Mayor Barry earned 61 percent of the citywide vote, to Carol Schwartz's 33 percent. (The remaining votes went to several candidates of smaller parties.) But Barry tallied only 15 percent of the Ward 3 vote to Schwartz's 76 percent. In Ward 2, where gentrification has transformed several neighborhoods from predominantly black to predominantly white, Barry beat Schwartz by only 29 votes. The mayor received devastating majorities in all other wards. Because Barry had carried both Ward 2 and Ward 3 with ease in previous general elections, his poor showing in 1986 was very likely due as much to white votes against him as to white votes for Schwartz.

Even as the 1986 campaign for mayor was unfolding, it was clear that while many whites focused their frustrations on the mayor, many blacks directed theirs not at Carol Schwartz but rather at the *Washington Post*. The *Post* began publishing its new Sunday magazine during the campaign, and the first issue sparked immediate opposition from numerous blacks. It carried stories that they deemed racist in tone, and thousands of copies of the magazine were piled in front of the *Post*'s headquarters in protest. The *Post* apologized that some readers had found the stories offensive but noted that they were only presenting the views of others, including some cab drivers who acknowledged that they refused to pick up young, black males wanting to go to some of the predominantly black, poorer sections of the city. The protesters continued to stack copies of the magazine at the *Post*'s entrance after subsequent issues—with little, if any, reference to racial topics—were published. Doubtless, the *Post*'s leadership in revealing the Barry administration's problems underlay the frustrations that many blacks were expressing, whatever the justification for their complaints about the magazine.

Race and Politics in the Mid-1980s

To an outsider it may be rather surprising that a mayor who won his third term by more than 60 percent of the vote should find himself embroiled in such controversy. With a majority-black electorate and a white population with many young, moderate to liberal voters, Barry faces a situation quite disparate from those in cities such as Chicago, Detroit, and Philadelphia, for example. There are no significant white, blue-collar or ethnic voting blocs in Washington, and the city's whites do not so directly compete with blacks for municipal jobs, services, and other forms of public largesse or patronage. Thus, by comparison with interracial problems of mayors in those cities, Mayor Barry's plight may seem rather mundane.

There is no doubt that frequent incompetence has occurred in some quarters of the District government and no doubt that the mayor must accept some of the blame. Neither has the city escaped corruption and dishonesty among some of its higher officials, and Mayor Barry, who has never been directly linked to these activities, is culpable at least on grounds of insufficient monitoring and oversight. What became apparent in 1986, however, was that black residents of Washington were likely to adopt a forgiving attitude about these matters. Whites, however, were more apt to question the mayor's integrity and his ability to govern.

Undoubtedly, at the extremes of racial stereotyping, there are some blacks who are convinced that whites want to reclaim the District government and some whites who believe that blacks are inferior and incapable of properly governing a city such as Washington. Nevertheless, it appears that these views are not widespread, and Washington's racial divisions, when compared with those of some other large cities, are modest indeed. Most blacks appear to have reelected Barry simply because, from their point of view, it was entirely practical to do so.

Barry is both black and a Democrat. His completed two terms have overseen numerous improvements in government services and management and in the quality of life in Washington. Furthermore, he is a known entity who has governed for eight years as mayor and served on the city council and school board for several years. He has affected the lives of thousands of blacks in the city, as well as the lives of many whites, all of whom have benefited in various ways from his administration. Blacks vote overwhelmingly for Democratic party candidates in Washington. Why, after all, would they take a chance on a relatively unknown, white republican, with no mayoral experience and very little by way of public record on which to base a voting decision? Taken in this light, the black vote for Mayor Barry, whatever the racial implications, was also entirely logical. Had there been irrefutable proof of significant violations of the law on the mayor's part and had black voting patterns remained unchanged, grounds for criticism would have been justified. This sort of scenario, remindful of white Irish support in the 1940s for Boston's Mayor James Michael Curley, even after his conviction in court, has yet to characterize the political preferences of Washington's black population.

As for white voting patterns, Barry correctly implied that most whites have a smaller personal stake in Washington's city government than do many blacks. Most of the city's whites work for the federal government, businesses such as consulting and law firms, trade associations, and cultural and public interest organizations. Thousands have migrated from other communities to Washington and are thus not natives. Unlike whites in other cities, many whites in Washington pay less attention to local matters and more attention to national concerns associated with their careers and their political and personal viewpoints. Seen in this light, the local issues of day-to-day life in the city take on secondary importance to many whites. Neither their personal livelihoods nor their pride is rooted in Marion Barry's continued service as mayor.

This is not to argue that there are no whites who are strongly interested in local political matters in Washington. Certainly, there are—just as there are some blacks who have little concern about Washington politics. And as the mayor points out, many of these liberal whites are likely to live in "integrated" wards, where gentrification has taken place. But white voter dissatisfaction with Mayor Barry in 1986 probably had far less to do with racism and far more to do with the simple fact that whites had less to lose than most blacks if Mayor Barry failed to achieve reelection. Impatient with charges of dishonesty among District officials, fed up with evidence of incompetence in some District agencies, and suspicious that the mayor had committed unlawful acts, many whites voted in a pattern that, for them, was also entirely pragmatic. Why take a chance on another four years of Mayor Barry if there was reason to believe that dishonesty and incompetence in government would continue under him?

Whatever one's views about Marion Barry's competence or honesty, there are several facts that should not be overlooked. First, there is nothing new about city governments with officials who are convicted of wrongdoing. It has happened in virtually all large city governments, yet rarely have city chief executives been found guilty of knowledge about, let alone participation in, illegal activities. Second, mayors very often receive substantial contributions from business and real estate interests. Most are not unmindful of the implications of such support, and many influence public decisions from time to time in ways that favor business interests. Third, tension between city newspapers and city hall is as old as city newspapers and city halls. Mayors are often subject to criticism by the press, and aggressive investigative journalism is the essence of modern democracy. It is unfortunate in a city such as Washington, where blacks predominate in the local government and whites predominate in the mass media, that honest reporting of misdeeds and facts has taken on racial dimensions. But charges of media bias are original neither to Washington nor to the 1980s.

The rise of black hegemony in Washington local politics is analogous with the rise of bossism and the political machine in American urban society. It is difficult to ignore the similarities, for the nation's capital is merely participating in a process that, in other cities, has benefited previous generations of ethnic groups such as the Irish, Italians, Jews, and Poles. Just as charges of ethnic favoritism, incompetence, patronage, and dishonesty once plagued Irish-controlled city halls in Kansas City, Cincinnati, Chicago, Boston, and New York, for example, so also do they arise today in varying degrees in cities with black mayors, such as Atlanta, Philadelphia, Chicago, Los Angeles, and Detroit. So far, at least, Mayor Barry's administration has been shown to be no worse than, and perhaps moderately better than, most of the previous or current municipal administrations in cities in which a racial or ethnic minority has risen to power.

That many of Washington's blacks simply smile and shrug when questions about Mayor Barry's honesty arise (as reported in the *Washington Post*) is certainly no departure from the attitudes of generations of voters elsewhere who kept members of their own ethnic groups in office despite charges of corruption.

In 1986 it is undeniable that the coalition of black and liberal white voters that Mayor Barry developed in earlier years has been diminished to no small degree. The mayor took office in January 1987 with the most compelling racial division in the city since before the Home Rule Act took effect. Whatever the aspirations for the advent of the "Chocolate City" were in the 1970s, they seem quite remote today. Then again, so do the paranoiac fears of a "white takeover" of government. Nevertheless, the 1986 mayoral elections in Washington clearly demonstrated that the old black–liberal white coalition that undergirded the first eight years of the Barry administration had eroded.

If this was an unhappy outcome, perhaps the candor that arose over racial differences in expectations about city government was a more positive turn of events. Mayor Barry was correct in pointing out that many whites depart from many blacks in the degree to which they feel they benefit from public services. Chapter 6 explored this issue in the city's school system, pointing out the growing frustrations of white parents in gentrifying areas who find themselves looking more carefully at the character of public education. The next section examines the implications of differing racial expectations about the schools in Washington.

Race, Perceptions, and Public Education

Because most white families in the city have different perceptions about the educational needs of their children than do most black families, it is difficult, if not impossible, for the public school system to reconcile the wishes of the two groups. Most whites who live in Washington are at least second- or third-generation members of the middle class; blacks are much more likely to be poor or to have only recently risen to middle-class status. Whites usually seek to equal, if not exceed, the rather more privileged circumstances of their own backgrounds. Because Washington tends to attract people with prestigious educational credentials, the expectations of many whites for their children's education are quite high.

While there are some blacks who share these goals, there are many more from underprivileged backgrounds for whom merely obtaining a high school diploma is a cherished accomplishment. Between these two extremes are black families who are rising on the socioeconomic scale and whose expectations about the public schools are more discriminating than those of poor people but not as exacting as those of affluent whites. Therefore, the District's public schools must cater to the widely varying abilities and expectations of these socioeconomic and racial groups.

The school board has wrestled for years with the lingering hopes of the Chocolate City Dream. Throughout most of the 1970s it concentrated its efforts on the needs of poor and black children. Torn by ideological and philosophical differences, with some of its members showing distrust of white educational aims, the board inspired little confidence from white parents during the early 1970s. In the late 1970s, with new members elected to the board and the appointment of school superintendents Vincent Reed and later Floretta D. McKenzie, the emphasis shifted from social experimentation to a back-to-basics approach to learning. The backbone of this approach was the requirement that each student master certain basic skills at each grade level before being passed to the next grade. No longer were pupils to receive "social promotions," a practice based in part on the desire to preclude their traumatization at having failed.

Nevertheless, while this strategy was applauded by many parents in Washington, it would have far greater benefits for many black children than for most whites, especially at the higher-elementary, junior high, and high school levels. Relatively privileged white children are better equipped to draw from one another and from family life to master basic skills in reading, spelling, arithmetic, and writing. Thus, the common complaint among white parents, and to a lesser extent among blacks, is that their children are not challenged by the District school system.

At the bottom of this problem are disparate perceptions among white and black parents about educational needs, if not disparate pedagogical philosophies. There is of course agreement among some whites and blacks about their children's schooling. But socioeconomically, the two races are separated by one or more generations of family success, and added to this are the lingering effects of racial discrimination against blacks. Thus, it will be difficult, and perhaps impossible, for the District's public educational system to effectively serve the needs of poor blacks, middle-income blacks, and middle- to upper-income whites. But if the out-migration of the last two groups to the suburbs is to be stemmed, it will require the explicit recognition that separate school curricula based on educational ability will be necessary. Although this policy will undoubtedly result in some (perhaps a majority of) classrooms with largely white or largely black attendance, it is probably the only way to increase middle-class support for the public school system. Indeed, if the Six Schools experiment is any indication, such a policy may already be unfolding. On top of this, middle-class parents, black and white, will have to feel that their children are safe in the public schools and that interracial hostility is absent.

The fact that the political structure of the city is shifting along racial lines raises questions about whether and to what degree the educational expectations of white parents will become more salient. If the white population continues to stabilize and if blacks continue to migrate to the suburbs in substantial numbers, it is conceivable that whites, rising in influence, may place greater pressure on the mayor and city council to allocate greater resources to the school board. The election of two white former school board members to the council could presage a new set of priorities. Collective lobbying by whites in the revitalizing core, as well as by whites in the northwest, might urge the council to attach budgetary strings requiring the school board to implement more programs catering to the expectations of white parents. For many white families who cannot or do not wish to send their children to private schools, continued residency in the city will depend largely on the appropriateness of public schools to their children's needs.

A recent manifestation of white parents' views about school spending was a proposal by parents to help finance construction of a multipurpose school and community center at the Horace Mann Elementary School in an affluent neighborhood of northwest Washington. After trying for several years to convince the school board to build the center, at this writing neighborhood parents have raised $150,000 through individual donations. Pledging to borrow much of the balance from a bank, they have succeeded in gaining school board approval for the project. (The District government has agreed to apply for a federal government grant to help finance the center's construction.) The center would become the property of the Board of Education. That these parents have been willing to go outside the school board and finance a public facility out of their own pockets is one measure of the frustration some feel about school board spending priorities.[30]

At least one writer has suggested the rising tide of concern among middle-class parents about school spending policies. Juan Williams has foreseen possible tension over school spending between white and black middle-class families on the one hand and childless people on the other.[31] He hints at a future in which blacks and whites may exert political power more on the basis of class interests than on the basis of race. One could infer from Williams's analysis that to the extent that affluent whites and blacks can reach accommodation on issues related to the public schools, they may influence the direction of Washington's population patterns in the future.

Still, no less an authority on public school policy than Professor Gary Orfield is doubtful about the likelihood of significant efforts by school boards to cater to the educational expectations of white gentrifier families in revitalizing cities such as Washington:

> Central-city school districts whose resources are growing far more slowly than their costs cannot afford new programs or new teachers. Typically, they face an annual choice about what to cut. In this climate it is unrealistic to expect the districts to come up with resources for programs to attract whites in a few schools. Black and Hispanic educators, fighting hard to address the needs of minority children, are hardly likely to divert resources to special programs for affluent whites in communities where minorities are being displaced.[32]

Orfield's perceptions, based on a study of 12 urban school districts, undoubtedly have strength. He cites the school board's rejection of the Capitol Hill site for Washington's academic high school (subsequently named Banneker High) as an example of the suspicions many minority school officials have for programs that might benefit affluent households.[33] Yet he recommends that school systems such as Washington's organize families in gentrifying neighborhoods and build better information channels as the primary means of attracting and holding white students in neighborhood elementary schools.[34]

Unfortunately, Orfield's prescription, while necessary, is not sufficient, at least insofar as Washington is concerned. With vastly superior educational provisions readily available in Washington's suburban and private schools, white families are highly unlikely to succumb in significant numbers to entreaties to enroll their children in inner-city elementary schools purely on the basis of organizing techniques. His proposal is based on an apparent presumption that because many whites are misinformed about the educational achievements of their neighborhood public schools, merely improving information flows and organizing through neighborhood groups will turn the tide. Other observers, too, have made this mistake.[35]

The truth, however, is that parents are all too aware that there are significant differences in school expenditures, teacher quality, curricula, test scores, and other factors between city public schools and the alternatives. Both the Peabody School on Capitol Hill and the Six Schools experiment have relied in part on resources and expenditure patterns not typical of most Washington elementary schools. Most important, ability grouping has played a part in the organization of these schools and helps to explain why some white and black middle-class parents have been willing to try them out.

Adding fuel to these fires is the fact that Mayor Barry sends his 6-year-old son to a private school. Worse yet, he repudiated his 1978 campaign statement that District of Columbia elected officials had a "moral responsibility" to send their children to city public schools. Calling that declaration a "tactical direction" during his 1986 reelection campaign, he changed course, announcing that he felt all parents should be free to send their children wherever they want.[36] Hence, middle-class blacks and whites may reason, If the mayor will not send his kid to public school, why should I?

However the issues surrounding Washington's public schools evolve in the future, it is important that school administrators not act in a vacuum. Because many new parents in the city—gentrifiers or not—are aware that suburban school districts are generally more highly rated, they will compare city-suburban choices carefully. Perhaps the most promising resolution of the disparities in public education between Washington and its surrounding jurisdictions would be that of metropolitanization.[37] Certainly, the evidence suggests that busing and magnet school programs that are able to cross jurisdictional lines have the best chance of reducing "white flight." In other words, when white parents (and perhaps some middle-class, black parents) become aware that black-white school ratios under such a program are not widely different between Washington and its suburbs, it is conceivable that some will choose to remain in the central city. Not only does metropolitanization permit a better balancing of white-minority pupil ratios in individual schools, it may also pave the way for interjurisdictional sharing of resources, effecting cost savings.

Orfield describes a metropolitan school desegregation system in the Wilmington, Delaware, area that had measurable effects on white parents in revitalizing sections of the central city:

> Integration of central-city schools by busing in suburbanites spurred increased white enrollment from the integrated neighborhoods. Officials of the merged district report that local realtors now sometimes market housing in central-city neighborhoods on the basis of the part of the suburbs a neighborhood is paired with. Homeseekers choose a convenient, historic neighborhood and still have well-integrated schools.[38]

However, it is difficult to be sanguine about the prospects for metro-politan solutions to city-suburban school problems in the national capital area. In part, this is due to the fact that this would involve not only the federal city but also educational systems in two states—Maryland and Virginia. The politics of such an effort are beyond comprehension. Yet with the vast majority of black residents and public school pupils residing in Washington and Prince George's County, with many Prince George's County blacks working for the District and federal governments, and with many blacks in both jurisdictions having social and family ties that tran-scend the boundary between the two jurisdictions, it is not inconceivable that a partnership between city and county could be forged. Moreover, moderate to liberal Montgomery County might be persuaded to partici-pate if busing distances were not too long, changes in county school racial mixtures were not excessive, and specialized opportunities were available for students in District schools.

Until such extensive approaches to resolving urban-suburban school problems are considered, however, public policy will be limited to intra-jurisdictional efforts. Within this context, Chapter 11 examines Prince George's County, where any resolution of public school conditions will necessarily possess racial dimensions. The political characteristics in the county are probed, and the increasing role of blacks in local and state politics is documented.

11

Race, Politics, and Public Education
in the Suburbs

In one respect, the political position of minority populations in Washington's suburban jurisdictions is at an earlier stage of development than that in the District of Columbia. While blacks have taken firm hold of the city's political structure, they are only beginning to assume power in the suburbs. As yet, they are a numerical minority in all suburban counties, although their vastly rising presence in Prince George's County has put them in the running for greater influence there. Hispanic and Asian populations are considerably smaller, and their representation in elected positions throughout the suburbs is minuscule.

As of mid-1984 there was one black on the ten-member Fairfax County school board. At the same time, three of the nine school board members in Alexandria were black. When the only black member of the Montgomery County school board resigned to take a position on the county executive's staff, the board appointed another black to replace her. Two blacks sat on the nine-member Prince George's County school board. There were no minority county executives in the Washington suburbs and only a handful of minority county council members. Recently converting to a ward-based election system, Prince George's County now has two blacks on its nine-member county council, both from areas adjacent to the District of Columbia where substantial black in-migration has occurred.

Just as blacks have achieved majority status in the District of Columbia, so also have whites maintained their predominance in the suburban jurisdictions. But where minorities have made noteworthy population gains—principally in Prince George's and Arlington counties and in Alexandria—their political influence has grown. More important, there is the likelihood that as racial balances shift further toward minority populations, their representation in elective and appointive offices will increase. Again, Prince George's County provides the most informative case study. Before considering the county's political dynamics, however, it is important to develop a more concentrated view of racial change than was possible in Chapter 7.

Racial Shifts in Prince George's County, 1970–1980

In 1970 Prince George's County had 561,476 whites and 91,808 blacks, who made up 84.9 percent and 13.9 percent of the county's total population, respectively. By 1980 there were 391,427 whites (58.8 percent) and 247,860 blacks (37.3 percent) living there.[1] Nothing so dramatically illustrates the impressive shift in racial composition as these statistics. Over the decade white population declined by 30.3 percent, while black population rose by 170 percent. Furthermore, the stark contrast in the direction of change for the two races is underscored when the Capital Beltway is used as a geographical reference point (see Map 11.1). Dividing the county from north to south, this circumferential highway has arisen as the sharpest demarcation line in delineating where blacks and whites have settled. Although the white population has decreased on both sides of the beltway, whites living to the west or inside (closest to the District of Columbia) dwindled from 337,535 in 1970 to 176,501 ten years later, a drop of 47.7 percent. At the beginning of the decade, 60.1 percent of the white population in the county was living inside the beltway, but at the end only 45.1 percent was doing so. Conversely, the white population outside the beltway, although having declined by 9,015 people during the decade, rose from 39.9 percent to 54.9 percent of all whites. Blacks inside the beltway, on the other hand, increased from 69,392 to 184,454, a rise of 165.8 percent. They made up 75.6 percent of blacks in the county in 1970 and 74.4 percent in 1980. However, the black population outside the beltway rose by 40,990 people during the 1970s, a gain of 182.9 percent.[2]

These data show not only that the white population dwindled by about one-third during the preceding decade but that the black population soared by several times that fraction. If these trends continue, of course, blacks will eventually outnumber whites, probably sometime in the early 1990s. Clearly, the white population was diminished most severely inside the beltway, where blacks increased so dramatically that they were in the majority in that area by 1980. While blacks were still vastly outnumbered by whites outside the beltway at that date, their numbers inside the beltway were rising steeply, while the white population was declining.

Much of the rise in the county's black population is due to spillover or black out-migration across the District of Columbia boundary into the

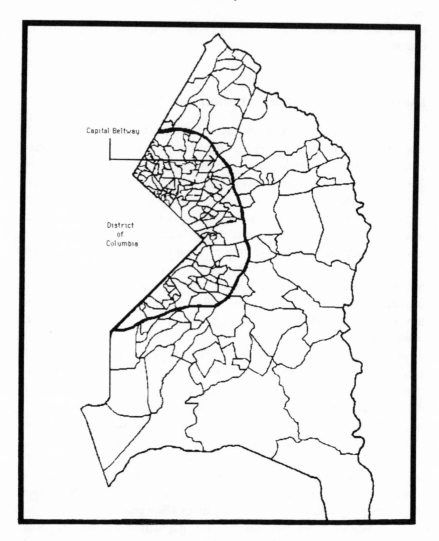

Map 11.1   Prince George's County, Maryland (showing census tracts)
Source: Prepared by Dennis E. Gale.

inner beltway section. One study of the period from 1975 to 1980, for example, found that about 86 percent of black out-migrant households from Washington relocated to Prince George's County, while only 12 percent of their white counterparts did so. White mover households were about evenly distributed between the Maryland and Virginia suburbs, while almost 95 percent of black mover households relocated to the Maryland suburbs.[3] Similar findings about the sizable differences between the two racial groups in mobility and settlement patterns around Washington have been found in other studies.[4] Moreover, household incomes and the education and occupation of household heads among whites were substantially higher than those among blacks, indicating socioeconomic disparities that help to account for some, although doubtless not all, of the differences in locational decisions. Thus, just as Washington's blacks and whites have settled largely in segregated patterns, so also have their counterparts in the metropolitan area and in the county.

As we proceed to examine the political chemistry of racial change in Prince George's County, we can see that a continued shift in the balance between blacks and whites is virtually certain. With many middle-class blacks in the county drawing on past political experience in Washington, where their numbers are decisive in most election contests, Prince George's is likely to become the scene of the metropolitan area's most critical struggle for enhanced black political power.[5] As the next section will show, this process is already underway and, moreover, is reaching to the level of state politics.

Prince George's County Politics

By early 1984 not only were there 2 black members on the county council and 2 others on the school board in Prince George's County, but both bodies were chaired by blacks. In addition, 1 of the county's 7 Maryland state senators and 5 of 21 state delegates were black. With approximately one-third of the county population made up of blacks and over one-half of the public school enrollment made up of minorities, it would not be surprising to find a black conspiracy theory among whites similar to the white conspiracy theory among some blacks in Washington. But if many whites in Prince George's County believe that there is a deliberate move afoot among blacks to take over county politics, their suspicions have not taken on the proportions of the white conspiracy theory in the District of Columbia. Perhaps this is due to the fact that the county has no minority counterpart to Washington's massive white reinvestment pattern. Whereas whites have influence over the city's economy disproportionate to their numbers, blacks have nothing approaching this influence over the county's economy.

Nevertheless, blacks in the county have made no secret of their desire for greater political power. Issues such as school busing, affirmative action in public employment, and alleged police brutality have begun to press home the importance to blacks of increasing representation in elective and appointive offices. This pattern is in marked contrast to that in Washington, where since home rule began, white candidates for political office have never attempted to publicly organize support on the basis of their minority racial identity in the city. In short, both the symbolic and practical importance of rising black political power in Prince George's County far exceeds that of rising white political gains in Washington. Not surprisingly, there appears to be less credence given to the belief that minorities in Prince George's County are seeking to wrest power from the majority white population.

To be sure, there are whites who believe in a racial conspiracy; racial incidents have occurred in the county that are reminiscent of those perpetrated by the xenophobic Ku Klux Klan and American Nazi party in other parts of the nation. But these tend to be isolated, infrequent occurrences that tell little about broader political beliefs. They do not seem to underlie a black conspiracy theory among whites comparable to the white political conspiracy theory that has circulated among some blacks in the District of Columbia for several years.

Until very recent times black candidates running for office or organizing Democratic party affairs found it very difficult to attract effective participation from within the county's black residency. Whatever the causes of black political apathy, it is clear that many families felt few ties to the county's polity because they had lived previously in Washington. Theirs was the indifference that many newcomers bring to a new local government and political climate.

Some Prince George's County blacks profess political allegiance to the District of Columbia, and especially to its black-dominated government.[6] If they work in the city, especially for the District government or the public schools, they are likely to feel even stronger ties. (Until recently, District law discouraged employment of non-District residents, although many employees lived in the suburbs before the law was passed, and others simply ignored it.)

In spite of these patterns, several forces have gradually chipped away at the apathy of black residents in the county. Occasional racist acts such as cross burnings and painted epithets have been one factor.[7] But the publicized incidents have become infrequent, and blacks are much more aware of relations between black residents and the county's criminal justice system. A more common source of irritation, the justice system, especially its police force, is sometimes the crux of racial tensions.[8] Although black police officers have risen in number from 33 (4 percent) in 1975 to 170 (19 percent) ten years later, the force is still predominantly white. As the county's black population grows and its rate of black arrests rises, some black leaders question whether blacks are unfairly treated by police. Incidents in which black suspects have been beaten, wounded, or killed during arrest procedures, while numerically very small, have attracted enormous attention from the press and from black civic leaders. Charges have been made that arresting officers have used racially derogatory language. Police have insisted that young blacks, some from deprived backgrounds, have grown in numbers, that they are more likely to resent questioning or commands by white officers, and that tensions inevitably result.

Political sensitivity among blacks in Prince George's County has been heightened by matters such as these. But other evidence has emerged that blacks are gradually becoming more integrated into county politics. By the end of 1983, for example, there were 7 blacks on the county's Democratic Central Committee, a 22-member body. (One Asian American, the only other member of a minority, was also on the committee.)[9] Newer members, some of whom were black, chafed at the seniority system used by county Democrats to fill state legislative vacancies. They argued that the county's mostly white legislative delegation, traditionally deciding who would be appointed to the vacancies, had too much power. Some members stressed that the committee should not merely defer to convention. While the issue was not strictly one of conflict between the races, it was undergirded by the aspirations of some blacks to redress what they viewed as the county's racially imbalanced political structure.

Race, Politics, and the Jackson Primary Campaign, 1984

It took the 1984 presidential primary campaign of a charismatic leader, the Reverend Jesse Jackson, to propel Prince George's County's black Democrats to participate in the nuts and bolts of voter registration drives and fund-raising campaigns. In March 1984 a "Convention of Black People" was convened in the county just as the Jackson campaign was beginning to make progress in a local voter registration drive. Among the topics discussed by the approximately 300 participants were police protection, political empowerment, the black family, education, and economic development. The fact that blacks were underrepresented in local government relative to their population in the county was discussed. Congressman Parren J. Mitchell addressed the convention, bringing it further prestige.[10] The convention stopped short of the aims of a political caucus, but it was one of the most noteworthy indicators of a rising consensus among county blacks about the possibilities that lay ahead.

By April 1984, 31,000 new voters had been registered in the county, especially in predominantly black precincts.[11] A spokesperson for the local Jackson campaign charged the county's election administration with "institutional racism" during the early months of registration, alleging that registration forms were deliberately being rationed out.[12] No evidence was produced that the administration was attempting to limit black voter participation, and the registration process proceeded without incident in the months that followed.

As it turned out, Jesse Jackson failed to win the Democratic presidential nomination. Yet, as expected, blacks in the county voted in record numbers to nominate him. More important for future black politics, however, voter registration in Prince George's County's largely black areas increased substantially by the time of the general election in November. For example, when compared with 1980 figures, registration rose from 2,841 to 4,250 in Palmer Park, from 958 to 1,581 in Glenarden, and from 2,310 to 3,346 in Carmody Hills.[13] Although Jackson failed to capture the Democratic presidential nomination, his participation helped to erode black apathy in the county. As a result, the nominee, Walter F. Mondale, was able to carry Prince George's County, one of only two jurisdictions in Maryland that he won in the election. (The other was the city of Baltimore.)[14]

While the high black registration came too late to motivate many black candidates to run for local and state offices in 1984 elections, members of Jackson's Rainbow Coalition, an outgrowth of the primary campaign in the county, were encouraged to organize for future elections. By November 1984 at least five blacks had expressed interest in running for local or state office in 1986. At a political gathering of county Democratic officials held right after the November elections, it was clear that black participation in county politics was on the upswing. Similarly, black political activists in the Democratic party have begun to press for increasing black representation on several state-appointed citizens' committees.[15]

Race and Politics, 1986

Prince George's County's 1986 elections were the first real test of black political strength since the 1984 Jackson primary attempt. In the intervening two years black residents had been quietly organizing voters, pressing for increased participation in Democratic party affairs, and making plans to field candidates. There was little doubt that the popular white county executive, Parris N. Glendening, would be reelected. A liberal on most issues, he had reinforced his ties to black voters by appointing black officials to his administration and by supporting programs and positions popular with many blacks. Still, few voters expected that the county's second most powerful office, that of the state's attorney, would become the pivotal point for black political gains in 1986. The white incumbent, Arthur A. Marshall, Jr., had occupied the office for an impressive 24 years, making his mark as a tough prosecutor and a law-and-order symbol among voters. Having successfully prosecuted Arthur Bremer, the man who attempted to assassinate presidential primary candidate, George Wallace, Marshall had figured prominently in many of the county's most widely publicized criminal cases. To many, his tenure as state's attorney was an immutable law of political life in the county. Nevertheless, Marshall's popularity in law enforcement matters had not carried when he took on other political challenges. Over the years, voters turned down his bids for Congress, the county executive's office, and the circuit court bench. It may have been his repeated attempts to extend his reach outside of law enforcement that hurt him most in 1986. After basketball star Len Bias died of a cocaine overdose at the University of Maryland, located in the county, Marshall criticized Coach Lefty Driesell, suggesting that he be fired. He also wanted the university to review its academic requirements for athletes after it was learned that Bias had been failing in most of his courses. Doubtless, some voters viewed the state's attorney as meddling in affairs that were not within the purview of his office and making political hay out of the tragic event, which was especially devastating to Washington-area blacks.[16]

The results of the Democratic primary in September 1986 left Marshall's chief challenger, Howard University law professor Alex Williams, with a slim margin of victory. He won by 52 percent of the vote to Marshall's 48 percent. A black, Williams confined his criticisms of Marshall largely to his professional performance. He swamped Marshall in the largely black precincts inside the beltway and managed to garner enough of the white vote to clinch his margin of victory. There were about 2,000 votes separating the two candidates.[17]

Marshall blamed County Executive Glendening and Congressman Steny H. Hoyer, both Democrats, for sacrificing him. Earlier, the Jackson-inspired Rainbow Coalition had pressed Glendening to help elect at least one black to high office in the county. Marshall said he was asked by

Glendening to pursue a circuit court judgeship so that Williams could run for the state's attorney's office unopposed. Refusing, he noted, he lost support from Glendening and Hoyer, both of whom championed Williams for the post. Glendening countered, stating that it was not the Rainbow Coalition he discussed with Marshall and that he wanted only to add more blacks to county political offices, not specifying any office in particular as a target.[18]

Williams went on to run against the white Republican candidate, David M. Simpson, a prosecutor in the state's attorney's office, in the general election. The racial issue arose again during the campaign, when it was learned that the county's Fraternal Order of Police (FOP) organization, supporting Marshall in the primary, endorsed Simpson thereafter. With a mostly white membership, it was joined by the District of Columbia's FOP chapter, also predominantly white. Apparently unprecedented locally, this interjurisdictional political alliance among mostly white police officers was a highly controversial action. The District FOP's president pointed out that about 1,000 members of his organization lived in Maryland and thus had an interest in the election's outcome.[19] But, of course, this did not explain what business a police organization in another jurisdiction had in political affairs in Prince George's County.

Earlier, there had been some dissension between black and white members of the District's FOP when the group endorsed Carol Schwartz, a white Republican, against Mayor Marion Barry, a black Democrat, in the District's mayoral primary. Thus, its support for Simpson became its second effort to elect a white over a black. The county's Black Police Officers' Association quickly countered with an endorsement of Williams. Its membership included about 57 percent of all black officers in the county police department.[20]

Endorsements aside, Williams triumphed over Simpson in the election, with 61 percent of the vote to Simpson's 39 percent. Neither man made an issue of race, and both voiced regret that it had arisen. But Prince George's County's black electorate made an unmistakable statement with William's victory, capturing an office theretofore the source of some of the county's chief racial tensions. Most certainly, the triumph had its roots in the successful black voter registration drive during the Jackson nomination bid, a critical turning point in the county's evolution. As the black population there continues to rise, County Executive Glendening is well aware that his political vulnerability will increase accordingly. Indeed, he lost no time after his reelection in 1986 in promoting several blacks in his administration to higher positions. Chances are excellent, he is aware, that blacks in the county will repeat the political history of neighboring Washington, where blacks have enjoyed political hegemony since the mid-1970s.

Race, Perceptions, and Public Education

However black candidates fare in future elections, voting patterns will be affected largely by how blacks and whites perceive the overall quality of life in Prince George's County. There appear to be large disparities in racial perceptions on this issue. A survey of county residents in 1983 found that 49 percent of blacks but only 29 percent of whites felt that the county was a better place to live than other localities in the Washington metropolitan area; 17 percent of blacks and 30 percent of whites thought it was a worse place to live.[21] Blacks, who tend to have resided less time in the county than whites, often compared it with Washington, emphasizing the county's cleaner environment, better schools, and racially mixed population. Whites discussed rising crime, declining schools, and increasing taxes. Some whites pointed out that the county had declined over the past 15 years, corresponding to the period of rising black residency. The "slums" of southeast Washington, adjacent to the county and mostly populated by blacks, were thought to be a bad influence. Even as blacks are increasing their political power in Prince George's County during the second half of the decade, the survey reveals that there are still substantial racial differences in outlook about public issues in the county. Hence, it is by no means certain that blacks and whites will cooperate routinely on some issues such as minority public employment and the perceived mistreatment of blacks by county police. In this regard county blacks find themselves in a somewhat different position than that of Washington's black community.

With a clear electoral majority in Washington's political structure, District blacks have the leverage to determine the course of some legislation, policy decisions, and budgetary matters. Of course, neither the mayor nor the city council typically exercises authority exclusively in racial terms. For example, it is rare that city council votes are split along racial lines. Cooperation between whites and blacks on the council and within the executive branch is routine in Washington. But the knowledge that blacks have the potential to control decisions probably helps to discipline whites to accept a reasonable degree of horse-trading in issues that confront the city.

In Prince George's County, on the other hand, unless blacks achieve a majority on the county council, they will probably find that differing perceptions among black and white voters make it difficult to realize important progress on issues critical to blacks. Nor are they likely to elect a black county executive with the ease with which Washington blacks elected mayors Walter Washington and Marion Barry. Yet their victory in the state's attorney's race suggests the possibilities.

Nevertheless, the issue of public education, a major concern among many county blacks, may be one on which blacks and whites agree. In 1978 a referendum supported the adoption of fiscal restraints that were designed to limit property-tax liabilities for county property owners. Public services were cut back or altered to reduce spending. A survey of residents in 1983 found that, although there was still considerable support for property-tax limitations, residents were most sensitive to public educational quality. In fact, of all county services, the most respondents (almost one-half) felt that educational of spending had been cut back since 1978:[22]

> Two-thirds said they favored increased spending for public education. Not surprisingly, 82 percent of those with children in public schools took the same view. But in a county where two of every three households have no direct stake in the schools, 60 percent of those without school-age children said they, too, want more money spent, and 42 percent of them believe schools have been hurt by the property-tax limit.[23]

The survey did not report attitudes by race, but 35 percent of respondents were black and 61 percent were white. No other public service was perceived to have declined to the extent of the public schools. These findings suggest, then, that education is not only one of the most salient issues among county residents, it is an area where there is a good deal of consensus among blacks and whites that improvements are needed.

The county's public schools have been affected by racial migration patterns in ways that are similar to those in Washington. In both jurisdictions middle-class whites have been leaving, many partly as a result of dissatisfaction with public education. But Washington has been losing middle-class blacks as well, and most of these have chosen Prince George's County as a source of improved instruction for their children. There are no signs yet that blacks are forsaking the county as whites have been doing. But it is known that black as well as white enrollments in private schools in the county have risen in recent years. Thus, if present trends continue, it is conceivable that shifting racial and demographic patterns will lead to not only a majority-black population in the county but one in which the issue of public educational quality takes increasingly higher precedence.

Yet even if minorities, and especially blacks, someday outnumber whites in the county, the new ward system of elections for the county council and school board could hamstring blacks from achieving further political gains. Today they are concentrated largely in two wards located inside the Capital Beltway and contiguous to predominantly black southeast and northeast Washington. Blacks from both wards were sitting on the county council and school board in 1984. (The remaining seven wards were represented by whites.) Unless black residents are able to sizably increase their presence in other wards, they are unlikely to realize further numerical representation on the two bodies. A return to an at-large system of elections would undoubtedly dilute black voting strength and perhaps lose black positions on the council and board.

But a combination of ward and at-large elections, such as the District of Columbia's, if adopted, could encourage black candidates to campaign in predominantly white wards. This would require candidates capable of appealing to issues such as education in terms that bring consensus rather than parochialism, a problem that now plagues the ward-based election system.[24] It could diminish the influence of racial considerations in county politics as at-large politicians—white or black—would be forced to find the common threads in public issues. Finally, a partial at-large system could become a good training ground for grooming black candidates for county executive, as well as for state legislative and judicial positions. At least one black state senator has already called for a combination of ward and at-large elections.[25] Furthermore, such a system already exists in neighboring Montgomery County.

12

The Future of Metropolitan
Washington

In the preceding chapters we have explored the growth and development
of the core of Washington and the suburbs surrounding the city. We have
been concerned with the physical, economic, and demographic characteristics of change as well as the manner in which these forces have been expressed in racial and political terms. We have drawn heavily on issues
pertaining to public education for insights into these matters. Throughout,
we have devoted most of our attention to the past and to the present. It
remains for us to question the implications of past and present for the
future of the Washington metropolitan area. Before undertaking that task,
however, it is important to review our major findings and to summarize
key trends and conditions related to inner-city revitalization and minority
suburbanization in the Washington metropolitan area.

Past and Present Trends: A Review

The revitalization process in Washington originated in Georgetown, the
capital's first neighborhood historic district. Evidence of the earliest stages
of property rehabilitation and community organization can be traced to
the mid-1920s. From Georgetown, the revitalization impetus spread to
Capitol Hill, Foggy Bottom, and Kalorama Triangle during the post–
World War II decades. Not satisfied that other inner neighborhoods would
similarly elicit private reinvestment and attract middle-class people, the
District government joined hands with the federal government and imposed the urban renewal template on the southwest area of the city. This
publicly controlled intervention succeeded in revitalizing the southwest
largely by erasing its physical and social identity. The excessive regulation
and rigid direction of redevelopment by governmental agencies à la south-

west renewal was never fully emulated in the remainder of the city's inner-ring neighborhoods. Rather, the Georgetown model, with slight modifications, provided the vision or concept that accounted for the regeneration of the city's second- and third-generation revitalization neighborhoods, largely through private-market dynamics. Government intervention in neighborhood change through the District's former urban renewal authority has been limited largely to neighborhoods affected by the 1968 civil disturbances. In these areas, however, the emphasis has been on structural rehabilitation, with limited clearance and redevelopment.

Revitalization in recent years has brought an infusion of relatively young, affluent, and highly educated households to the city's core. As recently as the late 1970s, most of these households were made up of single persons or families without children. Middle-class families with children were not a major part of the gentrification phenomenon. Nevertheless, in contrast with many other central cities in the United States, the District of Columbia has at least partially offset its out-migration of middle- and upper-income people through the gentrification process. Indeed, when compared with the rest of the city, the revitalizing neighborhoods have been disproportionately successful in retaining relative newcomers in the city. This condition may explain recent population estimates that found that the city had stopped losing population for the first time in several years.

Revitalization and Urban Form

From the broader perspective of urban form, one can identify a clear pattern of regeneration, which has largely transformed parts of Washington's central business district (CBD) and will probably spread throughout the CBD by the early twenty-first century. Surrounding the business center and the federal mall area is a ring of neighborhoods in various states of revitalization. In Georgetown, Foggy Bottom, and the southwest urban renewal area the process is essentially completed. In Dupont Circle, Capitol Hill, Adams Morgan, and Mount Pleasant, it is in advanced stages. In the area north of Massachusetts Avenue between Thomas Circle and Union Station, however, revitalization for the most part is in its germinal stages. Artist studios, a gay disco, and renovated dwellings have begun to appear in recent years.[1] Another section of the inner ring, located between Capitol Hill and the southwest, is almost certain to follow suit in the years ahead.

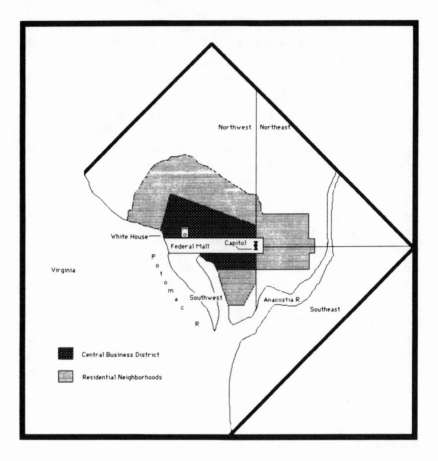

Map 12.1   The revitalized core of Washington (prospective)
Source: Prepared by Dennis E. Gale.

In addition to these sections is the West End, a portion of the city currently undergoing extensive office, hotel, and condominium redevelopment.

These trends point strongly to the conclusion that by the year 2000 most of the core of the nation's capital is likely to be renewed. It will be composed largely of a consolidated business district without the sharp geographical dichotomy based in part on race and class that existed previously. The business district will be enclosed by a ring of predominantly middle- and upper-class neighborhoods (see Map 12.1).

There is little in the literature of geography, sociology, or urban planning to provide a theoretical foundation for this phenomenon of renewal. But in one regard the city's inner-ring neighborhoods function much like those in Chicago described more than a half-century ago by Ernest Burgess.[2] His "Zone of Transition"—the ring of older neighborhoods around Chicago's Loop or central business district—was also the receiving ground for newcomers. But these were mostly poor immigrants from Europe and from rural American communities. Today newcomers to Washington's inner ring are decidedly different in socioeconomic dimensions. For most, residence in an older dwelling located in the inner ring of neighborhoods is by choice, not necessity. Many are homeowners rather than renters. Thus, we would expect that unlike Burgess's Zone of Transition residents, gentrifiers in Washington would have a greater commitment to continued residence in the inner ring. Rather than acting as a staging ground for future migration outward into the city's more affluent neighborhoods, the inner ring should become a more stable residential setting.

Yet this presumably desirable outcome is not without its social costs. Rapid declines in households with lower levels of education and working-class occupations in the city's inner ring of neighborhoods indicate the socioeconomic effect of gentrification. Substantial losses in housing supply, especially low- and moderate-income housing, in these areas are leading to a gradual resegregation by race and income. The first- and second-generation revitalization neighborhoods have shown us that this is the inevitable result of private reinvestment. Thus, unlike Burgess's Zone of Transition residents, who moved farther away from the city center in response to rising incomes and a desire to escape more recently arrived poor households, those leaving Washington's inner ring during revitalization are probably both less able to and less desirous of doing so. In short, many are being replaced—and in many instances, involuntarily—by people of higher socioeconomic status. This contrasts sharply with Burgess's classic model of succession, where out-migration from the Zone of Transition was more likely to represent upward "filtering" through the housing supply, a movement of rising opportunity rather than choiceless necessity.

Until comparatively recently, the old downtown proved to be more resistant to reinvestment than the surrounding inner-ring neighborhoods. Rather, new construction was deliberately diverted from the old retail and office center to a separate enclave largely west of Connecticut Avenue NW. Although various governmental planning documents lamely urged reinvestment in the old downtown, private capital was diverted overwhelmingly to the western portion of the CBD, an area that became the new downtown. Now made up mostly of office buildings with ground-floor shops, the new downtown is safely buffered from areas experiencing blight and rising minority populations; nearby white neighborhoods and major thoroughfares such as Pennsylvania, Massachusetts, and Connecticut avenues provided a cushion against these conditions. Meanwhile, the old downtown continued its downward spiral of generally poor property maintenance and lagging sales. The F Street retail area became known in Washington as the "black downtown," an identity that was only reinforced by the 1968 riots.

By the late 1960s two downtowns existed in the central business district of Washington—one, a newly built enclave of office buildings for a largely white, professional employment base and the other, an area of older, generally declining office structures and a retail center patronized mostly by black shoppers. The downtown of Washington had been dichotomized by race and, to a considerable extent, by land-use type and business sector. Only in the past half-dozen years has the reinvestment process spread eastward from the new downtown. Now it appears that the two downtowns will eventually be physically, if not socioeconomically, unified.

Minority Suburbanization

For anyone who has witnessed the renewal of Washington's core, the effect is striking. No less impressive, though, has been the rise in access to suburban living among racial and ethnic minorities in the metropolitan area. Yet the growth of minority suburbanization has not been uniform across all jurisdictions. It is highly concentrated in the inner-tier communities of Prince George's and Arlington counties and the city of Alexandria. Minorities are still underrepresented in Fairfax, Prince William, Loudoun, Montgomery, and Charles counties. Even within Prince George's County, with by far the highest percentage of minorities, blacks and other groups tend to be concentrated within the older suburbs inside the Capital Beltway. In short, black suburbanization tends to be most closely linked with spillover from northeast and southeast Washington; this condition suggests that blacks do not have the open access to the newer suburbs farther out that is enjoyed by whites, although there is evidence that blacks have penetrated farther into the newer suburbs than is the case in most Standard Metropolitan Statistical Areas.[3] Whether these patterns are due primarily to minority preferences, housing economics, or discriminatory banking and real estate practices, they have brought black access to the suburbs without bringing a notable level of racial integration. In short, suburban housing opportunities for minorities have led to much the same pattern of settlement that occurred in Washington during the 1930s, 1940s, and 1950s. As blacks have moved into white neighborhoods in larger numbers, panic selling has occurred and whites have moved farther outward. While there are exceptions to the "invasion-succession" syndrome in each suburban jurisdiction, racial settlement patterns persist in their tendency toward segregation.[4]

Moreover, it is clear that Washington's suburban blacks are considerably less well off than suburban whites. Measures of income, poverty, household structure, and education show that whatever its benefits, suburban residence can hardly be taken as proof that blacks have "made it" in the American economic system. This finding has special import, however, in the metropolitan region of the nation's capital. For it is in Washington, of all major American metropolitan areas, that blacks have achieved among the highest collective living standards. Even with these accomplishments, nevertheless, blacks still lag considerably behind whites in socioeconomic circumstances. If this is the case in the Washington metropolitan area, it does not bode well for blacks in many other urban areas, where opportunities are likely to be less in evidence. Thus, while rising black suburbanization is a positive signal about American society, there is still cause for real concern about its promise for the future of racial equality.

Future Directions: Politics and Planning

Over the past 20 years the political dynamics of race and geography in the Washington metropolitan area have produced important insights into the viability of the American democratic experiment. To be sure, there is no longer anything unique about a major central city governed by a minority mayor or councilpersons. Nor is it unusual to find growing minority populations and minority political influence in American suburbs. In Washington the shifting racial dimensions of population change have brought a new political order. Although blacks have hegemony in electoral might, elective office, and city employment, whites continue to assert their influence as minority voters. This situation, of course, is the inverse of that of most central-city polities in the United States. Yet whites continue to exercise disproportionate influence over the city's economy, a condition comparable to that of most major urban centers.

In Washington's suburbs it could hardly be said that a "new order" has taken hold. But in some jurisdictions blacks have begun to show representation on city and county councils, school boards, and public employment rolls. By far the most advanced of these is Prince George's County, where it is almost certain that blacks—and perhaps other minorities—will continue to increase their representation in elective and appointive offices, to say nothing of public employment. It is conceivable that they will hold an electoral majority in the county before the end of the century. As it is, the county stands among a handful of the nation's large suburban jurisdictions with noteworthy progress in the participation of blacks in governance.

In effect, Washington and Prince George's County are at two different stages in the evolution of egalitarian political participation. If it has not achieved the Chocolate City Dream, the District of Columbia has progressed dramatically toward the electoral enfranchisement of its entire population, both white and minority. A black mayor and a predominantly black City Council, School Board and city bureaucracy work routinely with a white minority on the city council, on the school board, and in the city bureaucracy. Prince George's County, on the other hand, has just begun to show signs of reaching toward a greater balance of political power between whites and minorities. Blacks sit on the county council and school board, and their numbers have increased among county government employees. They have made small but promising gains in representation in the state legislature and in the judiciary. But the black electorate in no way carries the numerical advantage of its Washington counterpart. Whites maintain both electoral and economic dominance in the county.

Yet it can be said with little distortion that almost every loss of a black voter from the District of Columbia is likely to be the gain of one for the growing black electorate of Prince George's County. For the city, with its apparently stabilizing white population, however, it is conceivable that white electoral strength could rise. Only a new wave of minority in-migration or of white out-migration from northwest Washington or the revitalizing core is likely to thwart this outcome. Over the long term, it would seem, the prospects for substantial black influence over local issues is at least as great in Prince George's County as in the District of Columbia.

A larger, more affluent, and better-informed black electorate is rising in Prince George's County as the white population is declining. Not only are there county offices to aspire to but black candidates can run for several state offices as well. As their numbers in the county electorate grow, they can expect to receive more favorable legislative and gubernatorial treatment in state appointments. Furthermore, the rising presence and seniority of blacks from Baltimore and other Maryland cities in the state legislature is likely to benefit blacks in Prince George's County. Black political aspirations in Washington, on the other hand, are considerably more circumscribed. Beyond the mayoralty there is no higher political office to seek, unless one prefers the relatively powerless position of nonvoting delegate to the House of Representatives or a judicial appointment. Although for several years a move has been afoot to achieve statehood for the District, by most accounts it is an effort unlikely to bear fruit. Therefore, Prince George's County not only offers blacks more opportunities for local and state elective and appointive positions to which to aspire, it offers greater potential for rising through the ranks to higher responsibilities.

Even with the restructuring of racial politics in the city and to a lesser extent in its inner-tier suburbs over the past decade, there has been little evidence of attempts to build new political alignments. The Metropolitan Washington Council of Governments (COG), a voluntary organization for cooperation between metropolitan jurisdictions, has been the primary forum for resolving issues. Growing out of earlier, less formalized organizations for metropolitan cooperation, COG has provided local governments the opportunity to reach compromises and achieve economies of scale in urban and regional planning, environmental protection, and public transit, among other issues. As minorities rise in political influence in some suburbs, it is conceivable, but by no means certain, that social issues such as publicly assisted housing, job training, and education could become the subjects of attempts to build factional alliances. If liberal whites and minorities, for example, increase their representation in suburban elected offices, the chance to join forces with District officials to redirect the COG's agenda may present itself. But the often more conservative agendas of the second-tier counties are likely to continue to inhibit such initiatives.

Nevertheless, insofar as minorities are concerned, the greatest avenues for intrametropolitan cooperation undoubtedly will be between Prince George's County and the District of Columbia. Black county politicians who are former residents of Washington may find it easier to reach accommodation with District officials on some bi-jurisdictional issues. Both the District and the county are heavily populated by Democrats. Furthermore, the emotional ties of many county blacks to the city of Washington are strong, and thus it would not be surprising if the future brought new efforts to build political alliances between the two local governments. We will return to the theme of city-suburban cooperation, but first we must examine recent public planning efforts for insights into the future of the Washington metropolitan area.

The Central City and Its Future

As discussed in Chapter 3, the city of Washington has had no dearth of plans for its growth and development. Since World War II there have been several plans prepared, and innumerable reports bearing on the city's future have been completed. Most of these were prepared by the District's early planning agency, the National Capital Park and Planning Commission, a federal body. But as we have seen, most earlier plans are now dated. And, to be sure, none of them was able to predict the rise of private-market revitalization, which has transformed much of the city's center since the late 1960s.

Nonetheless, it is useful to analyze planning efforts related to Washington's future that have been prepared since the city achieved home rule and established its own planning office in the mid-1970s. Consider, for example, the matter of population forecasting. For years Washington's population loss has been a topic of concern for planners. Not surprisingly, there has been a tendency to look to the future with the hope that population will stabilize or begin to increase. For example, a study by the District government in 1976 predicted that the 1985 city population would drop to between 736,000 and 764,500, varying according to differing assumptions about household size.[5] However, even by 1980 the decennial census found that population had decreased considerably further, to 636,000 people (later adjusted to 638,300 by the Census Bureau). More recently, the District's 1982 Comprehensive Plan forecasted population based on the 1980 census findings. It projected a 1985 population of 639,100.[6] (By 1990 it was expected to rise to 643,300.) But recently released estimates of the city's population by the federal Census Bureau placed the 1985 population at 626,000. Thus, the city's population estimate again, was higher than Census Bureau findings. (The bureau did find that population rose between 1984 and 1985 by about 1,000. Still, even if this trend holds, it is unlikely that the city's population will increase to the District's projected 643,300 by 1990.)[7]

Although there is reason to view the District's Comprehensive Plan population forecast with special caution, its predictions about the socio-economic character of the city's residents may be more accurate. The plan forecasts a loss of 4,200 of the city's poorest households and a gain of over 25,000 of its high-income households between the years 1977 and 2000.[8] Additionally, it predicts a gain of 5,200 moderate- and middle-income households and a loss of 3,700 upper-middle-income households.[9] The implication of these figures is an increasingly affluent population profile by the year 2000. If the figures are essentially accurate, they indicate that the city's need for subsidized services such as medical care, food assistance, and public housing should decline. Meanwhile, a higher-income profile in the District should portend higher per capita revenues from taxes. All in all, the socioeconomic forecast anticipates a wealthier Washington.

But what of the poor? What do these figures suggest about them? The plan accounts for losses of low-income people through two forces: declining household size (that is, having fewer children) and upward mobility (that is, rising to moderate- and middle-income status). Although the former assumption seems plausible, the latter does not. With vast cutbacks in federal and local welfare budgets in recent years and an employment market requiring more educated workers, it is not clear that upward mobility is a promising likelihood for significant numbers of the city's low-income families.

Surprisingly, the plan says little, if anything, about *outward mobility* of the poor to the inner suburbs. Yet the least-expensive median housing costs for a jurisdiction in the metropolitan area are in adjacent Prince George's County. In recent years small numbers of low-income households —mostly black—have moved into older housing across the District line, and there is little reason to suspect that this trend will not persist, if not increase. As the low- and moderate-income housing supply in Washington continues to diminish through abandonment, private-market revitalization, and expanding nonresidential development, it seems likely that many people in the city's poorer enclaves in northeast and southeast Washington will spill over into Prince George's County. Mostly black, these households will probably replace blacks and whites of moderate-income circumstances, who in turn are likely to continue pushing farther into Prince George's County. Therefore, while the plan is probably correct in assuming a decline in the city's poor population through smaller household size, it seems to err in predicting that upward mobility will also play a substantial role. Outward mobility, an unpopular subject in metropolitan politics, is likely to have a stronger effect on Washington's poor population.

Whatever the causes, the projection that collectively Washington will have a more affluent population is probably sound. Of course, future circumstances such as rising in-migration of foreign households, especially those consisting of undocumented aliens, could upset these outcomes by stabilizing or increasing the city's poor population. Catastrophic economic or political conditions in other countries have almost always affected American urban population dynamics. Nevertheless, given current trends, a wealthier Washington, with the out-migration of some of its poor to the suburbs, appears to be the most likely future trend.

Just as important, the plan predicts a moderately declining upper-middle-income residency in the city. Here, though, losses are expected to be due both to out-migration and to upward mobility. Thus, the Comprehensive Plan foresees a continuation of suburbanization as a factor in the city's loss of upper-middle-income families. The loss of more households in this income strata is probably likely, although the plan may again underestimate decreases caused by out-migration and overestimate those caused by upward mobility. As discussed earlier, rising birth rates among the city's middle- and upper-middle-income families, especially in the revitalizing communities, could contribute to demands on the public schools that cannot or will not be met by the school board. This factor, coupled with the increased out-migration of middle-income blacks in recent years, would seem to result in more upper-middle-income losses from suburbanization than from rising affluence.

Coupled with the plan's forecasts about population are those dealing with employment. The plan predicts a net gain of 110,000 (16.6 percent) employees working in the city between 1980 and 2000.[10] If this figure is even remotely accurate, we can expect that the years ahead will bring a shift in emphasis from the city's function as a residential center to its function as an employment locus. Until the 1950s Washington's prevailing pattern was growth, both in employment and population. Since then, this relationship has been changing. While employment has ebbed and flowed, the general trend has been upward; meanwhile, population has been declining since the post–World War II years, although the rate of decline appears to have slowed in recent years and there were signs of population stability by the mid-1980s.

If the plan is incorrect in assuming significant population increases over the next 15 years and it is essentially correct in projecting substantial growth in employment, the balance between employment and population will continue to shift. Employment facilities will take up a greater share of space in the city, and employment matters will play a greater role in city government affairs such as planning. In practical terms this portends the continued destruction or alteration of housing, especially that located adjacent to employment centers such as the central business district. In place of residential land uses, one would expect more employment facilities such as government and private offices and hotels. Unless the housing stock lost to these forces is replaced by new construction outside the central core (that is, mostly through demolition of existing structures and development of higher-density dwellings), the city will continue to suffer a diminishing housing supply. Given trends in private housing investment, especially rental housing, substantial new construction in the city seems implausible. The difficulty of adding housing is further compounded by growing opposition to new development from neighborhood preservation groups. Federal tax policy revisions by Congress in 1986 may also discourage new investment in housing. Furthermore, continued federal and local reluctance to invest public funds in building housing will contribute to the shifting identity of the nation's capital as an employment center rather than as a place of residence.

In Chapter 3 we pointed out that the District's Comprehensive Plan has been widely criticized for its initial failure to relate its various strategies and policies on housing, transportation, and other planning issues to specific geographical consequences. In other words, it lacked a map showing future land-use patterns. This omission was deliberate on the part of the city's Office of Planning and Development but was rectified as a result of city council pressure. Still, the map that resulted made little effort to distinguish precisely between varying types of residential and commercial land-use patterns. Thus, citizens could not determine whether a low-density, residential land-use pattern, for example, meant single-family detached homes, town houses, or garden apartments. The map also indicated certain types of land uses (for example, residential) where in fact differing uses (for example, hospital or gas station) were already in place. The Office of Planning and Development indicated that these discrepancies would be resolved when the last stage of planning, the preparation of detailed small-area plans, was completed.

Thus, it is difficult to predict what form the final version of the Comprehensive Plan will take and therefore, how its population, employment, and housing forecasts, strategies, and policies will be manifested in revised land-use configurations. Nonetheless, it is evident in the deliberations thus far that a central issue will be the location of space for business expansion on the periphery of the central business district and in certain neighborhood commercial corridors. Because the District government expects, and indeed ordinarily encourages, such expansion, it is likely that it will often occur in the paths of least resistance. As pointed out earlier, one sector that is likely to be designated for such growth is north of the CBD along Massachusetts Avenue NW and west of Union Station. Today this neighborhood is characterized by low-income housing, some signs of gentrification, vacant lots, and underutilized buildings. Immediately to the south the new convention center will undoubtedly exert growing pressure for primarily office, hotel, and retail commercial redevelopment. Residential uses are likely to dwindle, an outcome that is in keeping with the above observations about the balance between population and employment in the city.

The Metropolitan Area and Its Future

Just as Washington has revised its Comprehensive Plans over the years, so also have the surrounding suburban jurisdictions. Each county, for example, has its own planning commission or board with a professional planning staff. It is beyond the scope of this study, however, to provide a full review and discussion of each community's plans for the future. But since 1965 the Metropolitan Washington Council of Governments has been the primary metropolitan planning organization for the Washington metropolitan area. It is a voluntary body, its council made up of public officials from each of its constituent governments. It is not a state or local government and has no powers of taxing or regulation. Instead, like many metropolitan and regional organizations in the United States, its influence is advisory and its primary mission is to achieve consensus on public issues among local governments. Its tendency on planning matters is to develop metropolitan growth policy "from the bottom up." That is, it attempts to reach generalized agreements among jurisdictions without requiring that they commit themselves to a single mapped metropolitan land-use plan. Instead, it tries to convince local governments to manifest COG planning policies in their official planning documents and programs. The aggregation of these local plans amounts to the COG plan.

Over the past decade the COG has pursued a Metropolitan Growth Policy Program, which includes cooperative forecasting efforts among participant governments, assessments of the effects of new development, and "fair share" agreements. The last item involves the allocation of new metropolitan development and growth among jurisdictions through negotiation under COG auspices. When the Metropolitan Growth Policy Program statement was adopted by the COG board in 1980, it was the first comprehensive planning document of the council.[11] Again, however, implementation of the policy depends on local government cooperation. As localities have competed more vigorously for new economic development in recent years, idealism over fair-share allocations has slipped.

One of the most helpful outcomes of the Metropolitan Growth Policy Program, however, has been its periodic forecasts of future population and employment. For example, the 1984 forecast predicts that with the incorporation of Calvert, Stafford, and Frederick counties into the Standard Metropolitan Statistical Area in 1980, the population in the metropolitan area will reach almost 4 million by the year 2000.[12] It predicts population stability for the city of Washington by the year 2005. In the suburbs it projects a gain of 284,000 people for Loudoun, Montgomery, Prince George's, Charles, Prince William, Fairfax, and Arlington counties and Alexandria city. Calvert, Frederick, and Stafford counties are expected to add about the same population, 282,000, albeit in a smaller land area.

Like the District's Comprehensive Plan, the COG's forecast calls for continued decline in average household size but at slower rates than during the 1970s. It also projects a slower household formation rate than in the 1970s. Finally, it expects slower growth in employment than was predicted in earlier COG forecasts. It predicts that total employment will rise from 1.71 million workers in 1980 to between 2.26 and 2.77 million (depending on which growth scenario one accepts) in 2010. Three out of four new jobs are expected to be created in the economy's information sectors, such as data processing and communication.[13]

While Washington is likely to remain the largest single locus of employment, the COG's forecast expects that the city will not keep pace with the rate of growth of the surrounding region. If this prediction proves accurate, it suggests that many Washington minorities who move to the inner suburbs will place themselves closer to some of the most promising areas of future employment growth. By living in Arlington, Montgomery, and Prince George's counties, for example, they will find themselves and their children better able to commute to work not only inward, to the District, but also outward, to newly emerging employment centers around the beltway and beyond. Counties now actively compete for economic development, especially in office and the so-called high-technology fields. To the extent that educational achievement can keep pace with the requirements of these industries, minority future employment and income prospects will doubtless be enhanced by living outside the District. But even in service-sector work, such as in franchise food outlets, a field that minorities have entered in notable numbers, the suburbs have far outpaced the District in employment growth.

The Future of Inner-City Revitalization
and Minority Suburbanization

While existing public plans and studies provide insights into the future of metropolitan Washington, they are noncommittal about the twin forces with which this book is primarily concerned. Yet the preceding review helps to provide the context for a consideration of the future directions of inner-city revitalization and minority suburbanization. To a considerable extent, both forces were driven by a post–World War II phenomenon— the baby boom. Born in the decade after the war, members of this generation represented a major "bulge" in the population stream. This later manifested itself in the form of a sizable increase in the number of urban newcomers in the late 1960s and the 1970s. Both blacks and whites in this generation were benefiting from a meteoric rise in the availability of education, especially postsecondary education. Blacks took advantage of War on Poverty programs and Civil Rights Movement victories, gaining unprecedented access to college education, public and private employment, and urban housing. Urban areas such as Washington, with its high proportion of white-collar employment opportunities, drew the baby boomers in substantial numbers.

Arriving in Washington in competition with other groups, the baby boomers placed new demands on the housing market. Housing theretofore relegated to the poor and working-class families in older, inner neighborhoods took on a new appeal to thousands of whites. Most of these people spent their childhoods in suburbs or small towns and thus found a new challenge and appeal to inner-city living. Most blacks, on the other hand, with no such childhood experience, wanted to taste the fruits of suburban life; for many, there was little attraction to living in the same nineteenth-century housing their parents had hoped they would escape.

But the 1980s have brought the realization in Washington and similar metropolitan areas that the "bulge" of blacks and whites in their twenties and thirties is passing. Future numbers in these age cohorts will be considerably smaller. Thus, there is reason to predict that the *rate* of urban revitalization and minority suburbanization could decline somewhat in the next 15 years. While both phenomena will continue, they are likely to do so at a less impressive rate than in the 1970s.

We must also recall that minority suburbanization has included not only American blacks but Hispanics, Asians, and Asian Americans, among others. Although our data on these "other minorities" are less informative than those on black Americans, it appears that a substantial share of suburbanization by the former is due to the recent immigration of people from nations suffering economic and political difficulties. Should national immigration policies change, permitting increased flows of foreigners to enter the United States, we might experience a continuation in the earlier rate of minority suburbanization. Alternatively, if numbers of undocumented aliens continue to grow, the same outcome could occur.

As for the forces these two population subgroups are likely to impose on the Washington metropolitan area, we have already pointed out the implications for public education. With recently increasing birth rates among white families, especially those living in revitalizing areas of the city, there will undoubtedly be new expectations about educational quality. If these go largely unmet, it is probable that many whites will follow the lead of earlier generations of whites and current generations of black, middle-class families, migrating to the suburbs for the schools. The twin effects of continuing black out-migration, coupled with a new wave of white out-migration, could further impair the city's population balance. The result would be greater erosion of the District's population of predominantly middle- and upper-middle-income families. Moderate-income families and upper-income households made up of singles or childless couples would compose a larger share of the city's population. (Indeed, this outcome is given tacit expression in the population projections of the District's Comprehensive Plan discussed above.)

If there is a new surge of white out-migration from Washington in the late 1980s and 1990s and it is accompanied by continued black out-migration, suburban jurisdictions are likely to feel the pressure. Even at this writing, several communities are reporting new increases in public school enrollment due to rising birth rates. But it is not clear how much of the growth in enrollment is due to in-migration, especially from Washington. Whatever the case, Washington's blacks are likely to continue moving primarily to Prince George's County, with smaller numbers migrating to Montgomery, Fairfax, and Arlington counties and the city of Alexandria. Very few whites are likely to move to Prince George's County, however. Instead, they will probably emulate earlier generations of middle- and upper-middle-income whites, moving to Montgomery, Fairfax, and Arlington counties and the city of Alexandria. Even in these four communities, however, whites and blacks are unlikely to substantially alter the largely segregated residential patterns of the past. The heavy concentration of blacks in Prince George's County, of course, will only exacerbate the conditions of metropolitan racial imbalance.

One response to persistent black and white out-migration from Washington would be an *educational compact* between the city's public school system and one or more of the suburban systems. Under this arrangement, each jurisdiction would create a magnet high school with a specialty. For example, Washington might establish a school of the arts (perhaps located at its existing Duke Ellington School) and Montgomery County, a school of science. Children of families living in these jurisdictions would be allowed to attend high school in either jurisdiction. No further taxes or fees would be imposed for this privilege. Specialized curricula and faculty could be developed at each school to enhance academic excellence and prestige. Competitive entrance standards might be imposed. Not only could such a program offer an antidote to racially imbalanced school attendance patterns, it could reduce the incentive for Washington families to leave the city for the suburbs. Doubtless, many families would be less inclined to move out of the city, given attractions such as easy access to the downtown, museums, and galleries, if they were able to enroll their teenagers in a public high school (regardless of location) of sterling scholastic reputation. Perhaps even some families contemplating private school for their children might be attracted to such a public school alternative. Presumably, an educational compact would be most feasible for families living within a few miles of the District of Columbia's boundaries. Pupils living in locations where extensive commuting would be necessary (Rockville, or Damascus, Maryland, for example) would be less interested in attending school in Washington.

Proposals such as an educational compact point to the problem of encouraging interjurisdictional cooperation between city and suburbs. To date, such cooperation between Washington and its suburbs has been limited to issues such as sewage waste disposal and employment. Conventional public services such as education are left almost entirely to individual local governments. Perhaps it is local politicians, fearful of losing control over budgets or the power of service provision, who are to blame for the sorry record to date on interjurisdictional sharing of appropriate public services. Perhaps public employee unions have objections. Whatever the reasons, it is clear that racially segregated residential patterns in the Washington metropolitan area will not be solely the result of family income and housing supply. Differential quality of public services such as education, compounded by local government inertia and lack of creativity, will continue to play a role in this tragic social imbalance.

Appendix, Notes, and Index

Appendix

Methodology

Washington census tracts corresponding to areas (primarily residential) undergoing active revitalization during the 1970s were aggregated into a single analytical unit termed "Revitalizing Areas" (Map 5.1). Included were tracts which encompass neighborhoods such as Dupont Circle, Adams Morgan, Mount Pleasant, Logan Circle and Capitol Hill. All of these are well established gentrification sections. In addition, tracts that were less well recognized as reinvestment areas were added. These were identified by the author (a resident of Washington since 1971) based on his familiarity with Washington revitalization dynamics dating to 1969. Sources of information included reconnaissance visits to numerous neighborhoods, discussions with real estate businesspersons and systematic review of articles in the *Washington Post*, all undertaken during the late 1970s.

Nevertheless, one section of the city which is not technically a gentrifying area was included in the study area. The Southwest Urban Renewal Area underwent redevelopment during the 1960s and 1970s. Because the primary social effects were felt during the 1970s and because these effects are very similar to those of gentrification, it was decided to add the census tracts composing the Southwest Urban Renewal residential neighborhood. The gentrifying areas were primarily affected by private market forces, with the emphasis on rehabilitation of the existing building stock; conversely, the Southwest underwent revitalization through heavy government regulation and investment and the almost complete demolition of its existing environmental fabric. But both gentrification and Urban Renewal brought substantial physical, economic and social changes. The present analysis concentrates on measuring the collective effects of both forms— gentrification and redevelopment—of neighborhood revitalization.

The following census tracts in the District of Columbia were included in the Revitalizing Areas:

27.1	60.1
27.2	60.2

28	61
37	63.1
38	65
39	66
40	67
42.1	69
42.2	70
43	80.1
50	80.2
52.1	81
53.1	82
55.1	83.1
55.2	83.2

All census tracts in the city not listed above were included in the Remaining Area portion of the analysis.

The U.S. Bureau of the Census made no significant changes in the boundaries of these tracts between 1970 and 1980. Thus, the 1970 and 1980 tracts are identical for analytical purposes.

The sources of data are: *Census of Population and Housing, 1970*, Census Tract Final Report PHC (1), U.S. Bureau of the Census, Washington: The Bureau, 1972, and *Census of Population and Housing, 1980*, Summary Tape File 3A, U.S. Bureau of the Census, Washington: The Bureau (producer and distributor), 1983.

Notes

Chapter 1

1. Thomas S. Stanback, Jr., Peter J. Bearse, Thierry J. Noyelle, and Robert A. Karasek, *Services: The New Economy* (Totowa, N.J.: Allanheld, Osmun Publishers, 1981); Robyn Swaim Phillips and Avis C. Vidal, "The Growth and Restructuring of Metropolitan Economies," *Journal of the American Planning Association* 49 (Summer 1983): 291–306.

Chapter 2

1. Statistics presented in this section were taken from the 1950, 1960, 1970, and 1980 U.S. decennial *Census of Population and Housing*, U.S. Bureau of the Census (Washington, D.C.: U.S. Government Printing Office).

2. "Population, Households and Housing Unit Characteristics of Metropolitan Washington, 1980," COG Census Report 2, Metropolitan Washington Council of Governments, Washington, D.C., 1982, p. I-8.

3. Ibid., p. I-9.

4. Lawrence Feinberg, "Older Mothers," *Washington Post*, January 15, 1983, p. A1.

5. "Population, Households and Housing Unit Characteristics," pp. I-11, I-17.

6. Ibid., pp. I-13, I-14.

7. Ibid., pp. I-15, I-16.

8. Ibid., pp. I-24, I-25.

9. *Provisional Estimates of Social, Economic and Housing Characteristics, Census of Population and Housing*, PHC 80-S1-1, U.S. Bureau of the Census (Washington, D.C.: U.S. Government Printing Office, 1982), table P5, pp. 46, 49.

10. George Grier and Eunice Grier, *Metropolitan Washington: Leader in Changing Lifestyles* (Washington, D.C.: Greater Washington Research Center, 1982), table 20, p. 43.

11. Ibid., table 22, p. 46 and table 21, p. 44.

12. Lawrence Feinberg, "Which Is Richer?" *Washington Post*, March 22, 1984, pp. C1, C4.

13. Karlyn Baker and Jack Eisen, "The Economy Takes It Easy on Residents of Area," *Washington Post*, October 10, 1982, pp. C1, C3.

14. Janice Hamilton Outtz, *Data Book for the Greater Washington Region* (Washington, D.C.: Center for Municipal and Metropolitan Research, 1979), table 14, p. 25.

15. Frances Sauve, "City Housing Costs Outpace Paycheck Increases," *Washington Post*, November 18, 1976. See also Martha M. Hamilton, "Homeowners Now Pay Third of Income on Mortgages," *Washington Post*, September 16, 1979, p. C1.

16. *Jurisdictional Profiles* (Washington, D.C.: Metropolitan Washington Council of Governments, 1982), pp. 12–17.

17. Ronald Kessler, "Number of Poor Families Down in D.C., Up in Suburbs," *Washington Post*, February 9, 1984, p. C4.

18. Ibid.

19. Grier and Grier, *Metropolitan Washington*, pp. 25–26.

20. Eunice Grier, *Understanding Washington's Changing Population* (Washington, D.C.: Washington Center for Metropolitan Studies, 1961), pp. 10–12.

21. Ibid.

22. Lawrence Feinberg, "D.C. White Exodus Reversed in '75–'80," *Washington Post*, June 12, 1984, pp. B1, B7.

23. Lawrence Feinberg, "D.C. Population Holding Steady," *Washington Post*, January 24, 1985, pp. A1, A6. See also Charles Fishman, "Fairfax Gains, District Loses in Population," *Washington Post*, March 28, 1984, pp. C1, C4.

24. *Federal Employment and Federal Facilities* (Washington, D.C.: National Capital Planning Commission, 1982), p. 2-1.

25. Ibid., p. 2-3.

26. Ibid., p. 2-7.

27. *Greater Washington: The Association Capital* (Washington, D.C.: Metropolitan Washington Board of Trade, undated), p. 1.

28. Stephen S. Fuller and Andrew H. Shapiro, *The Changing Economy of the Washington Area* (Washington, D.C.: Greater Washington Research Center, 1983), table 6, pp. 23–25.

29. Ibid.

30. Ibid.

31. Ibid.

32. Thomas S. Stanback, Jr., Peter J. Bearse, Thierry J. Noyelle, and Robert A. Karasek, *Services: The New Economy* (Totowa, N.J.: Allanheld, Osmun Publishers, 1981).

33. "Washingtonians at Work, 1980," COG Census Report 6, Metropolitan Washington Council of Governments, Washington, D.C., 1983, table 2, p. 6.

34. *Greater Washington: The Association Capital*, p. 1.

35. Peter Perl, "COG Area Gained 23,300 Jobs in '83," *Washington Post*, March 15, 1984, p. B1.

36. Martha M. Hamilton, "Jobless Rate Down in 1983," *Washington Post*, February 15, 1984, p. B1.

37. Stephen J. Lynton, "Study Finds Jobs Lag near Metro Stations," *Washington Post*, September 12, 1984, pp. C1, C6.

38. Lawrence Feinberg, "Help Wanted: Suburbs Seek to Fill Jobs," *Washington Post*, August 23, 1984, pp. A1, A28.

39. Ibid. See also "Fairfax Puzzles over Disinterest of D.C. Laborers," *Washington Post*, May 21, 1985, p. A1.

40. Lynton, "Study Finds Jobs Lag," p. C6.

41. Stephen J. Lynton, "Subway Proves Job Boon to Suburban Commuters," *Washington Post*, April 19, 1984, p. C5.

Chapter 3

1. *A Living Downtown for Washington, D.C.: Planning Concepts* (Washington, D.C.: Government of the District of Columbia, Comprehensive Plan Publications, 1981), p. 10.

2. Ibid., p. 12.

3. For a comprehensive account of race relations in the District of Columbia up to the mid-1960s, see Constance McLaughlin Green, *The Secret City* (Princeton, N.J.: Princeton University Press, 1967).

4. *A Living Downtown*, pp. 9–10; *A Plan for the Year 2000: The Nation's Capital* (Washington, D.C.: National Capital Park and Planning Commission and National Capital Regional Planning Council, 1961), p. 84.

5. *Washington's Central Employment Area: 1973*, Informational Series Report 3, (Washington, D.C.: National Capital Planning Commission), p. 10.

6. Ibid., p. 16.

7. *A Plan for the Year 2000*, p. 84.

8. Ibid.

9. *A Living Downtown*, p. 46.

10. Ibid., p. 6.

11. *Downtown D.C.: Recommendations for the Downtown Plan, Mayor's Downtown Committee* (Washington, D.C.: Government of the District of Columbia, Comprehensive Plan Publications, 1982), p. 28.

12. Jerry Knight, "Downtown D.C. on the Verge of Spectacular Rebirth," *Washington Post*, July 9, 1978, p. F1; "Downtown Is Back," *Washington Post*, October 23, 1986, p. A22.

13. Charles A. Krause, "$42 Million Hyatt Hotel Opens on Capitol Hill," *Washington Post*, June 14, 1976, pp. C1, C6.

14. *Downtown D.C.: Recommendations*, p. 16.

15. Rudolph A. Pyatt, Jr., "New Luxury Hotels Popping Up All Over," *Washington Post*, (Washington Business), April 16, 1984, p. 32.

16. *The Proposed Comprehensive Plan for the National Capital* (Washington, D.C.: National Capital Planning Commission, 1967), append., p. 206.

17. Jerry Knight, "Business Leaders Urge Downtown Management," *Washington Post*, January 27, 1981, pp. D6, D7.

18. Wendy Swallow, "D.C. to Rethink Downtown Historic District," *Washington Post*, October 9, 1984, p. B3.

19. *Comprehensive Plan for the National Capital: District of Columbia Components* (Washington, D.C.: Government of the District of Columbia, Comprehensive Plan Publications, 1982). See also Wendy Swallow, "D.C. Land-Use Fight Due to Begin," *Washington Post*, January 26, 1985, pp. F1, F12, F14 and Wendy Swallow, "Zoning Discrepancies Are Found in Newly Adopted Land-Use Plan," *Washington Post*, January 26, 1985, F1, F11.

20. Martha M. Hamilton, "Troubled Streets: A Walking Tour of the Civic Center Site," *Washington Post*, July 21, 1977, p. D.C.4.

21. Barbara Vobejda, "Old-Time Coffee Shop Hangs On Amid Progress," *Washington Post*, March 8, 1984, pp. 1, 6; Karlyn Baker, "Businesses Face Relocation,

High Rent," *Washington Post*, July 4, 1978, pp. C1, C6; Eric Pianin, "Businessmen Decry Latest Boost in City Assessments," *Washington Post*, March 15, 1984, pp. 1, 4.

22. Peter Perl, "Topless Bar Loses Liquor License," *Washington Post*, July 19, 1984, pp. C1, C4; Michel McQueen, "Purging Porn," *Washington Post*, February 26, 1981, D.C.1–2; Jerry Knight, "Downtown Development to Scatter Porno District," *Washington Post*, August 9, 1978, pp. D8, D13.

23. Sheilah O'Connor, "Gas Stations Dwindle in Downtown Area," *Washington Post*, October 11, 1984, pp. 1, 4.

24. Ed Scullen, "Neighborhood Movie Houses Going West," *Washington Post*, November 15, 1984, pp. 1, 4.

25. Rudolph A. Pyatt, Jr., "A Development Beacon," *Washington Post*, October 20, 1984, pp. D1, D2.

26. Sandra G. Boodman, "Sholl's Cafeteria Building Sold, Popular Eatery Faces Shutdown," *Washington Post*, May 1, 1984, pp. B1, B4.

27. Sandra Evans Teeley, "Poll Says Shoppers Prefer Suburbs to D.C.," *Washington Post*, June 15, 1983, pp. C1, C8.

28. Arthur S. Brisbane, "For Suburbanites, District No Longer Key Attraction," *Washington Post*, January 6, 1985, pp. A1, A10.

29. Susan S. Fainstein, Norman I. Fainstein, Richard Child Hill, Dennis R. Judd, and Michael Peter Smith, *Restructuring the City: The Political Economy of Urban Redevelopment* (London: Longman, 1983), pp. 169–245.

Chapter 4

1. A full account of the shifting fortunes of Georgetown and the city of Washington during the late eighteenth, nineteenth, and twentieth centuries can be found in Dennis E. Gale, "Restoration in Georgetown, Washington, D.C., 1915–65" (unpublished Ph.D. dissertation), George Washington University, Washington, D.C., 1982. This section of Chapter 4 draws its documentation entirely from that study.

2. Louis Justement, *New Cities for Old: City Building in Terms of Space, Time and Money* (New York: McGraw-Hill Book Co., 1946), p. 98.

3. Elizabeth Kohl Draper, "Progress Report on the Restoration of Capitol Hill Southeast," *Records of the Columbia Historical Society* 51–52 (Washington, D.C., 1951–1952): 134–137.

4. Ibid., p. 135.

5. Ibid.

6. Robert J. Lewis, "Capitol Hill," *Evening Star*, November 19, 1960, p. B1.

7. George Beveridge, "City's Foggy Bottom Seen Test Ground of Urban Renewal," *Sunday Star*, October 23, 1955, p. A32.

8. Robert J. Lewis, "Foggy Bottom," *Evening Star*, October 22, 1960, p. B6. See also William W. Nash, *Residential Rehabilitation: Private Profits and Public Purposes* (New York: McGraw-Hill Book Co., 1959), pp. 9–25.

9. Suzanne Berry Sherwood, *Foggy Bottom, 1800–1975*, G.W. Washington Studies No. 7 (Washington, D.C.: George Washington University, 1978), p. 32.

10. Mary Goddard Zon, "The Kalorama Triangle," *Washington Star Sunday Magazine*, March 17, 1963, p. 4.

11. Penelope Lemov, "Southwest: Twenty-six Years of Renewal," *Washington Post*, August 13, 1977, p. D4.

12. Daniel Thursz, *Where Are They Now?* (Washington, D.C.: Health and Welfare Council of the National Capital Area, 1969).

13. *Housing and Redevelopment: A Portion of the Comprehensive Plan for the National Capital and Its Environs*, Monograph 3, (Washington, D.C.: National Capital Park and Planning Commission, 1950), pp. 10–23.

14. *A Plan for the Year 2000: The Nation's Capital* (Washington, D.C.: National Capital Planning Commission and National Capital Regional Planning Council, 1961), p. 96.

15. Ibid.

16. *Washington Present and Future: A General Summary of the Comprehensive Plan for the National Capital and Its Environs*, Monograph 1, (Washington, D.C.: National Capital Park and Planning Commission, 1950), pp. 13–17; *A Plan for the Year 2000*, pp. 88–89, 106–107.

17. *Community Renewal in the District of Columbia* (Washington, D.C.: Government of the District of Columbia, Office of Community Renewal, 1968), pp. 20–21.

18. Ibid., p. 7.

19. J. Thomas Black, "Private-Market Housing Renovation in Central Cities: A ULI Survey," *Urban Land* 34 (November 1975): 3–9; Phillip L. Clay, *Neighborhood Renewal* (Lexington, Mass.: Lexington Books, 1979).

20. Chris Hamnett, "Social Change and Social Segregation in Inner London, 1961–71," *Urban Studies* 13:261–271; Hal L. Kendig, *New Life for Old Suburbs* (Sydney: George Allen and Unwin, 1979), pp. 125–129; David Ley, "Inner City Revitalization in Canada: A Vancouver Case Study," *Canadian Geographer* 25 (1981): 124–148; Dennis E. Gale, *Neighborhood Revitalization and the Postindustrial City* (Lexington, Mass.: Lexington Books, 1984), pp. 109–150.

21. See, for example, Shirley Bradway Laska and Daphne Spain, "Anticipating Renovators' Demands: New Orleans," in Shirley Bradway Laska and Daphne Spain (eds.), *Back to the City* (New York and Oxford: Pergamon Press, 1980), pp. 116–137; S. Gregory Lipton, "Evidence of Central City Revival," *Journal of the American Institute of Planners* 43 (April 1977): 136–147; Dennis E. Gale, "Middle Class Resettlement in Older Urban Neighborhoods: The Evidence and the Implications," in Larry S. Bourne (ed.), *Internal Structure of the City* (New York: Oxford University Press, 1982), pp. 313–328.

22. David Goldfield, "Private Neighborhood Redevelopment and Displacement: The Case of Washington, D.C.," *Urban Affairs Quarterly* 15:453–468; Jeffrey R. Henig, *Gentrification in Adams Morgan*, G.W. Washington Studies No. 9 (Washington, D.C.: George Washington University, 1982), pp. 18–24; Eileen Zeitz, *Private Urban Renewal* (Lexington, Mass.: Lexington Books, 1979), pp. 39–45; Dennis E. Gale, "Neighborhood Resettlement: Washington, D.C.," in Laska and Spain (eds.) *Back to the City*, pp. 95–115.

23. Gale, "Neighborhood Resettlement", p. 100.

24. Gale, *Neighborhood Revitalization*, pp. 77–79.

25. Henig, *Gentrification in Adams Morgan*, pp. 22–23.

26. Gale, *Neighborhood Revitalization*, pp. 68–72.

27. Ibid., pp. 72–77.

28. Barrett A. Lee, Daphne Spain, and Debra J. Umberson, "Revitalization and Racial Change: The Case of Washington, D.C." (unpublished paper), 1984, pp. 16–21.

29. "Apartment Conversions, March 1979," *Housing Problems, Conditions and Trends in the District of Columbia* (Washington, D.C.: District of Columbia Department of Housing and Community Development, 1979), pp. 8–9.

30. *The Conversion of Rental Housing to Condominiums and Cooperatives* (Washington, D.C.: U.S. Department of Housing and Urban Development, 1980).

31. Ibid., append. 1, pp. 359–383.

32. See, for example, Cynthia Gorney, "The Selling of 15th Street NE," *Washington Post*, October 7, 1976, p. A14.

33. Linda Wheeler, "The Bright Side," *Washington Post*, June 17, 1984, pp. B1, B6.

34. Tom Precious, "Theatergoers Find Center Stage at 14th and T Sts. in Washington," *Washington Post*, August 30, 1986, pp. E1, E4.

35. Marcia Slacum Greene, "HUD Assails D.C. Loan Program," *Washington Post*, July 18, 1986, pp. A1, A14.

Chapter 5

1. Shirley Bradway Laska and Daphne Spain, "Anticipating Renovators' Demands: New Orleans," in Shirley Bradway Laska and Daphne Spain (eds.), *Back to the City* (New York and Oxford: Pergamon Press, 1980), pp. 116–137; Frank F. DeGiovanni and Nancy A. Paulson, "Household Diversity in Revitalizing Neighborhoods" (unpublished paper presented at the national conference of the Association of Collegiate Schools of Planning in Chicago on October 23, 1982), tables 1, 2.

2. Eileen Zeitz, *Private Urban Renewal* (Lexington, Mass.: Lexington Books, 1979), pp. 39–41; Jeffrey R. Henig, *Gentrification in Adams Morgan*, G.W. Washington Studies No. 9 (Washington, D.C.: George Washington University, 1982), pp. 21–22.

3. Dennis E. Gale, *Neighborhood Revitalization and the Postindustrial City* (Lexington, Mass.: Lexington Books, 1984), pp. 59–82.

4. Ibid., pp. 59–62.

5. Laska and Spain, "Anticipating Renovators' Demands," p. 120; Henig, *Gentrification in Adams Morgan*, p. 24; Zeitz, *Private Urban Renewal*, pp. 44–45.

6. Gale, *Neighborhood Revitalization*, pp. 63–65.

7. Ibid., p. 11.

8. Ibid., pp. 68–69.

9. Laska and Spain, "Anticipating Renovators' Demands," p. 119; Dennis E. Gale, "Neighborhood Resettlement: Washington, D.C.," in Laska and Spain (eds.), *Back to the City*, p. 100.

10. Gale, *Neighborhood Revitalization*, pp. 77–79.

11. *Housing Problems, Conditions and Trends in the District of Columbia* (Washington, D.C.: District of Columbia Department of Housing and Community Development, 1980), pp. 8–9.

12. For studies of the net effects of gentrification on central cities, see, for exam-

ple, Larry H. Long and Donald C. Dahmann, *The City-Suburb Income Gap: Is It Being Narrowed by a Back-to-the-City Movement?* Special Demographic Analyses CDS-80-1, U.S. Bureau of the Census (Washington, D.C.: U.S. Government Printing Office, 1980) and Kathryn P. Nelson, "Urban Economic and Demographic Change: Recent Shifts and Future Prospects," in Robert D. Ebel (ed.), *The Changing Economic and Fiscal Structure* (Greenwich, Conn.: JAI Press, 1985).

Chapter 6

1. Dennis E. Gale, "Neighborhood Resettlement: Washington, D.C.," in Shirley Bradway Laska and Daphne Spain (eds.), *Back to the City* (New York and Oxford: Pergamon Press, 1980), pp. 98-99.

2. "City Views," *Washington Post*, September 8, 1977, p. D.C.5.

3. Lawrence Feinberg, "White Enrollment in City's Public Schools Takes Sharp Drop," *Washington Post*, January 6, 1982, p. C7. It should be noted that as of May 1985 the District of Columbia public school system was projecting a slight increase in school enrollments for the ensuing autumn semester. But racial breakdowns were not announced. See Sandra Evans, "School Enrollment Expected to Rise," *Washington Post*, May 23, 1985, pp. C1, C6.

4. William Alonso, "The Population Factor and Urban Structure," in Arthur P. Solomon (ed.), *The Prospective City* (Cambridge, Mass. and London: Massachusetts Institute of Technology Press, 1980), pp. 33-44.

5. Ibid.

6. Lawrence Feinberg, "Older Mothers," *Washington Post*, January 15, 1983, p. A22; Lawrence Feinberg, "Number of Births Up in District," *Washington Post*, August 17, 1986, pp. D1, D6.

7. Gale, "Neighborhood Resettlement," pp. 98-99.

8. Unpublished statistics made available to the author by Mr. Warren Morse and Mrs. Josie Dyson of the District of Columbia Department of Human Services, Vital Records Branch, Research and Statistics Division.

9. "Student Membership in Regular Elementary and Secondary Day Schools by Schools, by Grades, by Race, by Sex, and by Regions," District of Columbia Public Schools, Division of Quality Assurance, Report for November 1980, pp. 11-17, 26-31, 37-42, 49-57 and Report for December 1983, pp. 13-19, 27-32, 40-45, 54-62.

10. Ibid., Report for November 1980, pp. 18-21, 32-34, 43-45, 58-62 and Report for December 1983, pp. 20-23, 33-36, 46-50, 63-67.

11. Ibid., Report for November 1980, pp. 22, 35, 46, 63 and Report for December 1983, pp. 24, 37, 51, 68.

12. "A Summary of Reading and Mathematics Test Results as Measured by the Comprehensive Tests of Basic Skills, Grades 3, 6 and 9," District of Columbia Public Schools, May 1980, p. 2.

13. "A Summary of Student Achievement on the Comprehensive Tests of Basic Skills, Grades 3, 6, 9 and 11," District of Columbia Public Schools, December 1983. Author's computation from table entitled "CTBS Results, Elementary and Middle Schools, Grades 3 and 6," pp. 44-85.

14. Martha M. Hamilton, "Goal of Six-Schools Complex Is to Woo the Children Back," *Washington Post*, March 29, 1976, pp. C1, C5; Sheilah O'Connor, "After Ten Years, Six-Schools Cluster is Still Unique in City System," *Washington Post*, June 28, 1984, p. C1. For a comprehensive history of the Six-Schools complex see, Judith Denton Jones, "Six School Complex: A Successful Innovation in Washington, DC's Public Schools," unpublished manuscript, 1987, p. 320.

15. *Hobson v. Hansen*, 393 U.S. 801.

16. "A Summary of Student Achievement," pp. 44–85.

17. Richard E. Prince, "SW School Project Ends in Failure," *Washington Post*, July 30, 1976, pp. C1, C8.

18. Bart Barnes, "Old School Building Saved on Capitol Hill," *Washington Post*, April 10, 1980, pp. 1, 5.

19. Linda Wheeler, "Inner-City Pioneers Face a Schools Dilemma," *Washington Post*, September 9, 1982, pp. A1, A6, A7.

20. Ibid., p. A7. See also Ann Mariano, "Staying in the City," *Washington Post* February 19, 1984, pp. E1, E10, E12 and Gary Orfield, *Toward a Strategy for Urban Integration* (New York: Ford Foundation, 1981), pp. 50–51.

21. Ronald D. White, "Inner-City School Pushes SE Students to Achieve," *Washington Post*, February 12, 1984, p. A10.

22. Ibid. See also Orfield, *Toward a Strategy for Urban Integration*, pp. 51–52.

23. Dan Morgan, "The Emotional Debate over Private Schools," *Washington Post*, June 29, 1980, p. C5.

24. Ibid.

25. Sheilah O'Connor, "Wilson High Seeks Help of Realtors," *Washington Post*, May 17, 1984, pp. 1, 7.

26. Judith Valente, "Reed Proposes Academic High School Aided by Howard University," *Washington Post*, December 9, 1980, p. A1.

27. Ronald D. White, "Banneker Students, Parents Complain of Robberies, Assaults," *Washington Post*, January 28, 1984, p. C3.

28. Bernhart Mingia, "Police, Schools Gear Up for Protecting Students," *Washington Post*, June 28, 1984, p. C5.

29. Lawrence Feinberg, "A 'Crazy System' That Seems to Work," *Washington Post*, October 2, 1986, pp. C1, C11.

30. A study of 12 urban school systems found that white misperceptions about neighborhood public school quality were common and underscored the importance of school-community information campaigns. See Orfield, *Toward a Strategy for Urban Integration*, pp. 49–51.

31. *Comprehensive Plan for the National Capital: District of Columbia Components* (Washington, D.C.: Government of the District of Columbia, Comprehensive Plan Publications, 1982), pp. 200–206.

Chapter 7

1. Eunice Grier and George Grier, *Black Suburbanization at the Mid-1970s* (Washington, D.C.: Washington Center for Metropolitan Studies, 1978), pp. 25–32.

2. Lawrence Feinberg, "D.C. White Exodus Reversed in '75–'80," *Washington Post*, June 12, 1984, p. B1.

3. Verna E. Martin, "Socio-economic Characteristics of the Black Population of Metropolitan Washington, 1980," COG Census Report 4, Metropolitan Washington Council of Governments, Washington, D.C., 1983, p. xiv.

4. Ibid.

5. *Hispanic Population and Characteristics in the Washington, D.C. Metropolitan Area* (Washington, D.C.: Comprehensive Technologies International, 1981), illus. 3, p. 8.

6. John C. McClain, Jr., and Roger Wentz, "Population, Households and Housing Unit Characteristics of Metropolitan Washington, 1980," COG Census Report 2, Metropolitan Washington Council of Governments, Washington, D.C., 1982 fig. I-13, p. I-22.

7. *Hispanic Population*, ibid.

8. McClain and Wentz, "Population, Households and Housing Unit Characteristics," table 11, p. I-20.

9. James Welsh, *All about Living in the Washington Area* (Washington, D.C.: *Evening Star* Newspaper Co., Inc., 1969), p. 23.

10. Saundra Saperstein, "Maryland Probes Insurance Redlining; Firm Fined," *Washington Post*, August 1, 1978, pp. B1, B5; Barbara Vobejda, "Black Mayor Seeks to Save Racial Mix," *Washington Post*, April 7, 1984, pp. B1, B8.

11. Welsh, *Living in the Washington Area*, p. 22. See also Eugene L. Meyer, "Riverdale Resists 'Emergency' Real Estate Pitch," *Washington Post*, August 24, 1977, pp. C1, C2; Eugene L. Meyer, "Realtors' Role in a Changing Neighborhood," *Washington Post*, January 26, 1980, pp. E1, E11.

12. Robert B. Zehner and F. Stuart Chapin, Jr., *Across the City Line: A White Community in Transition* (Lexington, Mass.: Lexington Books, 1974), p. 12.

13. Joseph T. Howell, *Hard Living on Clay Street: Portraits of Blue Collar Families* (Garden City, N.Y.: Anchor Books, 1973), pp. 350–351.

14. Eugene L. Meyer, "Marlboro Meadows: A Case Study of Neighborhood Change in Prince George's County," *Washington Post*, January 19, 1980, pp. E1, E8.

15. Dennis E. Gale, George Grier, and Eunice Grier, "Black and White Urban-to-Suburban Outmigrants: A Comparative Analysis, 1975–1980," Occasional Paper 4, George Washington University, Center for Washington Area Studies, Washington, D.C., p. 8.

16. Ann Mariano, "Survey of Area Apartments Finds Rental Bias Common," *Washington Post*, September 30, 1986, pp. A1, A9.

17. Albert B. Crenshaw, "Prices Lower in P.G., Figures Show," *Washington Post*, January 5, 1985, pp. E1, E16.

Chapter 8

1. Albert Gollin, Mary Eileen Dixon, and Andrea E. Golden, *Social Patterns and Attitudes in Greater Washington, 1973/1975* (Washington, D.C.: Bureau of Social Science Research, Inc., 1975), pp. 40, 113.

2. Unpublished data from a survey conducted by the *Washington Post*, July 9–11, 1983, in Prince George's County, Maryland. Entitled the Prince George's "TRIM" Poll, the survey interviewed 1,048 randomly selected residents of the county. For a partial discussion of the survey's results, see Leon Wynter, "Blacks Are Happier Than Whites with Life in P.G. County, *Post* Poll Finds," *Washington Post*, August 8, 1983, pp. B1–B2 and Eugene L. Meyer, "Poll Shows Majority Favors Modification of Revenue Freeze," *Washington Post*, August 16, 1983, pp. B1, B3.

3. Table entitled "Racial/Ethnic Enrollments," Prince George's County Public Schools, Pupil Accounting and School Boundaries Department, Upper Marlboro, Md., 1985 (no text or pagination).

4. Set of tables entitled "Status of Desegregation: Special Report Percent Black, 1972–1984," Prince George's County Public Schools, Pupil Accounting and School Boundaries Department, Upper Marlboro, Md., October 1984, pp. 1–17.

5. Lawrence Feinberg, "Prince George's 'White Flight' Seen Linked to Busing Order," *Washington Post*, September 25, 1978, pp. A1, A7. For the results of a study of 23 school districts (including Prince George's County) that underwent school desegregation, see David J. Armor, "White Flight and the Future of School Desegregation," in Walter G. Stephan and Joe R. Feagin (eds.), *School Desegregation: Past, Present and Future* (New York and London: Plenum Press, 1980), pp. 187–226.

6. "Racial/Ethnic Enrollments."

7. Ibid.

8. "Summary of Civil Rights Survey, October 1972," Arlington County Public Schools, Planning, Management and Budget Office, Arlington, Va., 1972; "Summary of Civil Rights Statistics as of October 1983," Arlington County Public Schools, Assessment Office, Arlington, Va., 1983 (neither document paginated).

9. "Enrollment, Membership, Racial Breakdown, September 1974," Alexandria City Public Schools, Alexandria, Va., 1974; "Monthly Membership/Ethnic Summary (1983)," Alexandria City Public Schools, Fairfax County, Va., 1984 (neither document paginated).

10. "Table I, Student Ethnic Membership, 1984–85," and "Table II, Five-Year Ethnic Membership, 1980–85" (from an unpublished data report), Fairfax County Public Schools, Office of Records and Reporting Services, Alexandria, Va., 1985 (unpaginated).

11. "Status of Desegregation: Special Report Percent Black, 1972–1984."

12. Ibid. See also Leon Wynter, "Enrollment at P.G. Public Schools Drops," *Washington Post*, November 2, 1983, p. A1.

13. Wynter, "Enrollment at P.G.," p. A1.

14. Barbara Vobejda, "P.G. Would Shut 22 Schools for Racial Balance," *Washington Post*, May 15, 1984, pp. A1, A16.

15. Robert L. Green, Joe T. Darden, Joseph S. Drew, Jomills Braddock II, and Robert L. Crain, "Final Report on Desegregation of Prince George's County Public Schools, Submitted to Chief Judge Frank A. Kaufman, United States District Court for the District of Maryland," Prince George's County Public Schools, Upper Marlboro, Md., 1985.

16. Barbara Vobejda, "P.G. Desegregation Plan Offered," *Washington Post*, May 10, 1985, pp. A1, A12.

17. Sue Anne Pressley, "Eight P.G. Blacks Urge Changes in School Plan," *Washington Post*, June 7, 1985, p. C3.

18. Sandra R. Gregg, "Changes in Magnet Plan Asked," *Washington Post*, June 1, 1985, pp. B1, B5.

19. Barbara Vobejda, "Black P.G. Group Opposes Busing," *Washington Post*, April 15, 1985, p. D5.

20. Barbara Vobejda, "Judge Clears Way for P.G. Magnet School Desegregation Plan," *Washington Post*, June 8, 1985, pp. A1, A9.

21. Barbara Vobejda, "P.G. School Board Reaches Accord with NAACP on an Integration Plan," *Washington Post*, June 22, 1985, p. B8; Barbara Vobejda, "P.G. School Reorganization Promotes Black Officials," *Washington Post*, July 12, 1985, pp. A1, A13.

22. Victoria Churchville, "Some Racial Goals Met," *Washington Post*, November 18, 1986, pp. B1, B8; Barbara Vobejda, "Magnet Schools in P.G. Flooded by Applicants," *Washington Post*, June 26, 1986, pp. A1, A20.

23. Derived from data published in graphic form (no text) in the "Teacher Work-Life Survey," Prince George's County Educators' Association, Inc., Forestville, Md., 1985.

24. Lena H. Sun, "Busing Linked to Alexandria Racial Balance," *Washington Post*, January 12, 1984, pp. B1, B7. For a history of school desegregation in Alexandria, see Mark Howard, "An Historical Study of the Desegregation of the Alexandria, Virginia City Public Schools" (D. Ed. dissertation), George Washington University, School of Education, Washington, D.C., May 9, 1976.

25. "The Superintendent's Proposed Elementary School Redistricting Plan," Alexandria City Public Schools, Alexandria, Va., 1984.

26. Lena H. Sun, "Alexandria Quota System Hits Some Minority Students," *Washington Post*, June 20, 1984, pp. C1, C5. At this writing an evaluation of the first year of operation provides positive although inconclusive evidence of the effectiveness of the magnet school. See the interim reports on the "Science Lab" program and on the "Mastery Learning in Mathematics" program (photocopies), Alexandria City Public Schools, Office of Planning, Research and Evaluation, Alexandria, Va., 1985.

27. Leah Y. Latimer, "Magnet School Lacks Drawing Power," *Washington Post*, October 27, 1986, pp. D1, D7.

28. Elsa Walsh, "Some Chevy Chase Parents Try Busing Despite Earlier Vow," *Washington Post*, September 28, 1983, pp. C1, C6; Elsa Walsh, "Montgomery Eyes Altering Schools' Racial Makeup," *Washington Post*, January 24, 1984, p. C1.

29. Leah Y. Latimer, "Arlington Schools to Review One-Way Busing of Blacks," *Washington Post*, October 9, 1986, pp. B1, B7.

30. Lawrence Feinberg, "More Money, Staff Change Little for Average Students," *Washington Post*, December 4, 1983, pp. A1, A16.

31. "1983–84 Annual Report of Standardized Test Scores," Fairfax County Public Schools, Department of Instructional Services, Fairfax, Va., 1984, p. 30. See also Lawrence Feinberg, "Math Scores Show Increase in Virginia SATs," *Washington Post*, September 28, 1983, pp. C1, C6.

32. Paul Hodge, "Fairfax Minority Students Lag," *Washington Post*, January 14, 1984, pp. A1, A22.

33. See "Minority Students' Academic Performance: A Preliminary Report" and "Addendum to Preliminary Report on Minority Students' Academic Performance," both prepared by the Fairfax County Public Schools, Department of Instructional Services, Annandale, Va., 1984.

34. D'Vera Cohn, "Minority Progress Seen at Fairfax Schools," *Washington Post*, October 17, 1986, p. C3.

35. Ann Koch, "Black Scores Lag in Arlington," *Washington Post*, September 6, 1986, p. A22.

36. Leah Y. Latimer, "Arlington Panel Approves Program for Black Students," *Washington Post*, November 7, 1986, p. B3.

37. Joy A. Frechtling, Kathleen M. Hebbeler, and Steven M. Frankel (eds.), "Summary of MCPS Data on Differences in Minority and Majority Performance and Participation," Montgomery County Public Schools, Department of Educational Accountability and Division of Instructional Evaluation and Testing, Rockville, Md., 1983, pp. 1–111.

38. Elsa Walsh, "Minority Students Shortchanged, Says Montgomery Panel," *Washington Post*, August 24, 1983, pp. C1, C7.

39. "Report of Results of the College Board Admissions Testing Program (the Scholastic Aptitude Test)," Prince George's County Public Schools, Office of Evaluation and Research, Upper Marlboro, Md., 1984, pp. 4, 13.

40. Walsh, "Minority Students," p. C7.

41. Lawrence Feinberg, "Alexandria Desegregation: Problems Persist," *Washington Post*, January 22, 1979, pp. A1, A8.

42. "Number of Pupils Suspended by Race by School, 1979–80, 1980–81, 1981–82, 1982–83, 1983–84, 1984–85 School Years," Montgomery County Public Schools, Department of Educational Accountability and Division of Administrative Analysis and Audits, Rockville, Md., 1985, pp. 1–2.

43. Feinberg, "Alexandria Desegregation," p. A8.

44. Mary Jordan and Bridgette A. Lacy, "Parents, Staff Grapple with Racism Perceptions at Reston School," *Washington Post*, August 5, 1986, pp. B1, B5.

45. Patrick Welsh, "Blacks, Whites, 'Grits,' 'Punks' and Cliques," *Washington Post*, February 12, 1984, pp. B1–B2.

46. Ibid.

47. Elsa Walsh, "Honor Student Faces Race Problem," *Washington Post*, April 24, 1984, pp. A1, A6.

48. Ibid., p. A6.

49. Leah Y. Latimer, "'Native Flight' Upsets Schools in N. Virginia," *Washington Post*, March 27, 1984, pp. A1, A10.

50. Elsa Walsh, "Black Parents, Students Complain of Race Bias at Kennedy High School," *Washington Post*, May 11, 1984, p. 6.

51. Readers who wish to explore the complexities of race and education are urged to examine, *inter alia,* the following: Armor, "White Flight and the Future of School Desegregation," in Stephan and Feagin (eds.), *School Desegregation*; Charles Clotfelter, "Urban School Desegregation and Declines in White Enrollment: A Reexamination," *Journal of Urban Economics* 6, no. 3:352–370; James S. Coleman, Ernest Q. Campbell, Carol J. Hobson, James McPartland, Alexander M. Mood, Frederic D.

Weinfeld, and Robert L. York, *Equality of Educational Opportunity* (Washington, D.C.: U.S. Government Printing Office, 1966); Reynolds Farley, *School Integration and White Flight* (Ann Arbor, Mich.: University of Michigan, Population Studies Center, 1977); Joe T. Darden, Robert J. Griffore, Margaret A. Parsons, Julie Schmidt, and John H. Schweitzer, "Metropolitan School Desegregation in New Castle County, Delaware," Michigan State University, Urban Affairs Programs, East Lansing, Mich., July 1982, also available in Robert L. Green and Frances S. Thomas (eds.), *Metropolitan Desegregation* (New York and London: Plenum Press 1985); Christopher Jencks et al. *Inequality: A Reassessment of the Effect of Family and Schooling in America* (New York: Basic Books, 1972); G. Donald Jud, "Public Schools and Urban Development," *Journal of the American Planning Association* 51, no. 1:74–83; Gary Orfield, *Must We Bus?* (Washington, D.C.: Brookings Institution, 1978); Thomas F. Pettigrew and Robert L. Green, "School Desegregation in Large Cities: A Critique of the Coleman 'White Flight' Thesis," *Harvard Educational Review* 46, no. 1:1–53; Christine H. Rossell, "School Desegregation and White Flight," *Political Science Quarterly* 90, no. 4:675–695.

52. John Sansing, "Blacks and Whites in Washington: How Separate? How Equal?" *The Washingtonian* 22, no. 1 (October 1986): 157.

53. Ibid.

Chapter 9

1. Lawrence Feinberg, "D.C. Population Holding Steady," *Washington Post*, January 24, 1985, pp. A1, A6.

2. Ronald J. Johnston, *Urban Residential Patterns* (New York: Praeger Publishers, 1972), pp. 30–31.

3. See, for example, Robert L. Crain and Rita E. Mahard, "Minority Achievement: Policy Implications of Research," in Willis D. Hawley (ed.), *Effective School Desegregation* (Beverly Hills, Calif.: Sage Publications, 1981), pp. 55–84; Willis D. Hawley et al., *Strategies for Effective Desegregation: Lessons from the Research* (Lexington, Mass.: Lexington Books, 1983); Meyer Weinberg, *The Search for Quality Integrated Education* (Westport, Conn. and London: Greenwood Press, 1983).

4. See, for example, Nancy H. St. John, "The Effects of School Desegregation on Children: A New Look at the Research Evidence," in Adam Yarmolinsky, Lance Liebman, and Corinne S. Schelling (eds.), *Race and Schooling in the City* (Cambridge, Mass.: Harvard University Press, 1981), pp. 84–103; Martin Patchen, *Black-White: Contact in the Schools* (West Lafayette, Ind.: Purdue University Press, 1982); Harold B. Gerard and Norman Miller, *School Desegregation* (New York and London: Plenum Press, 1975).

5. Willis D. Hawley, "Increasing the Effectiveness of School Desegregation: Lessons from the Research," in Yarmolinsky et al. (eds.), *Race and Schooling in the City*, pp. 145–162; Robert L. Crain, Rita E. Mahard, and Ruth E. Narot, *Making Desegregation Work* (Cambridge, Mass.: Ballinger Publishing Co., 1982), pp. 68–73.

6. Joe T. Darden, Robert J. Griffore, Margaret A. Parsons, Julie Schmidt, and John H. Schweitzer, "Metropolitan School Desegregation in New Castle County,

Delaware," Michigan State University, Urban Affairs Programs, East Lansing, Mich., July 1982. See also Robert L. Green and Frances S. Thomas (eds.), *Metropolitan Desegregation* (New York and London: Plenum Press, 1985).

Chapter 10

1. Bill Peterson and David S. Broder, "Republican Senatorial Hopes Rise," *Washington Post*, November 10, 1983, p. A2.
2. Keith B. Richburg, "Most D.C. Residents Reject Residency Law, Poll Finds," *Washington Post*, January 25, 1981, pp. B1, B3.
3. Marion S. Barry, Jr., "The First Year—And What's Ahead," *Washington Post*, February 23, 1980, p. B1.
4. William Raspberry, "Coming and Going in the District," *Washington Post*, September 3, 1980, p. A12; Juan Williams, "Goodbye to the Chocolate City Dream," *Washington Post*, April 26, 1980, p. A15; Juan Williams, "City Hall Notebook: District Middle Class to Gain Political Clout?" *Washington Post*, May 5, 1982, pp. D.C.1, D.C.8.
5. Williams, "City Hall," p. D.C.1.
6. Milton Coleman, "City Hall Notebook: Musings on a New Generation of Businessmen," *Washington Post*, December 6, 1979, pp. D.C.1, D.C.12.
7. Bob Levey, "In the Neighborhoods; Our Town: Friendly, but in Flux," *Washington Post*, January 8, 1981, pp. 1, 6.
8. Dennis E. Gale, "Restoration in Georgetown, Washington, D.C., 1915–65" (unpublished Ph.D. dissertation), George Washington University, Washington, D.C., 1982, pp. 190–192.
9. Richburg, "Most D.C. Residents Reject Residency Law," p. B3.
10. John Mintz, "Barry and the Developers: A New Alliance," *Washington Post*, August 31, 1986, pp. A1, A46.
11. Ibid., p. A1.
12. Williams, "Goodbye to the Chocolate City Dream," p. A15; Pat Press, "Moving On Out," *Washington Post*, April 23, 1984, p. A13; Eric Pianin and Courtland Milloy, "Does the White Return to D.C. Mean 'The Plan' Is Coming True?" *Washington Post*, October 6, 1985, pp. D1, D2.
13. Press, "Moving On Out," p. A13.
14. Results of the May 2, 1984, primary are available in tabular form from the Government of the District of Columbia, Board of Elections and Ethics, District Building, Washington, D.C. See also Eric Pianin, "Jackson Victory in D.C. Shows Votes Polarized," *Washington Post*, May 3, 1984, pp. A1, A18.
15. Results of the November 6, 1984, election are available in tabular form from the Government of the District of Columbia, Board of Elections and Ethics, District Building, Washington, D.C. See also Marcia Slacum Greene, "Moore's Loss Is Blamed on Strategy," *Washington Post*, September 18, 1984, pp. C1, C6; Eric Pianin, "Carol Schwartz Found Support in NW and Capitol Hill Areas," *Washington Post*, November 8, 1984, p. A58; Isaiah J. Poole, "GOP's Carol Schwartz Headed for Council in Democratic D.C.," *Washington Times*, November 18, 1984.
16. Results of the November 6, 1984, election are available in tabular form from

the Government of the District of Columbia, Board of Elections and Ethics, District Building, Washington, D.C. See also Eric Pianin, "Schwartz Win Is Official," *Washington Post*, November 10, 1984, pp. B1, B6; Isaiah J. Poole, "Ray and Schwartz Win Seats in At-Large Race for City Council," *Washington Times*, November 7, 1984, pp. C1, C3.

17. Eric Pianin and Courtland Milloy, "Barry's Racial Defense Wins Some Backers," *Washington Post*, August 26, 1984, pp. A1, A16, A17. For a contrasting view, see Dr. Calvin W. Rolark, "Let's Talk," *Washington Informer*, August 8–16, 1984, p. 16.

18. Pianin and Milloy, "Barry's Racial Defense," p. A16; Eric Pianin, "Barry Criticizes Media for Publishing 'Unlawful Leaks,'" *Washington Post*, January 17, 1985, p. C5.

19. "Mr. Barry's Contract Concerns," *Washington Post*, September 20, 1985, p. A12.

20. Pianin and Milloy, "Barry's Racial Defense," pp. A16–A17; Rolark, "Let's Talk," p. 16.

21. Pianin and Milloy, "Does the White Return to D.C. Mean 'The Plan' Is Coming True?" p. D2.

22. Eric Pianin, "Barry Gets High Marks in Survey," *Washington Post*, January 12, 1985, pp. A1, A8; Pianin and Milloy, "Does the White Return to D.C. Mean 'The Plan' Is Coming True?" p. D1.

23. Arthur S. Brisbane and Tom Sherwood, "Barry Says He Misjudged Aides," *Washington Post*, October 29, 1986, pp. A1, A14.

24. Robert L. Asher, "Mayor Barry on Blacks, Whites and City Hall," *Washington Post*, October 26, 1986, pp. B1, B4.

25. Anonymous, "Happy Birthday, Part II," *Washington Post*, September 16, 1986, p. A14.

26. Joe Pichirallo, "Barry's Expenses Probed," *Washington Post*, August 21, 1986, pp. A1, A6, A8.

27. Brisbane and Sherwood, "Barry Says He Misjudged Aides," p. A14.

28. Arthur S. Brisbane, "Using the Power of Incumbency," *Washington Post*, October 31, 1986, pp. B1, B4.

29. Arthur S. Brisbane, "Business Giving Big to Barry Bid," *Washington Post*, June 13, 1986, pp. B1, B4.

30. Jeff Burbank, "Parents Bankroll School," *Washington Post*, June 27, 1985, pp. D.C.1, D.C.2.

31. Williams, "Goodbye to the Chocolate City Dream," p. A15.

32. Gary Orfield, *Toward a Strategy for Urban Integration* (New York: Ford Foundation, 1981), p. 49.

33. Ibid.

34. Ibid., p. 75.

35. Steven J. Diner, "Crisis of Confidence: The Reputation of Washington's Public Schools in the Twentieth Century," Studies in D.C. History and Public Policy, Paper 1, University of the District of Columbia, Washington, D.C., 1982, pp. 49–57.

36. Tom Sherwood, "Barry Disavows '78 Remark," *Washington Post*, October 30, 1986, pp. C1, C4.

37. Thomas F. Pettigrew, "The Case for Metropolitan Approaches to Public School

Desegregation," in Adam Yarmolinsky, Lance Liebman, and Corinne S. Schelling (eds.), *Race and Schooling in the City* (Cambridge, Mass.: Harvard University Press, 1981), pp. 163–181.

38. Orfield, *Toward a Strategy for Urban Integration*, p. 48.

Chapter 11

1. "Racial Composition of the Population of Prince George's County, 1970 to 1980," 1980 Census Information Bulletin 2, Maryland National Capital Park and Planning Commission, Prince George's County Planning Department, Upper Marlboro, Md., 1981, p. 4.

2. Ibid.

3. Dennis E. Gale, George Grier, and Eunice Grier, "Black and White Urban-to-Suburban Outmigrants: A Comparative Analysis, 1975–1980," Occasional Paper 4, George Washington University, Center for Washington Area Studies, Washington, D.C., p. 8.

4. George Grier and Eunice Grier, "Changing Residential Patterns of Racial Minorities in Metropolitan Washington, 1970–1980," Preliminary Report 3, Greater Washington Research Center, Washington, D.C., 1982; George Grier and Eunice Grier, "Black Suburbanization in the 1970s: An Analysis of Census Results," National Institute of Public Management, Washington, D.C., 1983.

5. Dennis E. Gale and Jeffrey Henig, "The Political Incorporation of Newcomers to Racially Changing Neighborhoods," *Urban Affairs Quarterly* 22, No. 3:399-419.

6. Michael Eastman, "Prince George's County Draws Black Middle Class Out from Washington," *Washington Post*, October 4, 1979, pp. D.C.1, D.C.4; Michael Eastman, "Affordable Dream Home in P.G.," *Washington Post*, October 4, 1979, p. D.C.4; Patricia Camp, "Up and Out," *Washington Post*, May 17, 1980, pp. A1, A9.

7. Larry Perl, "Mayor Asks Probe of Racial Graffito," *Prince George's Journal*, April 12, 1984, pp. A1, A7.

8. Gale Pastula, "Convention Urges More Black Action," *Prince George's Journal*, March 19, 1984, pp. A1, A9.

9. Michel McQueen, "P.G. Newcomers on Party Panel Getting Restless," *Washington Post*, November 21, 1983, pp. D1, D8.

10. Leon Wynter, "P.G. Blacks Hold 'Coming Together,'" *Washington Post*, March 18, 1984, p. B9; Pastula, "Convention Urges More Black Action," pp. A1, A9.

11. "Voter Statistics—Primary 1984" (computer tabulations), Government of Prince George's County, Bureau of Elections, Upper Marlboro, Md., May 31, 1984. See also Sandra R. Gregg, "Prince George's County Registers 31,000 New Voters; Many Are Black," *Washington Post*, April 11, 1984, p. B1.

12. Leon Wynter and Sandra R. Gregg, "Jackson Workers Say Vote Drive Hindered," *Washington Post*, March 27, 1984, p. B4; Chris Harvey, "Jackson Workers: County Stalling Effort," *Prince George's Journal*, March 28, 1984, pp. A1, A9.

13. Gwen Ifill, "Black Voters in P.G. Gain Clout," *Washington Post*, November 11, 1984, pp. B1, B4.

14. "Official Returns for General Election" (computer tabulations), Government of Prince George's County, Bureau of Elections, Upper Marlboro, Md., November 6,

1984. See also Ann C. Schappi, "Democrats, Incumbents Win; TRIM Modification Passes," *Prince George's Post*, November 8, 1984, pp. 1, 17.

15. Ibid.; Barbara Vobejda, "P.G. Blacks Look Ahead," *Washington Post*, January 15, 1985, p. B1; Michel McQueen, "P.G. Black Politicians Want a Bigger Piece of Patronage Pie," *Washington Post*, January 16, 1985, pp. B1, B8.

16. Susan Schmidt and Keith Harriston, "Marshall Defeat Tied to Bias Case," *Washington Post*, September 11, 1986, pp. A21, A26.

17. Ibid., p. A26.

18. Ibid.

19. Keith Harriston, "P.G. Police Split over Endorsements," *Washington Post*, October 4, 1986, p. B4.

20. Ibid.

21. Leon Wynter, "Blacks Are Happier Than Whites with Life in P.G. County, *Post* Poll Finds," *Washington Post*, August 8, 1983, pp. B1, B2.

22. Eugene L. Meyer, "Poll Shows Majority Favors Modification of Revenue Freeze," *Washington Post*, August 16, 1983, pp. B1, B3.

23. Ibid.

24. Michel McQueen, "A Changed P.G. Council," *Washington Post*, July 2, 1984, pp. B1, B7; Mary Ellen Webb, "Trotter Hopes to Change County Council Elections," *Prince George's Post*, January 12, 1984, pp. 3, 16.

25. Webb, "Trotter Hopes to Change County Council Elections," pp. 3, 16.

Chapter 12

1. Linda Wheeler, "Transformation of a Drug-Ridden Street," *Washington Post*, November 26, 1983, pp. B1, B7; Linda Wheeler, "Gay Bar 'Fantasies' Produces Dreams of Shaw Renewal," *Washington Post*, January 8, 1984, pp. B1, B7; Linda Wheeler, "Combat Zone: Cocaine, Killings Terrorize Hanover Place," *Washington Post*, May 17, 1984, pp. A1, A16.

2. Ernest W. Burgess, "The Growth of a City: An Introduction to a Research Project," in Robert E. Park (ed.), *The City* (Chicago: University of Chicago Press, 1925), p. 55.

3. Larry H. Long and Diana DeAre, "The Suburbanization of Blacks," *American Demographics*, September 1981, pp. 21, 44.

4. Barrett A. Lee, Daphne Spain, and Debra J. Umberson, "Revitalization and Racial Change: The Case of Washington, D.C." (unpublished paper), 1984, pp. 19, 24–25.

5. *1985—A Look Ahead: Population Forecasts for the District of Columbia* (Washington, D.C.: Government of the District of Columbia, Municipal Planning Office, July 1976), p. 27.

6. *Comprehensive Plan for the National Capital* (Washington, D.C.: Government of the District of Columbia, September 1982), p. 68.

7. Lawrence Feinberg, "D.C. Population Holding Steady," *Washington Post*, January 24, 1985, pp. A1, A6; Lawrence Feinberg, "D.C. Population Shows First Rise since 1963," *Washington Post*, January 22, 1986, pp. B1, B7.

8. *Comprehensive Plan*, pp. 72–74.

9. Ibid., p. 73.

10. Ibid., p. 75.

11. *Metropolitan Policy Guide, Summary Report* (Washington, D.C.: Metropolitan Washington Council of Governments, December 1980).

12. *Cooperative Forecasting Round III, Summary Report—1984* (Washington, D.C.: Metropolitan Washington Council of Governments, 1984), p. 26. See also the *Technical Report*, ibid., p. 110.

13. *Cooperative Forecasting Round III, Summary Report—1984*, pp. 7–8.

Index